James Wellard

BY THE WATERS
OF BABYLON

HUTCHINSON OF LONDON

HUTCHINSON & CO (*Publishers*) LTD
3 Fitzroy Square, London W1

London Melbourne Sydney Auckland
Wellington Johannesburg Cape Town
and agencies throughout the world

First published 1972

*This book has been set in Garamond type, printed in Great Britain
on antique wove paper by Anchor Press, and
bound by Wm. Brendon, both of Tiptree, Essex*

ISBN 0 09 111060 2

BY THE WATERS OF BABYLON

£65.

IRAQ.

ⓐ DB

Contents

Illustrations

Acknowledgements: all illustrations are from the British Museum with the exception of nos. 2, 3, 5 and 9 which are from the Radio Times Hulton Picture Library and no. 4 which is from the Ulster Museum and the Board of the University of Dublin.

Chronological Table

Continual wars between the city-states of Ancient Mesopotamia, from the Assyrian Assur in the north to the Sumerian Eridu in the south, meant that no nation was ascendant for more than a few hundred years at a time. Each of the principal kingdoms of Sumer, Babylonia, and Assyria rose, fell, and sometimes rose again over a period lasting from 3000 B.C. to 331 B.C. The following table gives the significant dates which will enable the reader to identify the various states or empires, their principal kings, and memorable historic events.

DATES (B.C.)

3000	SUMER: THE CITY-STATES Kish, Nippur, Adab, Lagash, Uruk, Larsa, Ur, Eridu
2500	
2400	DYNASTY OF AKKAD Sargon (*c.* 2350–2300) Manishtusu (2300–2276) Naram-sin (2277–2240)
2200	Seven other kings (2240–2200)
2100	THIRD DYNASTY OF UR Ur-Nammu (2113–2096) Shulgi (2096–2048)
2000	Ibbi-sin (2029–2006)
1900	THE FIRST BABYLONIAN EMPIRE Sumu-abum (1894–1881) Hammurabi (1792–1750) Samsu-iluna (1749–1712) Samsu-ditana (1625–1595)
1595	HITTITE CONQUEST OF BABYLON
1400	28 kings of Hittite origin

Foreword

Robert Koldewey, the German archaeologist who excavated Babylon between 1899 and 1917, described that metropolis as 'perhaps the most celebrated city in the world'. He could have added 'also one of the least known', for while the Tower of Babel, the Hanging Gardens, and the last great king, Nebuchadnezzar, were an integral part of Western folklore, the site of the city itself had been lost for over 2000 years, and not a vestige of even its mighty walls, once counted one of the Wonders of the World, remained above ground.

Yet the very name of Babylon is enough to arouse our wonder, probably because it plays such an important rôle in the Bible, which, it should be remembered, was until recently the principal source of pre-Hellenic history. And the manner in which Babylon and its kings are presented in the Old Testament make the place unusually fascinating, in spite, and perhaps because, of the hatred shown towards it by the Jewish chroniclers. Consequently, until Koldewey excavated the actual site of Babylon and the philologists translated the cuneiform records, the general public had only the vaguest notion of what the city was really like, what it contributed to the advance of civilisation, and why it has always evoked such a sense of wonder.

The writer on this vast subject has nowadays a plethora of material to choose from—notably the Babylonian documents themselves, the excavations of the last 150 years, and the collections of artefacts in national museums all over the world. In addition, there are many formal histories of Assyria and Babylonia, mostly written by professional Assyriologists and based on a mass of evidence which became available once the cuneiform

writing could be translated. In general these works have been
written for, and read by, specialists, which is understandable in
view of the difficulty of the subject. Indeed, it soon becomes
obvious that Assyriology has hitherto been very much of an
academic discipline, limited to the Mesopotamian archaeologists
and philologists, especially the latter, since they are the only
people who can read the tablets which are the principal source
of the Assyro-Babylonian history.

In contrast to the particularised studies of the specialists, the
purpose and scope of the following book is to present a general
picture of the political, social, and cultural history of Babylonia,
which is a term we shall employ to include the sister states of
Sumer and Assyria. Our task, then, is to show how this centre of
empire reigned as the greatest and richest city of the Middle East
from about 2500 to 331 B.C.—a life-span of over 2000 years.
During most of this time it maintained a high standard of
civilisation, surviving one conquest after another, absorbing its
conquerors because it was intellectually superior to them, and
exporting its culture throughout the ancient world. Its language
was the language of international diplomacy; its religion,
astronomy, astrology, and jurisprudence dominated the civilised
nations until the rise of Greece. What, then, was the secret of
this fabulous city's dominance?

We shall not, of course, find the answer in the Old Testament
account of the long struggle between Israel and Babylon, though
this account is important in view of the religious ties which the
Western world has with the Jews and through them with the
Babylonians themselves. But the Hebrew prophets with their
tirades concerning the wickedness of their enemies give no hint
of the secret of Babylon's greatness, so that historians have had
to wait until the nineteenth century to discover what that secret
was. The real story of Babylon, then, begins with the first
travellers to those lost worlds which lay under the mounds
between the Two Rivers, the Tigris and the Euphrates, and the
first excavators who opened them up to reveal the true history
of 'the most celebrated city in the world'.

Here a word needs to be said concerning the geography and
nomenclature of the region. First, the term 'Middle East' has
been used throughout this book in the sense given it by the older
geographers who divided the Orient into three zones—the Near

East, comprising the countries along the eastern borders of the
Mediterranean; the Middle East, including those in the general
region of the river valleys of the Tigris and Euphrates; and the
Far East, meaning those countries east of Afghanistan. Modern
geographers tend to quarrel with this classification on the grounds
that it is 'egocentric', being based on distances from Europe.
This, of course, is nonsense, since all regions of the world are,
and must be, relevant to some fixed position, as the meridians
are relative to Greenwich. So the Middle East in the following
pages always refers to the Tigris-Euphrates basin and roughly
includes the modern states of Iran, Iraq, Syria, Jordan, and
eastern Turkey. 'Near East' means the lands of western Turkey,
the Lebanon, and Israel.

The second term which might cause confusion is 'Mesopotamia', which has been used to mean different things from
Roman times onwards. Its literal meaning is, of course, 'the
land between the rivers', the rivers being the Tigris and the
Euphrates, the former rising in a lake in the mountains of
Kurdistan and thereafter flowing, with the aid of many tributaries,
1150 miles into the Persian Gulf; the latter rising in eastern
Turkey and flowing 1700 miles across Syria and Iraq to unite
with the Tigris before emptying into the same gulf. These two
great rivers, which were the direct cause of the rise of civilisation
in the Middle East, approach each other closely at Baghdad, so
that the lands to the north and south are naturally divided into
Upper and Lower Mesopotamia. The former was the terrain of
Assyria; the latter of Babylonia.

The spelling of Assyro-Babylonian names gives us the same
sort of trouble that we have with the transliteration of all Semitic
languages: the French spell them one way, the Germans another,
and the English still another. In addition, scholars are continually
revising their theories of phonetics, so that names spelt in one
form in the mid-nineteenth century have little resemblance to
the way they might be written today. Further, many Babylonian
proper names which are familiar to us from the King James
translation of the Old Testament appear in a bewildering variety
of forms in academic treatises: an example is Nebuchadnezzar
which is written Nebuchadrezzar, Nebu-kudur-ussur, Nabu-
kudurri-usur, Nebekuluchar, et cetera. But for the general
reader such pedantic nomenclature can have no significance at

all, particularly as the Assyriologists themselves have not yet
made up their minds as to which version of the Babylonian
king's names is correct.

The present writer has therefore decided to follow the con-
ventional spelling of proper names as far as possible, writing
Nebuchadnezzar rather than Nebuchadrezzar, or Nebu-kudur-
ussur. Similarly we write Ashurbanipal, Hammurabi, Ishtar,
Tiglath-pileser, in preference to whatever forms may be currently
in fashion among the academicians.

The difficulties of transliteration are also very complex in the
area of Arab, Turkish, and Iraqi place-names. Here again we have
used as far as possible the old versions as they have come down
to us in English. It seems as pedantic to write Bab-ilim for
Babylon, Urusilimmu for Jerusalem, as it would be to pronounce
the capital of France *Paree* when talking to another English-
speaking person. In general, then, we have followed the spelling
recommended by the Permanent Committee on Geographical
Names of the Royal Geographical Society. Obviously some
uniform system had to be devised in order to eliminate the
confusion which resulted in referring to the town of Basra as
variously Busra, Bassorah, Bussorah, Bassra, and so forth.

Finally, the author wishes to thank the Trustees of the British
Museum for the facilities made available to him in researching
and writing this book; the publishers who commissioned it;
and the editors of *Encounter* magazine for permission to use the
material contained in Chapter 8 and first published in that
journal in May 1971. The number of titles listed in the Biblio-
graphy at the end of this book is an indication of the debt he
owes to generations of professional Assyriologists.

BY THE WATERS OF BABYLON

I

Babylon Remembered

BABYLON—THE CITY and its empire—flourished for almost 2000 years, from about 2225 B.C. until its capture by Alexander the Great in 331 B.C. When the Greek conqueror of the world died there, Babylon could be said to have died too. But up to that time it had been the cultural capital of the civilised world; and even after its site was lost, buried under mounds of rubble, its existence was never forgotten. The very name has always had a magical sound to it. The Hebrews placed the Garden of Eden somewhere nearby. The Greeks wrote that it contained two of the Seven Wonders of the World. The Romans described it as 'the greatest city the sun ever beheld'. And to the early Christians 'Great Babylon' was the symbol of man's wickedness and the wrath of God. And so it was 'by the waters of Babylon' that the history of the Western world could be said to have begun.

Although it seems unbelievable that a metropolis of such size and splendour should have vanished from the earth—its outer defences alone were ten miles in circumference, fifty feet high, and nearly fifty-five feet deep—the fact is that by the first century B.C. nothing remained but its walls. For Babylon had been devastated so often that by this time it was abandoned except for a few refugees who made their homes in the rubble. The royal palaces had been looted, the temples had fallen into ruins, and the greater part of the city inside the walls was overgrown with weeds.

Yet this was the Babylon that the Greek historian Herodotus describes as the capital of a region richer in grain than any other country he had visited; 'while such is its size and magnificence that no other city approaches it'. He then gives the dimensions which later historians find it difficult, if not impossible, to accept,

B

fifteen miles square, or a circuit of sixty miles. If he is referring to
the walled city, this is undoubtedly an exaggeration, as the archaeologists have shown; but if he includes the suburbs, outlying
villages, and farms, his estimate may be roughly correct. In other
words, Babylon at its height might have been the size of Inner
London.

Later Greek travellers also speak of the immense proportions of
Babylon, though by the time of the Romans the city was gradually disappearing from the maps, and even from men's memories.
The last we hear of Babylon from the classical authors is quite
strange, for according to Zosimus, the historian of the reign of
Julian the Apostate, the city had been made into a wild-animal
park in A.D. 363: that is, a royal game reserve for the Persian king
Shapur I. Zosimus states that the walls still stood, though most of
the 360 towers spaced along the ramparts had fallen down. This
incredible fate, the metamorphosis of the largest city in the world
into a zoo, is also remarked upon by St Jerome, who heard the
news from a monk who came from Mesopotamia. Jerome's statement, in fact, corroborates the description given by Zosimus—
that by the end of the fourth century A.D. Babylon had been
abandoned to wild beasts.

We know this much then: that only the great walls still stood
in A.D. 400, a thousand years after they had been rebuilt by
Nebuchadnezzar. But with the fall of the Roman Empire and the
withdrawal of the legions from the Middle East even these triple
bastions collapsed, and nothing more is heard of Babylon, except
for references to its ancient splendour. The reason was, in part,
that this city, along with other centres of the pagan world, had
become for the new and triumphant sect of Christians a symbol
of man's wickedness and of God's wrath. Sodom and Gomorrah
were, of course, the classic examples; but had not Babylon, too,
been cursed by the prophet Isaiah and Nineveh anathematised by
the prophet Nahum? And this conviction that a jealous deity
determined the course of history and so destroyed the pagan
world with all its gods and most of its monuments partially
accounts for the indifference towards the fate of the great civilisations of the Middle East throughout the late Romano-Christian
period, the Middle Ages, and so on up to the eighteenth century.
It is as though Babylon, the city, its people, and its culture, having
been condemned by Jehovah himself, were therefore unworthy to

be remembered at all. The Bible itself said so, and the Bible was
'the History of Nations written by God who there points out to
us what He accounts of importance in history, and what insignificant. And of Babylon He speaks only with indignation.'[1] So writes
the widow of Claudius Rich, the first man in modern times to
make a methodical study of the site of the ancient capital of the
world.

Whether God was indignant with Babylon or not is a matter of
theology which historians and archaeologists are not competent
to answer; but to those like Mrs Rich, who felt qualified to speak
on the subject of divine dispensation, the prophecy of Isaiah was
convincing proof. For calling upon Jahweh as his witness, Isaiah
predicts a terrible fate for the ancient enemy of Judah:

> Every one that is found shall be thrust through; and every one
> that is joined unto them shall fall by the sword. Their children
> also shall be dashed to pieces before their eyes; their houses
> shall be spoiled, and their wives ravished. Their bows [i.e., of
> the Medes, the allies of Judah] shall dash the young men to
> pieces; and they shall have no pity on the fruit of the womb;
> their eye shall not spare children.
>
> And Babylon, the glory of kingdoms, the beauty of the
> Chaldees' excellency, shall be as when God overthrew Sodom
> and Gomorrah . . .

To which anathema Jeremiah adds his characteristic impreca-
tion:

> And Babylon shall become a heaps, a dwelling-place for
> dragons, an astonishment and a hissing, without an inhabitant.

It is not surprising, then, that we hear very little more of
Babylon after the last scanty references made to it by the classical
authors. To the early Christian Fathers, for instance, it was merely
a symbol of corruption, a name which they used as a code-word
for pagan Rome, the implacable enemy of the church. And during
the early Middle Ages scholars and statesmen alike were too
occupied with a new threat to Christendom to spare a thought for
symbolic enemies. Babylon was now a legend; the armies of Islam
a reality.

And so it was left to a Jewish scholar to ponder over the
whereabouts of Babylon, not so much out of historical or archaeo-

logical interest as out of curiosity concerning the scene of his people's early religious history. Rabbi Benjamin set out from his home in the north of Spain in 1160 to see the place where his fore-fathers suffered their exile 'by the rivers of Babylon, where we sat down, yea, we wept, when we remembered Zion, and we hanged our harps upon the willows in the midst thereof'. Benjamin trav-elled overland to Venice, where he took ship for Constantinople, and so reached Mosul in Iraq in 1161. The ruins of Nineveh lie near Mosul, and had probably always been known to the Jewish community of that city, but it is not certain that the rabbi visited them. Instead, he floated down the Tigris to Baghdad, where he found a colony of 20,000 Jews and another community of 10,000 in nearby Hillah; and here his hosts told him that both the Palace of Nebuchadnezzar and the 'burning fiery furnace' into which Hananiah, Mishael, and Azariah were thrown were still to be seen, though, they added, people were afraid to visit these places on account of the serpents and scorpions with which they were infested.[2] Moreover, the Jews of Baghdad claimed that the syna-gogue in which they worshipped had been built by Daniel him-self, which proves not that this temple was 1500 years old, but that the Jews had been in the vicinity of Babylon since the time of their conqueror, Nebuchadnezzar. The rabbi was also taken to see a structure which he calls 'The Tower of the Dispersed Genera-tion'—in other words, the Tower of Babel. He says that 'the base measures two miles, the breadth 240 yards, and the height 1000 feet'—which would make this monument a mere 250 feet lower than the Empire State Building, the highest structure in the world. He adds that 'the heavenly fire which struck the Tower split it to its very foundations'.

All this seems to indicate that Benjamin was misinformed and had not visited the site of Babylon at all, but had been shown some of the enormous mounds of earth and rubble which covered the Mesopotamian plain between the Tigris and Euphrates rivers. Indeed, there were so many ruins of ancient cities that it has taken a hundred years of systematic excavation to identify them, while the names of some are still in doubt. The first cartographers, for instance, were wholly unable to place Babylon and Nineveh accur-ately on their maps, so that if you had asked a geographer of the sixteenth century the whereabouts of Babylon, he would have said on the Tigris at a place called Baghdad, and he would have been just as wrong as the Rabbi Benjamin, who was, in fact, the only authority available. The explanation was that those few travellers who had made the journey across the Syrian Desert to the Euphrates and Tigris were extremely vague about what they had seen and where they had seen it. Typical of the confusion is the next reference in literature to the lost city made by the German botanist Leonhard Rauwolff, who travelled to Baghdad in 1575 and claims to have seen the ruins of Babylon some forty miles due west of Baghdad and sixty north of the actual site. Rauwolff says that one can still see 'the tower of Babylon which the children of Noah (who first inhabited these countries after the Deluge) began to build up unto heaven . . .'. But when he adds that this tower in inhabited by insects bigger than lizards, with three heads and spots of different colours on their backs, the reader begins to doubt his qualifications as a naturalist, let alone as a geographer.[3]

But, as we have remarked, the Mesopotamian plain between the Euphrates and the Tigris was covered with the rubble of a score of large cities of antiquity, and the old travellers had no means of knowing which was which. Moreover, the majority of them were not antiquarians, but, as in the case of the Englishman John Eldred, were typical merchants willing to risk their lives in seeking out new markets. Eldred chose the Middle East for his sphere of influence and so 'upon Shrove Tuesday, 1583, departed out of London in the ship called the *Tiger* in the company of six or seven other honest merchants'. As a result of his travels throughout the Middle East over a period of five years, he returned to England a very wealthy man, 'arriving safely in the river of Thames 26 March 1588 in the *Hercules*, which was the richest ship of English merchants' goods that ever was known to come into this realm'.[4]

Eldred's narrative of his travels is particularly fascinating, since he saw the Middle East in the heyday of the great camel caravans coming overland from India, he himself joining at Baghdad a caravan of 4000 camels laden with spices and other rich merchandise bound for Aleppo across the Syrian Desert. But his journey is of special interest to us for his account of the ruins of Babylon which he calls 'the olde tower of Babell' and claims to have seen 'sundry times' while crossing the plain between the Euphrates to the Tigris; but we know now that what he saw was the ruins of a Cassite city called Aqar Quf, whose ziggurat is still one of the

sights for the tourist in Iraq. The obituary on Eldred's monument
in the church of Great Saxham, Suffolk, is, however, quite accurate, since though he had not seen the site of Babylon itself, he had
certainly been in Babylonia, as the quatrain on his tomb informs
us:

> The Holy Land so called I have seene,
> And in the Land of Babilon have beene;
> But in that Land where glorious Saints doe live
> My Soule doth crave of Christ a Roome to give.

But the day of casual travellers like Rabbi Benjamin, Leonhard
Rauwolff, and John Eldred was over. The mysticism of the
Middle Ages was about to give way to the scepticism of the Age
of Reason. And in the privacy of their libraries and studies scholars were beginning to ask leading questions concerning the real
role of Babylon in the ancient world. Their inquiries led them to
even examine the historicity of the Bible which had hitherto been
the principal source of information about that fabulous empire.
Was the Old Testament's claim that Babylon and Nineveh had
been destroyed because of God's anger, evoked by their inherent
wickedness, justified? The theocentric view of history, in other
words, was now being challenged by men of the intellectual
stature of Voltaire, Rousseau, and Gibbon. The cool appraisal of
these new social philosophers, and particularly of the deists,
directly affected the study of history, as they questioned in turn
the function of religion, the divine right of kings, and even the
nature of the deity. And just as the astronomers had dared to say
that the Earth was not the centre of our universe, so the historians
declared that the Bible was no longer the indisputable source of
all knowledge, but rather only one more record in the long annals
of mankind.

Such was the new 'scientific' approach of Carsten Niebuhr and
his colleagues who had been sent out by Frederick V of Denmark
in 1760 to explore Egypt, Arabia, and Syria. These inquirers were
looking for facts, not legends. Niebuhr, therefore, when he found
numerous inscribed bricks lying around the great mounds at
Hillah on the Euphrates, deduced that this was the site of a great
Babylonian city, and probably of Babylon itself, since he had
already identified the site of Nineveh near the Tigris, opposite the
modern city of Mosul. Niebuhr, deprived of the help and com-

panionship of his colleagues, all of whom had succumbed to disease within the space of a year, was unable to complete his investigations of the Hillah site, but in the characteristic spirit of eighteenth-century learning he calls for his fellow-savants to continue his work.

His call was soon answered, for in 1771 the French astronomer and scientist Joseph de Beauchamp, a Benedictine priest, visited the mound of Hillah to which Niebuhr had drawn attention and also another mound called El Kasr (The Castle). It was under this mound that the greatest finds were to be made by the German archaeologist Robert Koldewey between 1899 and 1912. What Abbé de Beauchamp revealed in his letters home to his colleagues in France marked the beginning of a completely new science, one day to be known as Assyriology, the study of the Assyro-Babylonian-Sumerian civilisation. For the abbé was told by the workmen who were employed to dig for bricks in the Hillah mound that they had found large, thick walls and rooms containing clay vessels, engraved marbles, and bronze statues. One room was decorated with figures of cows on varnished bricks (the reference is obviously to the enamelled bulls later found by Koldewey along the length of the Processional Way); and other bricks, according to the workmen, showed pictures of lions, the sun, the moon, and so forth. All of these artefacts had been thrown aside as worthless to the builders, who simply wanted the hard, kiln-baked bricks. (They had wanted them, in fact, from Roman times and when Koldewey arrived on the scene in 1899 he found that the contractors building a dam on the Euphrates had been raiding the El Kasr mound for the past twenty years and were still raiding it while he was excavating the Tower of Babel.) Fortunately for later generations, the workmen regarded as worthless the clay and bronze statues and the inscribed cylinders which they threw on the rubbish heaps; and their complete ignorance of the value of these artefacts evidently affected Abbé de Beauchamp's judgment, for he says that he did not trouble to acquire any of these cylinders 'as I was assured there were too many of them for any one of them to have any particular value'.

But his view was not shared by those scholars back in Europe— the historians who were eagerly waiting for the vital clues without the opportunity of seeing for themselves these 'books of the Babylonians'. The British, on the verge of the great age of intellectual as well as imperial expansion, were especially eager to acquire some of these cylinders and inscribed stones and they went about procuring them in the characteristic fashion of the last decade of the eighteenth century. In short, the Director-General of the East India Company 'being informed that near the town of Hillah on the Euphrates, there exist the remains of a very large and magnificent city, supposed to be Babylon', instructed his representative at Basra on the Persian Gulf to procure a selection of the Babylonian inscribed bricks and to send them to London. The inscriptions arrived early in 1801, and from that moment began the methodical study of Babylonian history.

This development was largely due to the interest created by the publication of a little book called *A Dissertation on the Newly-Discovered Babylonian Inscriptions* by Joseph Hager, D.D. Dr Hager was a typical product of the new Europe which had been created first by the intellectuals, then by the French and American revolutions: that is, his education was both liberal and international and he himself a citizen of the world. Born in Germany, he was educated at Vienna, travelled all over Europe, wrote and spoke fluently German, French, Italian, and English and then decided to make Chinese his speciality. Typical, too, of the man and his time were the fierce intellectual battles he fought with his colleagues which led to his being forced to resign his post at the Bibliothèque Nationale and to quit Paris altogether. In the 1790s and 1800s men took matters of learning as seriously as they now take questions of politics. Indeed, scholarship was then placed higher than politics in the scale of human values, so much so that not even wars were allowed to interfere with the free exchange of knowledge, even if they interfered with everything else.

In this stimulating atmosphere of intellectual freedom Joseph Hager's theories as to the Babylonian language and the realisation that a lost civilisation was awaiting rediscovery passed quickly across frontiers to the universities and academies of every country in Europe. The learned doctor with his great knowledge of languages had been able to demonstrate three important and, indeed, essential facts about a language not a single word of which could yet be read.

1. that the nail-headed [i.e. arrow-shaped or cuneiform, as Babylonian letters are now called] characters were real char-

acters and not ornaments or flowers as previous scholars had supposed;

2. that these characters were used not only in Persia but before that in Babylon whose culture was anterior to that of Persia; and

3. that they were to be read horizontally and from left to right.

It was from such small clues that the mysterious language of a lost world was eventually deciphered.* And once a start had been made on reading the language, the search for the Babylonians themselves, for the sites of their cities, and the ruins of their monuments, became one of the goals of the great explorations of the nineteenth century.

* For a discussion of the history of the decipherment of Babylonian see Chapter 5.

The Excavators

THE SCIENCE OF ASSYRIOLOGY, then, can be said to have begun at the beginning of the nineteenth century when the scholars back in Europe started work on the formidable task of deciphering the cuneiform script, while more practical men out in the field set about measuring and mapping the mounds which were thought to mark the sites of Babylon and Nineveh. These men, of whom Claudius James Rich, as we shall see, was the pioneer, prepared the ground for still another type of explorers who called themselves 'excavators' which was, in point of fact, an appropriate term, since none of them belonged to the class of trained or professional archaeologists. These 'excavators', in contrast to the academicians of their own or of our time, were a special breed of men who could only have been produced in the particular circumstances of the first half of the nineteenth century. For just as the intellectual revolution inspired by the writings of Voltaire and Gibbon had resulted in freeing men's minds from prejudice and superstition, so the American and French revolutions seemed to release a tremendous current of energy which was to change the course of history. The subsequent period was, above all, the age of explorers, intellectual and physical—explorers not only of new countries, but of the old empires; and most of this exploration was undertaken by individual travellers who combined great intellectual brilliance with remarkable physical courage. And in the newly emerging field of Assyriology we find the same unusual personalities dominating the scene as we find in the field of geographical exploration—notably the penetration of the continent of Africa. The marvellous discoveries of these men—whose names are now almost forgotten—were often made at the expense of their lives, as a glance at the list of the 'African travellers' who died trying to cross the Sahara Desert will show. But the results of their work can be seen in the museums and libraries of the Western world, even if their findings and the books they wrote are now superseded. Certainly the early 'excavators', complete with pickaxes, shovels, and pith helmets, tend to be discounted or even condemned by the modern archaeologist with his innumerable scientific aids; and it is indisputable that the damage they did was often grave. Scientific archaeologists shudder when they think of Henry Layard and his contemporaries tunnelling like coal-miners through the palaces and temples of Nineveh and Babylon and even obtaining light for their subterranean excavations by the rough-and-ready procedure of sinking vertical shafts right through ancient monuments. What these diggers must have destroyed in their quarrying will never now be known, but it was conceivably more than they found.

In fact, the losses from one cause or another were appalling. Not only were thousands of Babylonian tablets, statuettes, inscribed bricks and cylinders smashed up by the untrained workmen's picks, but many of the treasures that were dug out of the mounds were irretrievably lost before they reached Europe. Typical were two instances of such disasters. In 1844 a consignment of over 200 cases of sculptures and reliefs sent down the Tigris on a fleet of rafts by Émil Botta, the first 'excavator' of an Assyrian site, sank *in toto* near the mouth of the Shatt-el-Arab due to an attack by river pirates or to some mismanagement on the part of those responsible for the trans-shipment of the consignment to France. The entire findings of over two years' excavations were thus lost, including sculptures and wall-slabs from the palace of King Sargon at Khorsabad. Similarly, Christian Rassam, Henry Layard's deputy at the Kuyunjik excavations of 1851, sent fifteen cases of artefacts taken from the site of Nineveh to Baghdad. The cases, as was usual at the time, were floated off down the Tigris on rafts, and, also as usual, were attacked by river pirates who wanted the wood, iron, and ropes of the rafts and certainly not the Assyrian antiques, which they threw into the river, never to be found again.

But these losses, grievous though they were, were as nothing compared with the destruction wrought by the gangs of workmen recruited by the excavators from the local tribesmen. It is even suggested that whole libraries of clay tablets may have perished as a result of the heavy-handed attacks on the mounds which hid the palaces of kings and the temples of the gods. This could well have been the penalty of the first enthusiastic eagerness to enrich the great national museums of their own nations. It was this attitude and the wholesale destruction not only of priceless artefacts but of essential historical data that led the Egyptologist Flinders Petrie to characterise mid-nineteenth-century excavation-sites as 'ghastly charnel-houses of murdered evidence'.

Strong words. On the other hand, we should not be too hard on these courageous, zealous, and well-intentioned 'excavators', for none of them claimed to be an archaeologist in any case: they were nearly all diplomats, soldiers, or political agents who undertook, often at their own expense and nearly always at the expense of their health, to do the rough preliminary job of exploration. And, even more important, the justification of their work was the spectacular nature of their finds—enormous statues, historical friezes, and impressive monuments. In other words, though they were not treasure-hunters in the same sense as the tomb-robbers of Egypt, they were certainly hunters for museum specimens, which sometimes amounted to almost the same thing, though dignified in the name of science. And perhaps rightly so, for the final result of their discoveries was the foundation of the science we know today as Assyriology; and what they achieved was due, let it be remembered, to their dedication, their courage, and sometimes the sacrifice of their lives.

The first of these pioneers was Claudius James Rich (1787–1820) who achieved in the few years he was permitted to live a lifetime of travel, study, and discovery; and like so many of his contemporaries who were at this fascinating period of history penetrating the unknown parts of Africa and Asia, he died young of one of the 'fevers'. He died, in fact, aged thirty-three, helping to combat an epidemic of cholera in the Persian city of Shiraz, not far from Persepolis which he had been exploring.

Claudius Rich, then, was typical of his age. The bastard son of a French girl (name unknown) and a British colonel, James Cockburn of the 35th Foot, he was brought up as befitted a young gentleman: that is, he was allowed to follow his own bent, which in his case was definitely towards intellectual attainments. In fact, Claudius Rich was a child prodigy by any standards, for at the age of nine he had begun to learn Arabic; and at the age of sixteen he was described as 'acquainted with many languages. . . . Besides Latin, Greek, and many of the modern languages, he has made himself master of Hebrew, Chaldee, Persian, Arabic, Turkish, and is not without some knowledge of Chinese, which he began to decipher when he was but fourteen.' Though such accomplishments may seem to us today to be almost incredible, they were actually not all that unusual—or not among those young men who were to become the pioneers of the new science of Assyriology. Nor is it surprising that such a gifted young man, who also had 'a most engaging personality and address', was promptly taken up by the East India Company. In those days—at the beginning of the nineteenth century—this Company was virtually a department of the British Foreign Office, and its representatives in the major trading cities of the East had diplomatic status. Moreover—and this again was typical of the era—the young men who took up posts throughout the Middle East, India, and China were not expected to devote themselves wholly to trade. The humdrum business of commerce was undertaken by subordinates and native clerks; the Company's appointees were encouraged to interest themselves in politics, diplomacy, and, if they were so inclined, in the history, geography, and civilisation of their region.

And so we find Claudius Rich, though only seventeen years old, sent by the East India Company to Cairo in order 'to perfect himself in Arabic and to acquire the skill in horsemanship and the use of the lance and scimitar in which the Mamluks were past masters'. These Mamelukes were the descendants of Christian slaves who, brought up as Moslems, were formed into a special fighting force which seized power in 1250 and placed its own sultan on the throne. Claudius Rich saw the last of these blood-thirsty mercenaries who were wiped out in an ambush by Mehemet Ali in 1811. But in 1804 the Mamelukes were still a military and political body to be reckoned with in the Ottoman Empire, and taking advantage of this, the young Englishman, disguised as one of them, wandered through Palestine and Syria *en route* to his next post which was at Bombay. In Bombay he married the eldest daughter of the Governor, Sir James Mackintosh, and shortly afterwards was appointed the East India Company's resident at Baghdad.

In those days the Residency in Baghdad was maintained in the old tradition of British imperialism, and here the twenty-four-year-old Claudius Rich lived like a Roman pro-consul of the second century A.D. His house was really a palace consisting of two large courts, surrounded by galleried rooms and walled terraces for sleeping at night in the open air. Under the terraces were vaulted cellars used as stables, store-rooms, kitchens, and offices of every description. On Mr Rich's staff were an English surgeon, an Italian secretary (Carl Bellino who, like his master, died young of a 'fever'), several interpreters, janissaries, grooms, servants, a company of Indian sepoys who sounded the regular calls of a military garrison, a small troop of Hussars, and the captain and crew of a yacht moored in the river. Such was the style of living for a British consul in the early decades of the nineteenth century, and it is no wonder that the painter James Silk Buckingham, who was staying at the Residency in 1816, writes: 'Mr Rich was universally considered to be the most powerful man in Baghdad; and some even questioned whether the Pasha himself would not shape his conduct according to Mr Rich's suggestions and advice rather than as his own council might wish.'[1]

So Claudius Rich, whose knowledge of oriental languages and fascination with the lost civilisations of the Middle East had brought him to this outpost of the British Empire, began his explorations, and, being 'the most powerful man in Baghdad', he conducted them in style, as he tells us in his diary under the date December 9th, 1811:[2]

> Set out this morning on an expedition to visit the remains of Ancient Babylon, accompanied by Mrs Rich, Mr Hine, and some friends. Our escort consisted of my own troop of Hussars with a galloper gun, a havildar, and twelve sepoys, about seventy baggage-mules, a mehmandar from the Pasha, and a man from the Sheikh of the Jirbah Arabs.*

Mr Rich and his party were not only well protected, then, but carried enough supplies to feast and picnic all along the way. And on December 17th, a week after setting out, as it was too windy for sketching, the party decided to dig into one of the mounds where the brick scavengers had reported finding a skeleton. The

---

* A *galloper gun* is a light field gun; a *havildar*, an Indian sergeant; a *mehmandar*, a courier appointed by the Pasha.

report of a skeleton was just the type of thing to excite the enthusiasm and curiosity of these amateur archaeologists.

Claudius Rich and company did not, of course, do the digging themselves, but supplied the local workmen with picks and shovels, and told them to go to it. The workmen accordingly burrowed down through the mound, scattering bricks and clay tablets left and right, until they found something they thought would interest the sahibs, which, on this occasion, was an underground room with a sarcophagus in the wall.

I stood by and observed them by the light of the marshall [= a torch, or flambeau], while they dug it out, standing on a ladder. They could only pull it out piece by piece; sometimes the bones came out with occasional pieces of the coffin. I could not find the skull, nor collect a perfect skeleton. In digging a little further we found the bones of a young child. . . .

One can imagine the scene—the breaking down of the wall of this family tomb, the shouts of the workmen, their comments as they passed up to the Englishman another handful of bones, their eagerness to find something valuable for him—with the result that the remains of some long-dead Babylonians were thrown away as worthless, probably along with the inscription which no doubt gave the names of the deceased. Such were the beginnings of archaeology in Mesopotamia.

But Claudius Rich was to make ample retribution for this little example of vandalism through his careful exploration of the country round Baghdad, reported and sent back to the savants in Europe in a detailed description of the terrain, with maps and plans of the mounds, sketches of the ruins, and a learned essay published in a Viennese journal. So while this talented young English scholar and traveller knew nothing of the many disciplines which now make up the science of archaeology, he did arouse a world-wide interest in Babylonian studies and is entitled to be remembered as a pioneer in Assyriology.

One result of his work was that a procession of gentlemen travellers so characteristic of the times made their way towards this fascinating and mysterious country of the *Thousand Nights and a Night*. One of those who visited Baghdad to enjoy the consul-general's lavish hospitality looked on the ruins of Babylon and Nineveh with the eyes of a painter, and it was this man, Sir Robert

Ker Porter, who gave the vanished Mesopotamian cities the glamour and excitement which they have never entirely lost. Indeed, Sir Robert's *Travels*, published in London in 1821, is a splendid example of all those beautifully printed and illustrated journals with which the major and minor explorers of the nineteenth century were to delight an eager public. Such books were to appear by the thousands towards the end of the Victorian era, and banal though the majority were, all had the advantage of describing a world which had not been reduced to conformity by the ease of modern travel and the Westernisation of peoples with a life-style of their own. For when Sir Robert Ker Porter was travelling in Georgia, Persia, Armenia, and Babylonia in 1817–20 the only means of visiting these countries was on horseback or on foot, and this leisurely mode of travel seems to determine the style and even the format of his and his contemporaries' books. Sir Robert's is a work of 1600 pages, or some half a million words, with very few of the 'purple passages' or the tedious moralising we are obliged to endure in later Victorian writers. Porter was writing about places which not more than a few score Europeans had seen, yet in which tens of thousands who could not afford to travel were intensely interested—places like Mount Ararat, Isfahan, Shiraz, Persepolis, Baghdad, Babylon, Nineveh, and all the curious people and places along the way. His book, moreover, is illustrated by scores of maps, plans, sketches, portraits, and the first accurate copies of a number of cuneiform inscriptions. It is the kind of book written by a man whose love of adventure had taken him in his twenties to the court at St Petersburg as the historical painter to the Czar of Russia; then to the court of the eccentric Swedish king Gustavus IV; then to Finland and Germany; next to Spain with Sir John Moore, whose death at Corunna he witnessed; and so back to Russia to marry a Russian princess. Nor were his travels and adventures by any means ended, for after the publication of his celebrated *Travels in Georgia* he was appointed British consul in Caracas, Venezuela, where he became 'very well known for his hospitality'. The extent of this popularity is seen in the disorder of his estate after his death, which, perhaps fittingly, was in a drosky on a summer's night in St Petersburg as he was returning from a farewell visit to the Czar Alexander I.

The importance of men like Claudius Rich, James Silk Buckingham, and Sir Robert Ker Porter to the world of scholarship in general and to the field of Assyriology in particular was that they generated enough enthusiasm by their books and drawings to arouse the interest of the non-academic world. Rich or influential men were now prepared to patronise those young adventurers who were prepared to undergo the dangers and privations of excavations in Mesopotamia, for the kind of highly organised scientific expeditions which nowadays conduct archeological digs was entirely unknown to the Victorians. Indeed, all the work on the Assyro-Babylonian mounds throughout the nineteenth century was done by lone explorers of whom Austen Henry Layard was the English prototype.

C

Layard in Babylonia

AUSTEN HENRY LAYARD, like Claudius James Rich, Sir Robert Ker Porter, and many other young English gentlemen of the period, began his career as a soldier of fortune, with just enough funds to get him to exotic places. He began his wanderings, in fact, by resigning from his uncle's solicitor's office in London and taking to the road—the road which eventually led overland to India. His route and manner of travelling were much the same as those followed today by that stream of young people in search of adventure beyond the confines of Western convention. But in the mid-nineteenth century the rewards, like the hazards, were greater. Layard was lucky. When his money ran out in Turkey he was able to persuade Sir Stratford Canning, the British ambassador in Constantinople, to employ him on various secret missions—which meant in those days wandering about disguised as a native or a pilgrim and picking up bits of gossip which helped the envoys write impressive reports to the Foreign Office in London. Spying in the modern sense had not been invented. An agent like Layard had no aids other than his knowledge of the local language and his good constitution. And, of course, military secrets were relatively unimportant. Intrigue, on the other hand, made life in the Orient both exciting and dangerous, as the following episode shows. Layard recounts it in his autobiography, the place being Constantinople, the year 1843, and Layard twenty-six years old.

He says that he was being rowed on the Bosphorus in a Turkish caique with another young diplomat called Alison when they saw some ladies in bright-coloured cloaks and heavy veils getting into an eight-oared barge moored at one of the imperial quays. Layard and Alison stopped to watch them, and they were, of course, seen by the ladies, one of whom deliberately lowered her veil to show a countenance which Layard describes as 'surpassingly lovely'. Moreover, this beautiful lady made a sign to the young Englishmen to follow her. This their boatman refused to do, particularly as a corpse suddenly bobbed up out of the water, in the boatman's opinion an ominous warning of the danger they were risking. So Layard was not able to speak on that occasion to the mysterious lady, who, however, had her own thoughts on the matter. And the following morning a heavily veiled woman called at Alison's house and though refusing to give her mistress's name, informed the two diplomats of where the 'surpassingly lovely' lady lived. They were invited to call on her in secret. The adventure, they well knew, was not without danger, but the memory of the lady's beauty was enough to persuade them to accept the invitation, so off they went to the 'Sacred Quarter' where the lady lived, down the street described to them, across a garden, and into a large mirrored room where their hostess reclined on a divan, unveiled. 'We had not been deceived by the glimpse she allowed us to see of her face,' says Layard, 'for she was young, extremely beautiful with large almond-shaped eyes, delicate and regular features, and a clear brilliant complexion. She was obviously of mixed Turkish and Circassian blood. She was surrounded by a whole bevy of pretty girls.'

Invited to sit down, the two Englishmen were given coffee and sweetmeats by the girls, while they answered a hundred questions put to them by their hostess whose name they still did not know. But neither Layard nor Alison had come to this harem to talk politics, and as the latter spoke excellent Turkish and could even tell jokes in that language, the party went with a swing, especially when the girls agreed to dance, which they did in formal fashion for a time until a real old romp started as the young ladies pelted each other with sweets and tumbled about the floor, shouting and laughing and encouraged by their mistress.

The Englishmen left after two hours of this delightful interview and promised to come again. But they never did. Calling on an old Italian woman who organised all the romantic liaisons of Constantinople, they learnt that their beautiful hostess was none other than the Sultan's youngest sister and that to visit such a royal lady secretly was to risk their lives. 'We therefore determined not to repeat our visit to our lovely friend,' writes Layard, 'despite her reproaches.'

The story has a strange ending, for it seems that the princess refused to submit to the strict Moslem code, even leaving off the yashmak in public and exhorting Moslem women to claim their rights as human beings. Apparently her rebellion was soon crushed, and Layard adds this sad valediction to the beautiful almond-eyed girl who enticed him to her house: *She disappeared from the scene, her vagaries were soon forgotten, and I do not know what became of her.*

In any case, there were to be no more romantic adventures for Layard, who had, in the meantime, been commissioned by Sir Stratford Canning to begin excavations at the site of Nineveh, in competition with the French consul at Mosul in Iraq, Paul Émil Botta, who had been digging away in the great mound of Khorsabad and had finally hit upon a treasure more valuable than gold. In short, Botta had stumbled upon the palace of one of the Assyrian kings, and his collection of sculptures and reliefs, including the great winged bulls, was already on its way to Paris. The French were now able to announce to the world that one of their agents had discovered Nineveh and the proof was soon to be on display in the Louvre. The work of the British pioneers was now to all intents and purposes forgotten, for explorers like Claudius Rich and Sir Robert Ker Porter had sent back nothing but descriptions and plans of the ruins of Mesopotamia: Paul Émil Botta had produced sculptures of bearded kings and mythological animals unlike anything that had been seen before. He had made the Nineveh and Babylon of the Bible a reality, and his findings in Europe of the mid-nineteenth century caused as much excitement among the general public as the moon-dust brought back by the astronauts was to produce 130 years later.

Yet by modern standards and methods of archaeology Paul Émil Botta's discoveries could only be categorised as the chance finds of an amateur antiquarian. To begin with, this Italian-born diplomat was not a trained excavator at all, but a physician. Appointed by the French Government to handle their consular affairs in Egypt, Botta dabbled in oriental languages, Egyptian antiquities, and the natural sciences. Before he was sent as consul to Mosul on the Upper Tigris he had wandered over many Arabian countries, even into the unknown regions of Yemen and

Saudi Arabia where he was looking for the capital of the Queen of Sheba. Like his British contemporary Henry Layard, he had the constitution to withstand the hazards of the Mesopotamian climate and the endemic diseases of the region—typhoid, cholera, dysentery, and the rest of it—diseases which weakened or killed thousands of Europeans who lived or travelled in the Middle East. Both Botta and Layard dosed themselves liberally with laudanum, the characteristic opiate of the nineteenth century.

Since Botta was excavating at Khorsabad (Dur-Sharrukin) north of Nineveh, Layard chose as his site Nimrud, twenty-two miles to the south of Mosul. Layard's difficulty was that the Turkish Pasha of the province was hostile; and although utterly indifferent to archaeology, this official was continuously informed by his spies as to what the Europeans were up to, where they were digging, what they were looking for, and what they found. Layard, therefore, decided not to inform the Pasha of his true intentions, but gave it out that he was wild boar-hunting. And so, bypassing the officials in Mosul, Layard floated off on a raft down the Tigris until he came to the mound known as Nimrud. He describes for us in his lively manner some of the compensations as well as the hardships of his adventure:

> I know of no more enchanting and enjoyable mode of travelling than that of floating leisurely down the Tigris on a raft, landing ever and anon to examine some ruin of the Assyrian or early Arabian time, to shoot game, which abounds in endless variety on its banks, or to cook our daily food. It is a perfect condition of gentle idleness and repose, especially in the Spring. The weather was delightful—the days not too hot, the nights balmy and still. We were warned that there were Arabs on the banks who would rob us and plunder us of our raft if we ventured to land, or would fire upon us if we refused to approach the shore. But we saw none of them. . . . But our raftsmen would not stop during the night for fear of marauders and thieves, and, as they averred, of lions who are occasionally, but very rarely, found so far north on the banks of the Tigris.

The landscape which Layard saw in 1845 obviously did not differ greatly from what the English merchant John Eldred had seen 300 years before, or, for that matter, what the traveller can see today if he takes a native ferry across the Tigris south of

Mosul. The difference, of course, is the amount and variety of wild life, which Eldred describes as exceedingly abundant and including 'wilde asses all white, Roebucks, wolfes, leopards, foxes, and many hares'. None of these animals would be seen between Mosul and Baghdad today, and even out in the desert, beyond the two great waterways, the gazelle, which were able to survive before the introduction into Iraq of the motor-car, have been finished off by sportsmen mounted on Land Rovers and armed with tommy-guns. The nineteenth-century hunters wiped out the little Mesopotamian lions which were not much larger than a big dog, enabling the Assyrian monarchs in their day to kill them at close range. As the Assyrian king Tiglath-pileser I tells us in an inscription: 'I killed 120 lions on foot with great courage, and I brought down 800 lions with my javelin from my chariot.'

But there is a still more significant change in the landscape of Iraq, a change as striking as the contrast between a lush, fertile countryside and an empty desert. The former was the condition of Mesopotamia in the Sumer-Babylonian period; the latter that of the Iraq Layard and his fellow-excavators knew. Babylonia, in short, was once the richest granary in the world; and this agricultural plenty was the result not simply of the rich alluvial soil laid down every year by the Tigris and Euphrates during the floods, but also of a highly sophisticated system of irrigation based on a network of canals, dams, and waterways. In addition, the land was tended with the love as well as the unremitting toil of the ancient farmers, because fat animals and a full barn meant plenty and prosperity for them. Symbolic of the importance of agriculture in Babylonia was the proud boast of the kings that they served their god and their people by keeping the canals in good repair.

With the fall of Babylon in 538 B.C., the complex irrigation system seems to have become neglected and by the seventh century A.D., when the conquering armies of Islam overran the region, the canals fell into decay, and the twin rivers, the Tigris on the east and the Euphrates on the west, periodically changed their courses altogether and flooded vast areas of the countryside at the time of the spring sowing. The end result of the collapse of the canal system, the divagation of the rivers, and depopulation, was that Mesopotamia, by the end of the nineteenth century, was one of the most dreary landscapes in the world, as infertile, but by no means as beautiful, as a true desert.

And just as the devastating annual floods of the Tigris and Euphrates urgently needed to be controlled by an irrigation system in order to make life reasonably secure both for the cultivation of the land and the organisation of social life, so the surrounding countryside had to be made safe from attacks by nomads and raids by bandits. It was safe during Nebuchadnezzar's time, but it wasn't when the early excavators were digging into the mounds which marked the sites of the ancient cities. The region had by then become the habitat of a number of impoverished tribesmen whose economy was dependent solely on their flocks and herds and on what they could exact from occasional caravans in the form of tribute. All the men of these tribes were armed with ancient muskets and swords, and since they were constantly feuding among themselves, it was extremely difficult for the excavators to know which of the sheiks to deal with over the business of hiring workmen and of receiving 'protection'. And over and above the dangers and difficulties of living in a lawless country, the field-workers were harried and harassed by a corrupt Turkish officialdom. We shall see in Chapter 4 how the American archaeologist Edgar J. Banks had to contend with conditions which entitle him to be ranked high among nineteenth-century explorers, along with his European colleagues Rich, Botta, Layard, Rawlinson, and the other early Assyriologists. We shall also see from the writings of these pioneers how desolate the Babylonian landscape had become since the decline and fall of the old empires. In fact, the dreariness of their surroundings may account for a certain melancholy amounting almost to desperation which occasionally underlies their narration of the constant trials and tribulations to which they were subjected. To begin with, they were very much alone, as the custom was to have just one man supervising an archaeological expedition, with the result that he often found himself isolated in some remote district with no company other than a hundred or so Arab workmen. Solitude was bearable during the day when the search was on and, with luck, the marvellous statues and cylinders and relics of a lost civilisation were unearthed. And in the evening, when the excavator sat outside his tent and watched the sun set over the mysterious Mesopotamian plains, he may at least have experienced a sense of mystic communion with the people whose records were spread out on the table before him. But how lonely the nights must have been, with the constant menace of bandits or of dissatisfied workmen, each armed with a musket or dagger!

Moreover, there were no marble columns or stone arches, as with Greek and Roman ruins, to show where a thriving community had once existed; there were only these vast mounds, sometimes with broken brick towers, to mark the site of cities with names like Kish, Nineveh, Babylon, Ur, Larsa, and Borsippa. These mounds stand up in the flat plains not unlike enormous rubbish tips taken from a builder's yard, and during the flood season, when both the Tigris and the Euphrates overflow their banks, the mounds are surrounded by lakes of water. So the landscape itself is inclined to be depressing, like those deserts which have neither the beauty of sand-dunes nor the greenery of oases to relieve them. The few people, too, who managed to survive in this abandoned country during the mid-nineteenth century were impoverished nomads from whom the excavators had to fashion some sort of a labour force to undertake the excavations, while, at the same time, serving as a private army to fight off raids from a rival tribe. During the 1889 excavations at Nippur by the Reverend John P. Peters, the first American to dig in Mesopotamia, two of the regional tribes laid claims to the mounds where he had set up his headquarters and each insisted on furnishing workmen to the exclusion of the other. The Rev. Peters attempted to pacify them, with little success; and it soon became obvious to this New York clergyman that further work might be impossible when on a night in April 1889 the Arabs made a frontal assault on his camp, burnt his tents and huts to the ground, robbed him of his firearms, money, horses, and food, and then disappeared into the desert.[1] Practically every single Mesopotamian excavator during the nineteenth century had a similar experience of treachery or violence at the hands of the vagrant tribes.

In addition to the dangers from the nomads, all of the fieldworkers fell gravely ill at one time or another, and a number of them died, including Claudius Rich, Carl Bellino, and Layard's artist, T. S. Bell. Yet despite the summer heat which reached over 120° Fahrenheit in the shade at Babylon in 1911, some excavators continued their work right through the hottest months of the year. The winter months could not have been much more comfortable, since Iraq from November to March is cold and damp, while in March the dust storms come sweeping across the eroded land from the Arabian Desert. The winds also often bring with them swarms of locusts.

It is scarcely surprising that Layard was to discover that his life as an excavator was not always as idyllic as his journey down the Tigris: on the contrary, it was full of dangers, hardships, and countless irritations. A man had to be young, brave, tough, and resourceful to stand it. He needed, in addition, enormous enthusiasm and ambition. Henry Layard had all these qualities, together with one other—a sense of fun which must have made him a wonderful companion, as Mr Alison of the British Embassy in Constantinople had found when the two of them called surreptitiously on the Sultan's sister. And so we find that Layard, after he had discovered the great winged and human-headed lions of Nimrud, although harassed by the suspicious Turkish authorities, could still 'see the funny side of it'; for he writes that when the enormous statues had been uncovered and at once identified by the natives as portraits of Nimrud himself, the Pasha at Mosul was not able to make up his mind as to whether Nimrud was a true prophet or a detested infidel; for, if the former, further excavations would be declared contrary to the laws of the Koran; and, if the latter, the statues would have to be destroyed *in situ*. Fortunately for Layard and for the British Museum which was eventually to acquire these magnificent Assyrian artefacts, the Pasha, the Moslem priests, and the councillors spent weeks trying to decide this question of Nimrud's status. And while they deliberated, Layard used to spend hours contemplating his statues, for he knew that he had found one of the greatest treasures of antiquity in a perfect state of preservation. It is no wonder that he sat gazing in the evening light at the splendid bearded heads conjoined to the beautifully carved bodies of winged lions, the whole covered with immaculate cuneiform inscriptions on every inch of free space along the twelve-foot torsos. The urgent problem now was to get his pair of winged lions back to Britain.

It was a problem that would have seemed insuperable to a lesser man. There were no roads, no carts large enough to carry stone statues weighing about forty tons, and bandits roamed the desert between Baghdad and Basra, the nearest port. In fact, there was only one possible route to the sea and Europe and that was by the two rivers, the Tigris and the Euphrates, the immemorial highways of the Middle East. But the only suitable boats available on these rivers were rafts made buoyant by inflated goat skins, almost exactly the same type of craft which Herodotus had described 2000 years previously; and on to these scarcely manageable ferries the priceless treasures of the excavators were loaded to go floating crazily downstream, frequently running aground or breaking up in the rapids. Strenuous efforts were made by the British to replace these primitive river craft with modern ships, and there did exist a steamship on the Tigris called the *Nitocris* which tried to get upstream to Nimrud, but was stopped by the rapids fifty miles above Baghdad. This left the steamer another fifty miles to go before reaching Layard and his winged lions. The excavator himself, in the meantime, had the problem of moving his lions from the mound of Nimrud to the banks of the Tigris with nothing but a cart, a small crane, and a few blocks. In this he was much better equipped than his colleague Botta, farther up river at Khorsabad, for Botta had nothing at all in the way of tackle to lift and transport his huge bulls found in the palace of Sargon. The Franco-Italian excavator had had to improvise and eventually to build a waggon with enormous wooden wheels and home-made iron axles which needed 500–600 men to pull it; and even 600 were not enough at times to drag the waggon out of the mud, and one of Botta's bulls had to be left behind.

Layard was more fortunate. He tells how he accomplished the feat of moving his lions down to the Tigris in time for the spring floods. First, even when the great beasts had been successfully loaded on to their carts, the hundreds of men hired to pull them could not budge the load more than a few feet at a time. Whenever the carts stuck, says Layard, some innocent bystander was invariably blamed. The artist Mr Cooper, who was making drawings of the operation (they can still be seen adjacent to the statues in the Assyrian Room of the British Museum), was the first one to be accused of bringing the porters bad luck. His was the evil eye which sapped the men of their strength. Layard advised Mr Cooper to make himself scarce. Next the Arabs wanted an English lady who had come to see the fun to sit on the lion to improve the omens. Her presence enabled the carts to progress a little further. And so:

The wheels rolled heavily along, but were soon clogged once more in the yielding soil. Another evil eye surely lurked among the workmen or the bystanders. Search was quickly made, and one having been detected on whom this curse alighted, he was ignominiously driven away with shouts and execrations. This impediment having been removed, the cart drew nearer to the village, but soon came again to a standstill. All the Sheiks were now summarily degraded from their rank and honors, and a weak ragged boy having been dressed up in tawdry kerchiefs and invested with a cloak was pronounced to be the only fit chief for such puny men. The cart moved forwards until the ropes gave way under the new excitement caused by this reflection upon the character of the Arabs. When that had subsided and the presence of the youthful Sheik no longer encouraged his subjects, he was as summarily deposed as he was elected, and a greybeard of ninety was raised to the dignity in his stead. He had his turn; then the most unpopular of the Sheiks were compelled to lie down on the ground that the groaning wheels might pass over them, like the car of Juggernaut over its votaries. With yells, shrieks, and wild antics, the cart was drawn within a few inches of the prostrate men. As a last resource, I seized a rope myself and with shouts of defiance between the different tribes and amidst the deafening *tahlel* [ululation] of the women, the lion was at length fairly brought to the water's edge.[2]

We can see why Layard's account of his excavations called *Nineveh and its Remains* sold nearly 8000 copies on publication. In fact, the book became a best-seller throughout the Victorian period, and Layard was able to write to an acquaintance 'a new edition is in the press, and Murray [the publishers] predict a continual steady demand, which will place it side by side with Mrs Rundell's *Cookery*'. Despite the author's self-depreciation, *Nineveh* remains a classic of archaeological literature. Layard, the almost penniless hitch-hiker of twenty-two, had found fame and fortune at forty and no man had deserved them more. For with no training or experience in archaeology, and no knowledge of Assyriology, alone and unaided, with no tools other than spades and pickaxes, he had undertaken the excavation of a lost city under conditions of great hardship and constant danger, not only digging, and supervising his native workmen through the fearful summers of Iraq, but meticulously recording, accurately describing, and

beautifully drawing his immense number of finds. And he did all
this in the kind of dream world he had created for himself, as he
makes clear in his letters home to his mother:

> The life I am now leading is so monotonous that I really know
> not what to write to you. Fancy me in a mud hut in the centre
> of a deserted village, for my neighbours have wisely taken to
> their tents. I have no companions in misfortune and am rapidly
> losing the little I once knew of the English language. . . . I live
> among my ruins and dream of little else. For the moment my
> hopes, fears, and joys centre on them. . . .

But with the publication of *Nineveh*, Layard's hopes were suddenly realised and his fears dispelled, for he now found himself
famous and so popular with the general public that pressure was
exerted on the Treasury to make a grant of £3000 for further excavations in Mesopotamia. The British Museum allocated these
funds to Layard, who concentrated on the palaces of Sennacherib
and Ashurbanipal for the next year, after which he returned to
England, never to excavate again. In brief, Layard, now one of the
most renowned Assyriologists in the world, suddenly, at the age
of forty-four, abandoned his career as an archaeologist and entered politics. The changeover is significant in that it shows how
truly independent were the great excavators of the mid-nineteenth
century; but, even so, Layard's decision to run as a member of
Parliament for the borough of Aylesbury seems a rather tame
alternative to life on the banks of the Tigris. Not surprisingly,
this bold adventurer was as successful at politics and diplomacy
as he had been at archaeology and quickly achieved distinction in
his new career with his appointment first as a member of the Privy
Council in Gladstone's administration of 1868; then as British
minister at Madrid in 1869; and finally as ambassador to Turkey
in 1877. In 1880 he again made a radical change in his life, resigning from the foreign service and retiring to Venice where the
study of art in general and of Italian painting in particular occupied his remaining years. It is strange to see under his name in the
library catalogues works as diverse in subject and contents as
Discoveries in the Ruins of Nineveh and Babylon; *A Handbook of Rome*;
The Danish Question; and *The Madonna and Saints: in the Church of
S. Maria Nuova at Gubbio*.

Layard, together with Botta and Place, the French excavators, the Rassam brothers, Christian and Hormuzd, and Henry Rawlinson represents in the field of Assyriology the last and greatest of the explorer-archaeologists of the nineteenth century. They differed radically in their methods from the modern specialists, the obvious difference being that Layard and his contemporaries were really inspired amateurs while the new professionals hold no brief for 'inspiration'. The principal tool of the former was the spade; of the latter the trowel. And the nineteenth-century finds and publications were meant for the enlightenment and entertainment of the general public; those of our own times for the information of fellow-specialists. A strong hint of the professional archaeologists' disapproval of their predecessors is seen in the comments of Wallis Budge and Professor L. W. King, both of the British Museum's Department of Oriental Antiquities. The former has this to say of Layard:[3]

He was a man of tremendous energy, but he was neither a scholar nor an Assyriologist; and most of the information of a linguistic, historical, or learned character found in his books was supplied to him by Birch, Vaux, and Ellis of the British Museum, and by Rawlinson. The importance of the greatest treasure which he found at Kunyunjik, i.e., the inscribed baked tablets of the library of Nineveh, was not recognized until it reached England. Birch told me that Layard thought that the writing was a species of ornament and hardly deemed them worth the carriage to England. They were shovelled without any packing into old digging baskets which were tied up and put on rafts, and in this way they arrived with the larger objects at Basra where they were shipped to England. They suffered more from their voyage from Mosul to London than from the fury of the Medes when they sacked and burned Nineveh.*

Professor L. W. King was even more censorious and stated in the biography of Layard written for the *Dictionary of National Biography* that the famous excavator of Nineveh 'was without the true archaeologist's feeling', a curious and rather sour assessment of this early Assyriologist's achievements, since Layard surely had the feeling, if not the training, modern techniques, and sophisti-

---

* Wallis Budge's statements, so damaging to Layard's reputation, are dismissed as 'a pack of lies' by many Assyriologists today.

cated equipment for this work. Moreover, it cannot be denied that
what pioneers like Botta, Layard, and their colleagues had really
done was to rediscover Babylonia. The exploration in depth, the
detailed surveying, and the meticulous mapping of this lost empire
were still to come, to be undertaken by less spectacular explorers,
both archaeologists in the field and scholars in the libraries,
though few of their discoveries were to make newspaper head-
lines.

But when all is said and done, the fact remains that what Layard
had accomplished was to popularise not only Assyriology but
archaeology as well, and this even before Troy had been found by
Schliemann. For prior to the English excavator's discoveries digging up the past had been regarded as the rather eccentric pastime
of country parsons. In the seventeenth and eighteenth centuries,
for instance, British antiquaries were more interested in the Druids
and what they thought were druidical temples than they were in
the Romans and Roman remains. They were convinced that all
history, in so far as it interested the average educated man, had
been *recorded*, either in the Bible or by the Greek and Roman
historians, so that there seemed to be no point in digging in the
ground to know what happened in the past. Indeed, the excitement that Layard's finds at Nimrud caused was largely due to the
belief that they were positive, factual proof of the veracity of the
Bible concerning which doubts were beginning to be entertained.
Similarly, several decades later Schliemann's discovery of Troy
and Mycenae confirmed the historicity of the Iliad. It can, therefore, be said without fear of contradiction that men like Layard
and Schliemann changed the whole course of historical scholarship, even though they made no claims to scholarship themselves.

4

The First American Assyriologists

IT WAS INEVITABLE THAT the sensational finds of the first excavations in Mesopotamia were to make nearly all the subsequent digs in less renowned cities and sites something of an anticlimax, at least as far as the general public was concerned. People now expected an expedition to yield artefacts as prodigious as the winged lions, man-headed bulls, and great battle friezes dug out of the Assyrian palaces by Botta and Layard. The emphasis, in brief, was on size and rarity; interest waned as the nineteenth century drew to a close and the treasures brought from the dust of Mesopotamia became less spectacular. It was time for the amateur treasure-hunters to vacate the field to the professional archaeologists.

Before the modern 'scientific' school arrived on the scene, however, there was a period of transition during which orientalists, with more scholarship than the first excavators, though not, perhaps, a great deal more archaeological skill, began work on a number of new sites. German and American excavators now appeared for the first time in the field; the French-British monopoly in Assyria and Babylonia was ended. For up to the last decade of the nineteenth century all the actual field-workers had been either French or British (or agents of one or the other), and all the treasures they unearthed were the property of their national museums, the Louvre and the British Museum. It was only natural that the other nations should be envious, the Germans in particular, since their philologists had contributed so much to the decipherment of the Assyro-Babylonian language. Yet the Germans had scant share of either the spoils of the lost cities or of the prestige that rare museum exhibits could bring, simply because the British and

French had been able to exert enough influence on the Sublime
Porte virtually to keep them out of Mesopotamia.

The Germans finally got into the field in the 1890s, and when
they did so it was with the full support of the emperor, the government, and the universities. They immediately proved themselves
to be the most efficient and scientific of excavators, and they
changed the whole course of Middle Eastern archaeology. Their
great work was, of course, the Koldewey excavations at Babylon
between 1899 and 1917 which is discussed in a later chapter.

The other nation which looked longingly towards the Babylonian plains was the United States, particularly in view of the
religious significance that the discovery of cities and sites mentioned in the Old Testament had for the Bible-reading public. The
Americans hitherto had been at a considerable disadvantage in
the field, since they were geographically a long way away from
the Euphrates and Tigris and, most important, had neither the
orientalists nor the archaeologists to undertake the necessary
field-work. In fact, they did not enter the arena at all until 1889
when the Babylonian Exploration Fund of Philadelphia sent out
an expedition to Nippur under the directorship of the Rev. Dr
John P. Peters, a clergyman who had studied Semitic languages
at the University of Berlin and had persuaded a rich New York
spinster (reputed to be the wealthiest woman in America) to
finance the dig. Apart from his knowledge of Hebrew and the
Bible, the Rev. Peters had no special qualifications for the work,
his interests lying more with the internal affairs of the Protestant
Episcopal Church on the one hand and the politics of New York
City on the other: hence the subject-matter and title of his numerous publications—e.g. *The Annals of St Michael's* and *Labor and
Capital. The Dictionary of American Biography* says of him 'he was
quiet in manner, but displayed originality and determination in
the way in which he surmounted obstacles, both in his civic work
and in his enterprises as an explorer'.

Originality and determination in surmounting obstacles sums
up quite neatly the enterprises of all the early explorers in Mesopotamia, including those of the Americans, the most venturesome
of whom was Dr Edgar J. Banks, a member of the small group of
American scholars, most of them graduates of Harvard or Yale,
who went to Germany in the 1890s to study under the orientalist
Friedrich Delitzsch. Returning to the States in 1897, Banks saw

the practical as well as the scholarly advantages of being among the pioneer excavators of Babylonia and shrewdly chose as his site Mukayyar, the Arab name for the mound covering Ur of the Chaldees, the reputed birthplace of Abraham. The young scholar made it known that his project 'seemed to promise, at least to the Biblical archaeologist, results of unusual interest'. In short, he was well aware that the Bible was an excellent financial collateral for a non-profitable venture like archaeology, enabling him to organise an expedition to Ur and to raise $12,000 (worth five times that amount today), thanks to wealthy donors like John D. Rockefeller, who felt, rightly, that such a project could contribute to proving the historicity of Holy Writ.

But even with these sizeable funds (Layard was given $150 in 1846 to excavate Nimrud), Banks never did realise his ambition to excavate Ur and, in fact, was unable to put as much as a single spade into the Mesopotamian soil *for nearly three years*, during which time he waited in Constantinople attempting to get the necessary firman, or royal decree, permitting him to start his work. His account of his trials and tribulations is one of the most extraordinary and entertaining documents of archaeological literature.[1]

It presents him to us as an eager young American who had persuaded President McKinley to appoint him consul to Baghdad and who, under the aegis of diplomatic privilege, anticipated being allowed to visit the ruins of Babylon and to dig into the mounds of the ancient cities. But what Banks did not know or understand were the workings of a system so devious and so corrupt that it defied description. He had no way of knowing, for instance, that favours were not granted and permits not acquired in the Ottoman territories in the manner that they were in Washington D.C., and his bewilderment was great when he discovered that he was not only forbidden from excavating but even from visiting the historic sites. In fact, far from getting permission to dig at Ur within two weeks of his arrival, as he had been led to expect, he was still waiting for his firman to dig anywhere at all in Mesopotamia three years later.

He endured his tribulations with good humour and real fortitude, for he had gone to Baghdad with great expectations as well as the blessing of influential or wealthy compatriots like President W. R. Harper of the University of Chicago, Bishop Potter, Isidor Straus, and George Foster Peabody, who served as treasurer of

D

the Ur Expedition Fund. So sanguine were his sponsors that before he left the U.S. Banks was given a farewell dinner at which the place cards were written 'in the language of Nebuchadnezzar'; the bread was in the shape of Babylonian bricks; the great tray of ice-cream was the colour of the desert sand, with ice-camels marching across it; and the cake was a model of the Tower of Babel concealed within which were gifts ('antiquities fresh from Tiffany's') for each of the guests. Poor Banks was mortified when the assembled company raised their glasses to the success of the expedition and he discovered that the waiter had omitted to put a glass at his place. 'Did it portend failure?' he asks. It did.

However, Banks arrived in Constantinople on January 15th, 1900, fully expecting to be out in the field within a week or two. The application for the necessary firman had been made six months previously by President Harper in July of 1899. It had, of course, been pigeon-holed in the archives of the Ministry of Public Instruction ever since and, for all one knows, is still somewhere in the Turkish archives. In the meantime, Banks, with the help of the embassy officials, began the rounds of the various ministries, wining and dining numerous officials, and even learning Turkish so that he could appeal to them personally. They were all very polite and encouraging; and absolutely nothing happened. The American was, in fact, being given the treatment traditionally meted out to rich but unwanted foreigners. And so ten months after his arrival in Constantinople, almost every day of which he spent at one or the other of the ministries, Banks was finally informed that he would not be permitted to excavate at Mukayyar (Ur) because the mound was private property; then, when it was proved to be public property, he was denied permission on the grounds that the region was unsafe due to local bandits.

Banks accepted his defeat after almost a year's work with good grace and at once applied for a firman to excavate at Birs Nimrud, the site of the Tower of Babel, only to learn that he was too late, as this concession had been given to Dr Koldewey and the German expedition already excavating at nearby Babylon. Banks did not delay a moment: the day after learning about Birs he applied for permission to dig at Tell Ibrahim, the Biblical Cutha. The progress of this application was satisfactory for a time, especially after the American agreed to purchase the mound and present it to the Constantinople Museum on the termination of his work; but after several months' delay it was discovered that the Moslem prophet, Abraham, had one of his various tombs on top of the mound and that such a holy place could not, of course, be touched. Banks attempted to overcome these and similar objections by digging still deeper into his expedition funds to provide what he calls 'the usually eloquent baksheesh' and behold! in the course of time a firman to excavate Tell Ibrahim was actually granted, an event which the would-be archaeologist says he could hardly believe. He would have done better not to have believed it at all, for a couple of weeks later he received another communication from the Sublime Porte to the effect that a regrettable mistake had been made and that the certificate delivered to him, Dr Edgar J. Banks, had been wrongly addressed and was meant for somebody else. The American refused to accept this explanation, so the Turkish officials patiently started the process all over again, emphasising the usual difficulties of private ownership, holy ground, and so forth.

Banks now had to give up Tell Ibrahim along with Birs Nimrud and Ur. He reports that the committee in America was 'thoroughly discouraged' and advised him to come home. He was unwilling to give up, declined to accept any further salary, obtained a teaching post at Robert College, the American school in Constantinople, and began all over again, applying for still another firman, this time to excavate at a site called Bismaya, an unknown ruin so far out in the desert that nobody had bothered even to run trial trenches through it. Two and a half years had gone by since he had arrived in Constantinople and at this critical moment in his career he received a cable from Philadelphia which read: 'Ur Committee disbanded, funds distributed, withdraw application.'

It must have seemed like the end of all hope to a man who had spent so much time and effort and all of his private means in trying to realise his ambition. But not to Dr Banks. The fact was that he had succumbed to the exotic atmosphere of Constantinople where he was now settled down as a professor at Robert College and an official of the American legation. 'Whoever had really lived in the Bosphorus', he writes, 'always longs to return, for in spite of the filth and constant dangers and the semi-barbarism, the Orient possesses an irresistible charm.' No wonder, when he tells us that he used to visit the 'genial Englishman' Mr Frank Calvert, who owned the land on which were the ruins of Homer's Troy and who 'dug up for our entertainment an ancient Trojan grave and presented us with its contents'. Those were certainly the days for amateur archaeologists and treasure-hunters.

But Dr Banks's luck was to change, perhaps due to the decision of the United States Government to employ in the Near East the gunboat diplomacy which had been so successful in North Africa. Thus when it was reported (erroneously) that the American vice-consul in Beirut, a Mr Megelsson, had been assassinated while driving along the main street in his carriage, the public back home (namely, the more jingoistic congressmen and newspapers) demanded immediate redress for the death of this official and a squadron of the U.S. fleet, led by the flagship *Brooklyn*, Admiral Colton, was ordered to take up battle stations in the eastern Mediterranean. Later it was discovered that Mr Megelsson's death had been greatly exaggerated, and Dr Banks in his account of the affair rightly points out that the situation was embarrassing for the Department of State, and especially for Admiral Colton on his arrival at Beirut, on which all the guns of his battleship were now trained. It was embarrassing, too, for the Turkish Government which had no desire to start a war with the United States. In a word, all the parties concerned were at something of a loss to know what to do next, except Mr Megelsson 'who was busily collecting for a scrap-book the newspaper accounts of his own assassination'. Washington, in no position to admit that it had been ready to start a war on the basis of a bazaar rumour, now issued a dignified statement justifying the presence of American naval units in the Eastern Mediterranean as a token of peace and goodwill. It was diplomacy at its apogee.

The Turkish Government took the hint, interpreting this declaration as meaning that Americans demanded their fair share of the Middle East market, along with the British and French, who had held an almost complete monopoly from the sixteenth century onwards. Banks was evidently one of the first to benefit from this new attitude of the Turks, for when they learnt that Mr John D. Rockefeller had given $100,000 to cover the cost of a ten-year project for Biblical archaeology in the Middle East, it was not long before the American professor obtained his firman to excavate at Bismaya, 'the lost city of Adab'.

Banks's troubles were not, of course, over. He still had to deal

with the Sublime Porte in organising his expedition; and as soon
as it was known that an American of incalculable wealth and considerable inexperience was looking for help, the officials and their
entourage proceeded to think up ways and means of relieving the
professor of this surfeit of dollars. The word quickly passed from
the ministries to the embassies, and so to the bazaars, that a young
American had an immense fortune at his disposal, which he intended to spend digging holes in the ground. Now everybody was
anxious to be of service, including the Russian consul, who
begged the archaeologist not to lure away his interpreter, one
Latinik, an orientalised Austrian or Frenchman, pleading that this
man was indispensable to the consulate. Banks immediately
offered Latinik much higher wages than the Russians could afford,
and thereby relieved the Czar's representative of an incompetent
rogue everybody in Baghdad avoided. This same Latinik now
undertook to hire most of the other servants needed for the expedition, among them his friend, an unemployed carpenter, who
was signed on as cook. He also ordered the expedition supplies,
including a large consignment of canned lobster which had been
lying around in a warehouse for over a year and which no one had
dared to eat.

And so with his retinue and provisions Professor Banks set off
for his Babylonian site deep in the desert, so worn out by this
time that he used to faint at the end of a day's ride, a weakness
which had to be hidden from the Arabs. When he finally reached
Bismaya he was obliged to admit that the ruins were far from
impressive and his early attempts at excavating with thirty untrained and physically weak Arab tribesmen must have been exceedingly disheartening. In fact, when they could not find water
they threatened to desert. It was only Banks's large funds which
enabled him to control the situation by buying a train of camels to
carry water in skins across the desert. And so on Christmas Day
1903 Professor Banks began his excavations.

His methods, as one would expect, were of the pickaxe-and-
shovel variety. Gangs of nine diggers under the supervision of a
headman were scattered over the mounds of Bismaya and encouraged by the promise of double pay to look for antiquities.
The results can be imagined. For instance, an unopened tomb in
perfect condition was found, containing a corpse and seven clay
pots of various sizes and shapes. The body was evidently that of a

woman. However, the examination of the tomb and its contents
was left to the next day. When Dr Banks returned to the site to
photograph his find the walls had completely collapsed and the
tomb was merely another heap of rubble which the workmen
shovelled aside. The excavator had no idea of the age of this and
the other graves he opened up. In other cases of finds which he
could not explain, he tells us that he 'could but accept the theory
of the workmen'. Ignorance of Sumerian chronology (not surprising in 1903) and the too zealous methods of the inspired
amateur led Banks into many false assumptions which are easily
forgiven a man of such courage, modesty, and dedication.

Banks spent two years excavating at Bismaya, and there was
scarcely a day during all that time that he was not harassed and
often positively endangered by the conditions obtaining in Mesopotamia at the beginning of this century. He accepted all his trials
and tribulations, as he had accepted his three years' wait for his
firman, with great patience and good humour, so he was deserved-
ly lucky in many of his finds, especially since the Bismayan
mounds were reported in the press to be nothing more than the
ruins of an early Arab settlement of no archaeological interest.
Bismaya, to the contrary, proved to be the site of one of the oldest
cities of Sumer, yielding statues, vases, thousands of clay tablets,
the foundations of palaces, temples, and private homes, and
enough artefacts to make it finally possible to write a chapter in
the history of a civilisation 5000 years old.

No doubt Banks's most spectacular find was the statue of a king
he calls Da-udu, which he describes, rather rashly, as 'the oldest
statue in the world'. The king's name was actually Esar and the
age of the statue some 5000 years, so it was certainly one of the
earliest of Sumerian artefacts and undoubtedly one of the most
fascinating. Let the archaeologist himself describe how he found
the king:

At nightfall Haidan Bey and the Om Bashi were called from the
camp, and with Ahmed, Shia, the foreman of the gang, and
Abbas, the real discoverer, we remained behind until the flames,
rising from the camp fires, invited the last of the men to supper;
then we climbed down into the trench. With the curved blades
of the Arab knives we carefully dug away the hard clay from
about the white stone; the body was nude to the waist; then we

worked down the pleated skirt to the ankles and the feet. We were disappointed to find the feet imperfect; the toes were missing, but at the base of the statue Ahmed pried loose a dirt-covered stone, and as he rubbed the dirt away a toe appeared. In a moment other toes were found, and finally the feet were complete. . . . Then almost frantically we searched for the missing head, but it was nowhere to be found. When it became so dark that we could search no longer, and despairing of finding the head, we wrapped the statue in a great *abba* to protect it from the chill night air, so Ahmed said, but rather to secrete it from the prying eyes of the Arabs, and carried it to camp. And that was no easy task for the statue represented a corpulent old king.

In the seclusion of my tent we placed the king down and gave him a scrub, and he sorely needed a bath, for he had not had one for about six thousand years. . . . All that night the headless king, patiently and with folded arms, stood at my bed-side as if to guard me.[2]

Banks's statue, for which a few days later he found the head, measured eighty-eight centimetres in height and was sculpted from white marble. It is a magnificent example of early Sumerian art, not 6000 years old, as the American archaeologist hoped and believed, but probably dating from 3000 B.C. More important than its precise age is the school of sculpture to which it belongs, and there is no mistaking this. The bald round head, the large eye-sockets, the square shoulders, the naked torso, the pleated skirt, and, above all, the piously clasped hands, make this figure almost the prototype of Sumerian sculpture. Banks worked long and hard to translate the inscription on the right upper shoulder and came to the conclusion that the king's name was Da-udu (Hebrew Dawid, English David). He translated the three lines as

ESAR (MACH)	(The temple of) Esar, or Emach
LUGAL	King
DA-UDU	David
LUGAL	King
UD-NUN-KI	(of) Ud-nun-ki (= Adab)

The correct translation is 'King Esar, the mighty, King of Ud-nun-ki'.

Encouraged by such a splendid find, Banks and his gangs of

workmen dug rapidly all over the Bismayan mounds, and the rewards were immense: other important finds were scores of broken vases made of alabaster, white and yellow stone, porphyry, and onyx; Babylonian lamps of various ages; objects of ivory, copper, and mother of pearl; several small statues of kings and gods; cylindrical seals; and 2500 clay tablets. The tablets were disappointing from the literary point of view, for the general public, having by now been given the Babylonian Story of the Flood, the Epic of Gilgamesh, and some colourful historical inscriptions from the library of Ashurbanipal, were waiting for something equally sensational; and we must also remember that the Bismaya expedition was financed by John D. Rockefeller with the object of adding to Biblical, not Sumerian, studies. Banks's tablets, however, were mostly business contracts: there were no hymns, psalms, poems, or stories.

His explanation of this absence of literary texts is ingenious. He had found various shafts leading down to an ancient library and decided that these shafts were made by Assyrian excavators at the behest of Ashurbanipal, who, we know, sent out orders to all his agents throughout the land to collect the books of the ruined cities of Sumer. Adab by this time (640 B.C.) was already a sand-covered mound, the city beneath it having been devastated and depopulated for almost a thousand years. The Assyrian king's book-collectors, therefore, had to tunnel down into the lost library, where they undoubtedly took all the books of any value and threw the uninteresting tablets higgledy-piggledy on to the floor, which was where and how Dr Banks found them two and a half thousand years later. The objection to this theory, however, is how did the book-collectors know where to find the buried library?

Banks withdrew to Baghdad for the intolerably hot summer months when the temperature in the shade often rose to 115° Fahrenheit. He and his wife, he tells us, used to wander about the bazaars during the morning when the archaeologist kept his eyes open for antiquities of which there were hundreds for sale, some genuine, and many more false. The reproduction of pseudo-Assyrian artefacts was already a thriving industry in the alleys of Baghdad, and the merchants were always eager to improve the quality of their wares, so that when Banks spotted a particularly well-sculpted fake of an Assyrian king which even had faint traces of an inscription on the pedestal he was asked by the Persian craftsman of this statuette how one could improve one's work; for, said the Persian, though a number of his reproductions were now on exhibit in European museums, there was always something new to learn, especially from experts like archaeologists.

In the meantime, cholera was raging in Baghdad, with scores of people dying from the disease every day. Banks was now anxious to get his wife out of Iraq and back to the United States. Obviously Bismaya was no place for a woman. It was lonely, uncomfortable, and dangerous. In fact, when the archaeologist returned to the site in September 1905 he found that his camp had been rifled and looted and his little museum robbed of its most treasured exhibits, including the Sumerian statue of King Esar. The theft of this now-celebrated artefact was a heavy blow to a man who had worked so hard to obtain the sort of prize so coveted by archaeologists, especially as Banks was powerless to do anything about it. He was, in fact, accused of intending to defraud the government of a national treasure.

At all events, the statue was gone, and Banks never saw it again or even knew where it went—fortunately not to a private dealer, but eventually to the museum in Baghdad where it can be seen today. But that was not the end of the affair for the American, who, in consequence of the robbery, was forbidden all further excavations and obliged to pay off his workmen and to start back once again to Baghdad. It was a journey that few modern travellers would care to undertake, with all the waterholes dried up and contaminated by decaying fish, and what water there was shared by buffaloes and goats who lay or stood in the pools, or by men bathing naked and women filling their jars—all this with an epidemic of cholera in the district.

Banks eventually arrived back safely in Baghdad where the Turkish authorities refused to let him continue with his excavations at Bismaya: he was formally accused of being personally implicated in the disappearance of the Sumerian statue. An assistant who had just been sent out from Chicago to help in the expedition's work was now despatched to the site in order to keep the American option to excavate open. But this decision proved disastrous, for within six weeks of his arrival Mr V. F. Persons, the replacement, either had a complete nervous breakdown or (according to his own story) was given poisoned coffee to drink. In any case, Persons lay for several weeks on his bed, only half-conscious, his memory gone. Eventually he was brought back to Baghdad and shipped home to Chicago, a physical and mental wreck. Banks has this to say of him, and one can only read between the lines what he really thought of his new assistant:

> Mr Persons was an engineer, not an archaeologist or a linguist, and he was inexperienced in desert life and customs.[3]

It seems unbelievable that the Oriental Exploration Fund of the University of Chicago, which was now responsible for Banks's dig, should send out an engineer without any knowledge of even Arabic to work on a Babylonian excavation; but such was the case, indicating, perhaps, the attitude of the directors of the Fund towards the Bismaya project and its field-director. In line with this, Banks tells us that he received no communication whatsoever from Professor R. F. Harper, director of the Babylonian and Assyrian department of the Exploration Fund, for nine months after he, Banks, received the precious permit to begin work at Bismaya. His comment is: 'Monthly checks had been sent by the treasurer; one or two notes had come from President Harper [president of the University of Chicago and brother of Professor R. F. Harper], and surely I had not cause to complain of interference from home.'[4]

Can one hear a faint echo of the lonely American's real thoughts, 'and no cause to be grateful for encouragment either'?

All in all, Dr Banks's experiences in Mesopotamia were typical of those of all the nineteenth-century excavators: that is, loneliness, isolation in a lawless corner of the desert, continuous exposure to danger, disease, and irritations, lack of adequate equipment and even some necessities like dictionaries and textbooks, and, of course, insufficient funds. For despite John D. Rockefeller's munificent gift of $100,000, Banks was evidently severely hampered by the penny-pinching fashion in which the Exploration funds were doled out, as his letter attached to his *Fourteenth Report of Work in Progress* reveals:

> I cannot too strongly urge the necessity of more money immediately, for, apart from the extremely great success of the excavations, it is next to impossible to carry on the work with the sum now at my disposal. I have reduced the number of

watchmen to three and the soldiers to two for the purpose of cutting down my expenses, and for the same reason I have not purchased a house, which is a necessity. The workmen number about 120, and in case of an attack, which may occur at any day, it is not sufficient for protection. An increase of the workmen would decrease the dangers to which we are exposed. To prolong the work here after two years seems an unnecessary exposure of life and health, for there is no part of Mesopotamia more inhospitable than this. Personally I do not mind the dangers nor the fierce sandstorms, but I believe it is for the best interest of the University to complete the work here while we have the *irade* [i.e. the Turkish firman or permission to dig].[5]

A sad letter, though Banks did manage to survive the dangers and the fierce sandstorms, returning home to Chicago just in time, for he tells us that 'my health was leaving me'. Like Layard, however, whom he resembled in some respects (in his sense of humour and fun among other things), he regained his strength and lived to a ripe old age, dying in 1945, at seventy-nine. And again, like Layard, he left the field of Assyriology later in life and turned his attention to other more mundane matters. He became, in fact, first a director of a film company which made features and documentaries on 'sacred subjects', then president of an organisation called Seminole Films Co., Inc. Film work combined with travel, journalism, and the writing of popular books occupied him until he retired to Florida and joined the local Rotary Club where he was remembered for a time as a minor businessman and forgotten as one of the great pioneers of Assyriology.

The Decipherment of the Cuneiform Script

OF ALL THE ACHIEVEMENTS of the human mind, whether in the arts or the sciences, the decipherment of unknown languages ranks among the most masterly and the least recognised accomplishments of genius. To understand this for himself, the layman has only to examine for a moment an original inscription in any one of the ancient Mesopotamian languages—Sumerian, Babylonian, or Hittite. In the first place he can have no idea of the script, no clue as to whether it is alphabetical, syllabic, or pictographic. Secondly, it is impossible to know whether the text should be read from left to right, right to left, or from the top to the bottom of the columns. Where does one word begin or end? And, quite apart from these purely visual puzzles, the actual identification of the signs is as nothing compared with the problems of vocabulary and grammar.

So we see what the philologist is faced with in attempting to solve the mystery presented by an unknown language; and we see, too, why there are still a number of languages the key to which has eluded all the learning, skills, and years of effort of scores of specialists. The most notable example of such 'lost' languages is undoubtedly Etruscan, even though the alphabet in this case is perfectly straightforward and a few bi-lingual inscriptions give a hint of both vocabulary and grammar. And when it comes to pictographic languages like ancient Mayan the difficulties are much greater and even insuperable. The best the experts can do is to guess the meaning of the signs without being able to read a single sentence, assuming that we are dealing with a 'language' at all and not a series of mnemonics.

Naturally enough, the first travellers to the sites of the ancient

Babylonian and Persian empires could not make head or tail of the signs they saw cut into the stone pillars of the palace at Persepolis or lying about in the rubble of the Mesopotamian mounds. But the more educated of them did copy a few lines of the Persepolis inscriptions, while others sent home samples of Babylonian cylinder seals, clay tablets, and inscribed bricks. Yet the savants back in Europe could not at first agree as to whether the signs on these artefacts were letters or merely decorations; and even when the weight of evidence made it clear that they did represent a written language a controversy began as to whether they were derived from the Hebrew, Greek, Latin, Chinese, Egyptian, or even the Ogham script of Celtic Ireland. We can gauge the extent of the confusion in this description of the mysterious writings given by one Thomas Herbert, a secretary to Sir Dodmore Cotton, British ambassador to Persia in 1626. Herbert says of the cuneiform text he examined on the walls and lintels of the palace at Persepolis:

> Very faire and apparent to the eye, but so mysticall, so oddly framed, as no Hierogliphick, no other deep conceit can be more difficulty fancied, more adverse to the intellect. These consisting of Figures, obelisk, triangular, and pyramidall, yet in such Simmetry and order as cannot well be called barbarous.[1]

This Thomas Herbert, who was later to accompany Charles I as his attendant to the scaffold, was one of the first Europeans to visit Persepolis, to make a drawing of the ruins, and to copy an inscription in the cuneiform writing. Unfortunately for the learned men who set about studying this newly discovered script, the three lines which Herbert gives as an example of cuneiform were not taken from a single inscription, but two lines from one and the third from another. The actual characters, too, were not accurately reproduced, and this was true of the copies brought back by Italian and French travellers. And so one can imagine the confusion wrought by yet another bogus inscription, the so-called 'Tarku inscription' which was supposed to have been copied by Samuel Flower, an agent of the East India Company at a place called Tarku on the Caspian Sea. There never was any such inscription.[2] Samuel Flower, in short, had copied not an inscription, but twenty-three different isolated signs which he regarded as characteristic of the cuneiform script and each of which he separated by a full stop. Yet scholars tried for years to translate this hodge-podge of odd letters strung together without rhyme or reason, and several of them, including Eugene Burnouf and Adolf Holtzmann, both scholars of very great learning, claimed to have actually succeeded.

The confusion, muddle, and mistakes were, of course, inevitable, since neither the languages themselves nor the script in which they were written were identifiable. In fact, the Persepolitan inscriptions were actually written in three languages, a vital clue to decipherment which was at least glimpsed in the late eighteenth century by the two French scholars Jean Jacques Barthelemy and Joseph de Beauchamp. The great Danish explorer Carsten Niebuhr had also noted that the inscriptions on the window-frames of the palace of Darius at Persepolis, repeated eighteen times, were written in three different alphabets, but he failed to draw the all-important conclusion that the words, whatever the alphabets, were repetitions of the same text.

We can see, then, that until this fact was established and until the languages involved were identified, all attempts at translating the numerous written records coming out of the Middle East were largely an exercise in cryptography. And still the number of inscriptions available for study increased, until, with the discoveries of Botta and Layard, they ran into hundreds of thousands. In fact, 100,000 came from the library of Ashurbanipal's palace; another 50,000 were to emerge from the excavations at Sippar; many thousands more from Nippur; and so many from Lagash that the loss of 30,000 smuggled out by the natives and sold at the rate of twenty cents a basket load was hardly noticed. Tens of thousands of others still lie buried in the 2886 known *tulul,* or mounds, that conceal the ancient cities.

Obviously, the literature of a past civilisation is as important to our understanding of its people and their society as the monuments—perhaps even more important. And so the scholars who worked at the immensely difficult task of solving the mystery of the strange arrow-shaped characters were as essential to the science of Assyriology as the excavators, though it was the latter who received all the prestige, fame, and financial rewards. This can hardly surprise us since the study of the cuneiform inscriptions began as an exercise in cryptography and philology, neither of which sciences particularly interested the general public. And even when the first, or Persian, column of the great Behistun memorial of Darius was roughly translated by Professor Lassen of Bonn in 1845 this brilliant achievement was scarcely noticed by anybody other than scholars. The customary indifference of laymen to scholarship of this variety makes some specialists both chary and somewhat disparaging of those of their colleagues who receive too much public acclaim, for they remember that while a dilettante like Layard was growing rich and famous, a scholar like Edward Hincks, a pioneer of cuneiform decipherment, lived all his life in the seclusion of a rectory at Killyleagh, County Down, Ireland, his only reward for forty years of dedication to the decipherment of the lost Mesopotamian languages the Conyngham Medal of the Royal Irish Academy. It has been said of Hincks that 'he had the misfortune to be born an Irishman and to fill the obscure position of a country clergyman so that he was, no doubt, reconciled from the first to the inevitable sequence of disparagement and neglect'. The esteem in which he was held, even in learned circles, may be gathered from a single short paragraph allotted to him in the *Athenaeum* where he was permitted to explain one of the most far-reaching discoveries in the Assyro-Babylonian language. Yet in point of fact the contributions of Edward Hincks to our knowledge and understanding of Babylonian history are far more important than those of Layard. Why? Because the artefacts that the latter sent back from Nimrud actually told the learned world little that they did not already know. Herodotus had already described the magnitude of Babylon and its monuments and the Old Testament the power and glory of Nebuchadnezzar's empire, whereas Layard's digging had taught him so little that he even got the name of the place he excavated wrong: his 'Nineveh' is actually the Calah (Kalhu) of the Bible. His mistake was understandable since neither he nor anybody else could read the inscriptions which were the clue to the lost city.

It was, then, a long succession of scholars like Edward Hincks who made Assyriology a real science by their contributions towards the eventual decipherment of the mysterious wedge-shaped signs of the Assyro-Babylonian monuments. Naturally the public were unaware of, or indifferent to, their labours, for their findings were published in the obscure journals of this or that Royal Academy and were bound to be technical for all but the specialists. One could hardly expect laymen to be excited by Hincks's dis-

covery that 'if a primary consonant precedes *i* or *u*, when a second-
ary consonant existed of the same value as the primary one, and
appropriate to that vowel, an *a* must be interposed, either as a
distinct syllable or as a guna to the vowel'.

Yet it was the finding of such small and seemingly insignificant
clues by a country parson that finally led to the solution of what
at first seemed an impenetrable mystery. As we have pointed out
at the beginning of this chapter, the man-in-the-street has only to
stand in front of one of the bulls in the British Museum or the
Oriental Institute of Chicago and to examine the characters with
which the monster is covered in order to realise the magnitude of
the task which faced the first students of the Babylonian inscriptions. In fact, these scholars initially concluded that the language
was so difficult that the chances of ever properly translating it
were negligible; and Henry Rawlinson himself admitted that he
was so discouraged by the difficulties that he sometimes felt dis-
posed 'to abandon the study altogether in utter despair of arriving
at any satisfactory result'.

But as we find in the case of all unknown or half-known languages, there appeared on the scene a number of enthusiasts, several
of them men of good sense and considerable scholarship, who
essayed a translation even before the script, let along the syntax
and the morphology, of the dead language was understood.
Typical of them was William Price, the secretary to Sir Gore
Ouseley, Ambassador Extraordinary and Minister Plenipotentiary
from his Britannic Majesty to the Court of Persia in 1810–11.
William Price tells us that while the British Embassy was at Shiraz
he visited the ruins of Persepolis and copied 'with great care'
many of the inscriptions, including some which were so high up
that he had to use a telescope to see them.

> There is no clue to ascertain whether the characters are alpha-
> betic or hieroglyphic [Price writes], but they are formed of the
> arrow-head and resemble some impressions of bricks found in
> the vicinity of Babylon.[3]

He then adds a footnote with the statement that, 'having discovered some alphabets in an ancient manuscript, the author has
great hopes of their leading to the reading of these venerable
records'.

It is astonishing how often in the annals of misguided or bogus scholarship these mysterious manuscripts—which nobody else is ever allowed to see—turn up, usually in remote and inaccessible parts of the world. At all events, William Price, having acquired his 'ancient manuscript' and uninhibited by any of the rules of philology, proceeded to give the world what he calls a 'literal translation' of a clay cylinder in the Babylonian language as follows:

> The banks of avariciousness might be filled, were our vanity to be raised above the grape-stone, and our nation, unsheathed and divided, infamously exposed [to danger] under the triple crown.
>
> This would be a display of blue-beads and an empty throne. Happy the man who can show his grape-stone in this inn, uncorroded with evil: for sins committed here must be accounted for at the grand inn [of heaven]. . . .[4]

Since Price gives neither the original text nor explains his method of translation, we are in the dark as to how he arrived at these grape-stones 'which a happy man can show at the inn, uncorroded with evil'; and since we know nothing about his sources, we can only assume that his 'translation' came to him in a self-induced trance brought about by prolonged staring at the mysterious wedge-shaped characters of the Babylonian script. His delusion is not uncommon, and he belongs to a fairly numerous group of amateur cryptographers who have wrestled with obscure languages like Etruscan, Linear A, Mohendjo-Daro, Hassite, Hattian, Haldean, Hurrian, Lycian, Lydian, and so on.

Yet, interestingly enough, the first real breakthrough in the decipherment of the cuneiform inscriptions was made by an amateur orientalist Georg Grotefend, just as a hundred or more years later the breakthrough in the Greek script known as Linear B was made by the amateur hellenist Michael Ventris.

The German schoolmaster Georg Friedrich Grotefend (1775–1853) regarded the cuneiform writing as a cryptographical rather than a philological puzzle, and his approach to the problem of finding the 'key' was more mathematical than linguistic. He began by examining two Old Persian inscriptions and noting that a certain group of signs occurred three times in each of them. He now assumed that these signs stood for the word 'king', since it was known that Persian monarchs traditionally began their proc-

E

lamations with their name, followed by the formula 'great king, king of kings'. If this was so, then the first words of the inscription would be

X, great king, king of kings

and the complete royal formula would conceivably be

X, great king, king of kings, son of
Y, great king, king of kings, son of
Z, et cetera.

The formula, then, could be mathematically stated as

$$X < Y < Z$$

where X = the name of the son; Y = the name of X's father; and Z = the name of X's grandfather. Therefore, if one of these names could be read, the identity of the other two would automatically be established.

Grotefend knew that there were several celebrated son–father –grandfather genealogies in Ancient Persian history, e.g.:

Cyrus < Cambyses < Cyrus

But he saw that this trio did not fit the text he was studying, as the initial letter of these three names, Cyrus, Cambyses, Cyrus, was the same, which it was not in the cuneiform text he was working on. Similarly, the series Darius < Artaxerxes < Xerxes did not fit, as the name of Artaxerxes seemed to be too long for the middle name. Grotefend's inspired guess was that the genealogy was

Xerxes < Darius < Hystaspes

the inscription presumably reading in full:

Xerxes, great king, king of kings, son of Darius, great king, king of kings, son of Hystaspes.

Note here that the last name of the three does not, and should not, have the royal titles attached, since Hystaspes, though the founder of the royal line, was not himself a monarch and not therefore entitled to the honorific 'great king, king of kings'.

Grotefend's brilliant guess proved correct and he became the

first man to translate a cuneiform inscription and to give phonetic
values to the Old Persian symbols. Thus:

Persian:	⟨cuneiform symbols⟩						
Grotefend:	D.	A.	R.	H.	E.	U.	S
Correct reading:	D.	A.	Ra.	Ya.	Va.	U.	Sh

And so Grotefend was the first modern man to read the name
of a Persian king whom the Greeks called Darios (Latin, Darius)
in the cuneiform script.

But despite this epoch-making result, the contemporary scholars, especially in Germany, were neither impressed nor convinced,
and refused to publish Grotefend's findings in their academic
journals. He had, in fact, presented a paper outlining his methods
and findings to the Academy of Sciences in 1802. It was rejected
as the work of an amateur who was not an orientalist. Hence
Grotefend's discovery was not announced to the world until 1805
when it appeared as an appendix in a friend's book entitled
*Historical Researches into the Politics, Intercourse, and Trade of the
Principal Nations of Antiquity*. In his article, which was written in
Latin and called *Praevia de cuneatis quas vocent inscriptionibus persepo-
litanis legendis et explicandis relatio*, Grotefend essayed to translate
not merely the three Persian names (Xerxes, Darius, Hystaspes),
and the royal formula (great king, king of kings) but the rest of
the inscription. His translation is as follows:

> Darius, the valiant king, the king of kings, the son of Hystaspes,
> the successor of the ruler of the world, in the constellation of
> Moro.

The correct translation should read:

> Darius, the great king, the king of kings, king of the lands, son
> of Hystaspes, the Achaemenian, who built this winter palace.

Grotefend's guesses involving such curious matters as 'the
constellation of Moro' were the inevitable result of his ignorance
of oriental languages without a knowledge of which he was unable to proceed beyond the decipherment of names and the correct
translation of an occasional word like 'king' and 'son'. Indeed, it
was very soon obvious that these dead or forgotten languages of
the ancient Middle Eastern empires could only be properly understood (provided they could be translated at all) by the methods of

comparative philology. Thus, the key to the Old Persian spoken and written in the time of Darius, Xerxes, and the other 'great kings' is Avestan, the language of Zoroaster, the great Persian prophet of the seventh century B.C. Avestan, in turn, is very closely related to Sanskrit, and both of these 'dead' languages are known. Thus, an orientalist with a knowledge of Sanskrit, Avestan, and Modern Persian was far more likely to be able to understand and translate accurately the language of the Persepolitan and other inscriptions than a cryptographer like Grotefend, brilliant decipherer though he was. Similarly, a knowledge of Hebrew, Phoenician, and Aramaic was obviously going to be necessary once the Assyro-Babylonian language was ready for transliteration and translation.

And now, as the texts of the tri-lingual inscriptions in Old Persian, Elamite, and Babylonian arrived in Europe, there began one of those great co-operative ventures so characteristic of European learning during the eighteenth and nineteenth centuries. Even the political, economic, and military rivalries of the European states during the Napoleonic Wars and the subsequent period of imperialist expansion did not prevent scholars from continually communicating with each other across national boundaries and from unstintingly sharing their discoveries. The German, Danish, French, and English philologists were an international team in the pursuit of knowledge. They included the Dane Rasmus Christian Rask (1787–1832), who was 'comfortably master of twenty-five languages and dialects'; the Frenchman Eugene Burnouf (1801–1852), translator of Avestan and Sanskrit; the Germans Eduard Beer (1805–1841) and Jules Oppert (1825–1905), both Semitic scholars of enormous erudition (Oppert has seventy-two books and articles listed in the British Museum catalogue); Dr Edward Hincks (1792–1866), the Irish clergyman; and, greatest of all, the Father of Assyriology, the English soldier and diplomat Sir Henry Rawlinson (1810–1895).

Of these dedicated scholars, the last achieved the greatest fame, and rightly so, since his contributions to Assyriology are perhaps greater than any other single man's including his contemporaries. Rawlinson's fascination for us today when we have forgotten names like Rask, Burnouf, Hincks, and Oppert, lies in the extraordinary fullness of his long and active life—a life in which he was a soldier on duty in places like Afghanistan; a political agent in

Baghdad; an ambassador in Persia; a Member of Parliament; a trustee of the British Museum; and both the copier and translator of the inscription of Darius on the rock at Behistun.

Behistun! In some respects the most exciting ancient monument in the world—and still one of the most inaccessible. One has only to stand beneath the towering peak which rises almost sheer for 4000 feet and to gaze upwards at the fabulous memorial to Darius, Great King, King of Kings, to realise the magnitude of Rawlinson's achievement in merely copying the tremendous inscription. To begin with, the Behistun rock presents a challenge to be undertaken by only the most daring and experienced climbers, for as well as being equally difficult to reach from either above or below, the platforms from which the old Persian sculptors and inscribers must have worked have been cut away except for a short narrow ledge about eighteen inches wide below one of the inscriptions.

The rock-face of Behistun is covered by some ten columns or tablets of cuneiform writing describing in three languages the manner in which Darius came to the throne by killing his ten rivals. One language is Old Persian, another Elamite, and the third Babylonian. All three languages had disappeared along with the empires of the people who spoke them by the beginning of our era. Old Persian was, of course, the language of Darius himself and his successors, of his son Xerxes and his grandson Artaxerxes. Elamite (once called Scythic and then Susian) was the language of the population of south-western Iran, a people who appear and reappear in early Mesopotamian history as sometimes allies, sometimes enemies of first the Sumerians, then the Babylonians. They rose for a brief period as a great state and even an international power in the twelfth century B.C., but were finally reduced to a satrapy of Persia in the sixth century. But obviously the Elamite language, like the Babylonian, retained its historical and cultural significance and was used by the Persian monarchs in their commemorative inscriptions much as Latin, and sometimes Greek, are still used on English monuments.

Darius, then, meant his name and exploits to be remembered for as long as men could read, though he could never have dreamt that all three of the languages he used to glorify himself would be 'dead' less than six centuries after his reign. For to a Persian king the Middle East was the cultural centre of the world; here were

the great international capitals of trade and commerce, cities like
Babylon, Ecbatana, Susa, and Persepolis; and from here he ruled
an empire which extended from the cataracts of the Nile to the
Black Sea and from the shores of the Mediterranean to the frontiers of India. In the geographical centre of this empire, as it were,
stood Behistun, the last of the peaks in the Zagros range which
divides Iran from Iraq. It is the place where the great caravans
passed between ancient Ecbatana (modern Hamadan), capital of
Persia and Babylon, capital of Mesopotamia. They must have
paused here from time immemorial, because at the base of the
peak several springs provide a pool of crystal-clear water from
which every army, including that of Alexander the Great, drank on
their march from Babylonia into Persia, or vice-versa. There must
have been a caravanserai and a small town here in ancient days,
for according to Diodorus the mountain was a sacred place, which
may account for the legend of Semiramis having been here. For
Semiramis, mythical queen of Assyria, was supposed to have been
the daughter of a Syrian goddess, so the mountain may have been
her shrine; hence the reference to the 'Paradise' which Diodorus
says she built here. The Sicilian historian was, of course, recording a legend, the truth being that the location seemed ideal to the
Persian king Darius as a site on which to commemorate his victory
over the impostor Gaumata and the nine rebels who challenged
his authority. The sculpture shows Gaumata the Magian lying on
his back, his hands raised in entreaty to King Darius whose left
foot rests on the defeated man's chest. The nine rebels, who re-
joice in the names Atrina, Nidintu-Bel, Fravartish, Martiya,
Citrantakhma, Vahyazdata, Arakha, Frada, and Skunkha, are all
roped together by their necks. It is a scene typical of the time and
place.

    At the foot of the mountain there is the usual Persian tea-shop
where travellers can sit at a wooden table under an awning and
drink tea (or Coca-Cola) while studying the rock-face through
field-glasses, as Rawlinson studied it in 1834 through his telescope. This, in fact, was how he began copying the cuneiform
characters of the Old Persian text and eventually succeeded in
deciphering the names of Darius, Xerxes, and Hystaspes by almost
the same cryptographical methods Grotefend had used. Rawlinson was thus able to prove that the inscription was not made by
order of Semiramis, the semi-mythical builder of Babylon, or by

Shalmaneser, King of Assyria and conqueror of Israel, but by Darius who became sole master of the Persian Empire in 521 B.C. He also demonstrated that the great winged figure which hovers above the group of human figures is Ahura Mazda, the national god of Persia, and not an heraldic device as an earlier traveller had thought; or a cross hovering over the twelve disciples as reported by a Frenchman in 1809; or a portrait of Semiramis herself as related by Diodorus in the following passage:

> Semiramis having made a platform of the saddles and trappings of the pack-animals which accompanied her army, ascended by this path from the plain to the rock where she had caused her portrait to be sculpted together with those of a hundred attendant guards.

The statement that this legendary queen ascended 500 feet up the face of the rock by means of her animals' trappings was obviously absurd, but until Rawlinson actually reached the memorial nobody had been able to copy the sculptures and inscriptions in detail. Even so, the problem was not merely to climb the 500 feet up to the inscriptions, but to stay up there in order to examine and, of course, transcribe them, as Rawlinson was to discover when, in the summer of 1844, he climbed up to the narrow ledge which juts out below the rock-face on which the Persian text is inscribed.

Henry Rawlinson
and the Inscription of Darius

THIS PERSIAN TEXT IS cut into five columns of rock and is immediately below the sculpture of Darius, his two attendants, the ten impostors, and the god Ahura Mazda. To the left of the Persian text are three columns in the Elamite language; and above these three columns, written on two faces of an overhanging rock, the Babylonian text.

Rawlinson's first task, once he had reached the ledge, was to copy the Persian text; and in order to do this he needed ladders of varying length, for if the ladder was too short, he was unable to read the upper lines; and if it was too long, it was liable to teeter back and forth on the eighteen-inch ledge on which it rested. Rawlinson decided to solve this problem by standing on the top rung of a short ladder; by steadying his body and the ladder against the rock with his left arm; holding his notebook in the palm of his left hand and copying the text with his right. To those who suffer from vertigo, the mind boggles at the image of the tall Englishman perched on the top rung of an almost vertical ladder placed on a narrow ledge 500 feet up from the plain below. Rawlinson states in his famous description of his achievement: 'In this position I copied all the upper inscriptions, and the interest of the occupation entirely did away with any sense of danger.'[1]

By 'interest of the occupation' Rawlinson meant an almost self-sacrificial devotion to his oriental studies; for not content with copying the Old Persian text under these hazardous conditions he next attempted a nearly suicidal feat in order to reach the Elamite text, which, as stated above, consisted of three columns of text to the left of the Old Persian tablets or columns.

His problem was to cross a gap in the ledge which ran under-

CLAUDIUS JAMES RICH (1787–1820), right, a pioneer of Assyriology. As British Resident in Baghdad for the East India Company, he explored the sites of Babylon and Nineveh. He died of cholera in Shiraz, Persia, aged thirty-three.

AUSTEN HENRY LAYARD (1817–1894), left, excavated the rich sites of Nimrud and Kuyunjik and found the colossal man-headed lions and bulls now in the British Museum. At the age of forty-four, he abandoned archaeology for politics.

HENRY CRESWICKE RAWLINSON (1810–1895), right, the 'Father of Assyriology'. Also soldier, member of parliament, ambassador, and orientalist. His crowning achievement was to copy and translate the trilingual inscription of Darius, which led to the eventual decipherment of the Elamite and Babylonian languages.

EDWARD HINCKS (1792–1866), left, the Irish clergyman who devoted his life to the decipherment and elucidation of the cuneiform languages. He seldom left his rectory at Killyleagh, County Down and never received the recognition he deserved as one of the greatest orientalists of his age.

THE TOWER OF BABEL, left. Early travellers to Mesopotamia believed that this ruin of the ziggurat of Borsippa was the original Tower described in Genesis. There were once scores of such lofty temples throughout Sumer, Babylonia, and Assyria. The ziggurat of Babylon which Herodotus may have climbed in the fifth century B.C. was about 300 feet high.

A SUMERIAN OFFICIAL, right. This portrait of a nobleman who lived over 4000 years ago shows how free and naturalistic Sumerian sculpture was in comparison with the stiff, formalised art of the Assyrians and Babylonians.

GUDEA OF LAGASH, left, who lived around 2100 B.C., was a great builder of temples and his piety is shown in his clasped hands and his gaze fixed in rapt contemplation of the gods. Some thirty statues of Gudea survive, all of them portraying him in this reverent posture.

ASHURNASIRPAL II (883–859 BC),
right, one of the early kings of Assyria,
noted for his conquests and his cruelties.
This portrait is not so much a likeness of
Ashurnasirpal himself as a stereotype of
all the Assyrian kings who are made just
a little smaller than the gods and con-
siderably larger than their subjects.

BAGHDAD ON THE TIGRIS, below,
capital of the caliph Harun al-Rashid,
city of the Arabian Nights, and headquarters, together with Mosul to the
north, of the nineteenth-century archaeologists.

KING DARIUS HUNTING LIONS. The Assyrian sport of hunting lions from chariots was practised by the Persian kings, again as a symbol of royal invincibility.

LIONS COMING OUT OF A CAGE. This scene from the frieze found in the palace of Nimrud shows that the lions hunted by the Assyrian kings were trapped and then released. The lions, now extinct, were not much bigger than the mastiffs used to hunt them.

DYING LIONESS. Perhaps the most moving animal portrait of antiquity. This masterpiece is part of the Lion Hunt frieze found at Nimrud in the palace of the Assyrian king Ashurnasirpal II (883–859 B.C.) and now the treasure of the British Museum's Assyrian collection.

neath the inscriptions. The gap was about ten feet long over a
sheer drop: there was no way of climbing across, so Rawlinson
decided to use a ladder. Unfortunately, his ladder was too short,
so that only one side of it lay firmly on the opposite ledge while
the other side barely reached the ledge at all. His companions
managed to dissuade Rawlinson from crossing this so-called
bridge, as it would have obviously spun over as soon as his weight
was on the wrong side. Thereupon the explorer decided to put
the ladder across the gap by standing it on its side with the rungs
upright and to walk along it from rung to rung. But as soon as he
started across he discovered that the lower side of the ladder gave
way under his feet as the rungs (which the Persians do not clench)
sprung out of their sockets; and the appliance, except for the
upper side-piece, went crashing down the precipice, leaving
Rawlinson dangling in space as he clung to the swaying and
bending upper stave. Rawlinson's comment: 'Eventually, assisted
by my friends who were anxiously watching the trial, I regained
the Persian ledge, and did not again attempt to cross until I had
made a bridge of comparative stability.'[2]

But an even more difficult challenge awaited Rawlinson, one so
dangerous, in fact, that the local mountaineers said it was impossible. The challenge was to reach the Babylonian texts carved
on the two faces of the rock above the Elamite version. Some
idea of the appalling difficulties and dangers of this climb can be
seen from the fact that not only the 'cragsmen of the place', as
Rawlinson calls them, but the Englishman himself admitted that
the Babylonian Rock was unattainable. However,

> At length, a wild Kurdish boy who had come from a distance,
> volunteered to make the attempt, and I promised him a con-
> siderable award if he succeeded. The mass of rock in question
> is scarped [i.e., cut down vertically] and it projects some feet
> over the Scythic recess [i.e., the rock face on which the Elamite
> text is inscribed] so that it cannot be approached by any of the
> ordinary means of climbing. The boy's first move was to
> squeeze himself up a cleft in the rock a short distance to the
> left of the projecting mass. When he had ascended some distance
> above it, he drove a wooden peg firmly into the cleft, fastened
> a rope to this, and then endeavoured to swing himself across to
> another cleft at some distance on the other side; but in this he

failed owing to the projection of the rock. It then only remained for him to cross over to the cleft by hanging on with his toes and fingers to the slight inequalities on the bare face of the precipice, and in this he succeeded, passing over a distance of twenty feet of almost smooth perpendicular rock in a manner which to a looker-on appeared quite miraculous. When he had reached the second cleft, the real difficulties were over. He had brought with him a rope, attached to the first peg, and now, driving in a second, he was enabled to swing himself right over the projecting mass of rock. Here with a short ladder he formed a swinging seat, like a painter's cradle, and, fixed upon this seat, he took under my direction the paper cast of the Babylonian translation of the records of Darius. I must add, too, that it is of the more importance that this invaluable Babylonian key should have been thus recovered, as the mass of rock on which the inscription is engraved bore every appearance when I last visited the spot of being doomed to a speedy destruction, water trickling from above having almost separated the overhanging mass from the rest of the rock . . . to go thundering down into the plain, dashed into a thousand fragments.[3]

Rawlinson was right, of course, about the importance of the Babylonian text, for as part of the tri-lingual inscription it provided all the clues which the philologists needed to complete their grammars of Akkadian, which was the term finally agreed upon to define the two dialects—Babylonian and Assyrian—of the same language. After such an incredible feat of daring and skill it was only just that Rawlinson himself should have the distinction of being the first to translate the great Darius inscription, and his translation, made in 1847 from the Old Persian into English and Latin, is accepted by scholars today with no significant changes.

What is so exciting about the Rock of Behistun and Rawlinson's achievement is that this long inscription, unlike so many cuneiform documents which are merely records of commercial transactions, immortalises a piece of Persian history written with the splendid arrogance of the ancient oriental kings. It begins:

I am Darius, the Great King, the King of Kings, the King of Persia, the King of the Provinces, the son of Hystaspes, the grandson of Arsames, the Achaemenian . . . from antiquity are we descended; from antiquity hath our race been kings. . . .

And continues:

> Thus saith Darius the king: A man named Citrantakhma, a
> Sagartian, revolted from me and thus he spake unto the people:
> 'I am king in Sagartia, of the family of Cyaxares.' Then I sent
> forth a Persian and a Median army. A Median named Takhmas-
> pada, my servant, I made their leader, and I said unto him: 'Go,
> smite the host which is in revolt and doth not acknowledge me.'
> Thereupon Takhmaspada went forth with the army, and he
> fought a battle with Citrantakhma. Ahura Mazda [the national
> god of Persia] brought me help; by the grace of Ahura Mazda
> my army utterly defeated that rebel host and they seized Citran-
> takhma and brought him unto me. Then I cut off his nose and
> his ears, and I put out his eyes. He was kept in fetters in my
> court and all the people beheld him. Afterwards did I crucify
> him in Arbela.

The inscription informs us that Darius cut off the nose and ears,
put out the eyes, exhibited in public, and finally crucified five of
the nine rebels and slew the other four in battle. Being a very pious
man, he ascribed his victories over his enemies to the grace and
favour of the god Ahura Mazda, who is repeatedly thanked in the
phrase 'Ahura Mazda brought me help; by the grace of Ahura
Mazda my army utterly defeated the rebel host'. Ahura Mazda,
like all other gods, appears to have been on the side of the big
battalions, for the nine pretenders with weird names like Arakha
the Babylonian and Skunkha the Scythian were mostly regional
upstarts and no match for Darius with his large and well-trained
national army.

And thus the Persian monarch celebrated at Behistun his
victories in the civil wars that marked the beginning of his reign,
even taking care to leave some of the rock-face blank in anticipa-
tion of future triumphs. However, no more victories are recorded
at Behistun; nor would one expect to hear mention of the Greek
battles like that at Marathon where the Great King's army of
300,000 men was defeated by a force of 11,000 Athenians, leaving
6400 Persians dead on the battlefield for the loss of 190 Greeks.

By 1847 Rawlinson had copied and made a paper squeeze of the
whole of the Persian text, giving up his diplomatic career and 'all
the comforts of civilisation' to do so; in fact, 'doing penance', as
he later said, 'to attain a great literary object'. The literary object

was not only a translation of the Persian text, but the finding of the key to the Elamite and Babylonian languages. For the trilingual nature of the Behistun memorial made it as valuable to the Assyriologists as the Rosetta Stone to the Egyptologists; and just as the key to Egyptian hieroglyphs would have been greatly delayed and possibly not found at all without the help of the Greek translation on the Rosetta Stone, so all attempts at decipherment of the Elamite and Babylonian script remained purely speculative until Rawlinson made freely available to the world of international scholarship the three parallel texts of Darius's memorial.

Some idea of the difficulties still confronting the early decipherers of Elamite and Assyro-Babylonian can be seen from the fact that the philologists did not know who were the people who spoke these languages; whether the languages themselves were Indo-European or Semitic; and whether the script they were written in was alphabetic, syllabic, ideographic, or a mixture of all three. In fact, they could not even agree for a long time on what to call these two unknown tongues which we now call Elamite and Akkadian. The former of the two has had a number of different names in its day—Scythic, Median, Susian, Aloradian, Medo-Scythic, and Anzanish among others; and the family of languages to which it belongs is still being argued about, though few contemporary scholars would go so far as Professor Sayce who invented a new linguistic family he calls *Alarodian* in order to accommodate the Elamite. Needless to say, *Alarodian* remains a figment of the learned professor's imagination, the hard fact being that scarcely anything is known of the people who spoke the language apart from vague references in the Old Testament where Genesis lists 'Elam' as one of the children of Shem. Jeremiah and Isaiah, as expected, prophesy the dire destruction of Elam, along with Babylon and all other enemies of Israel. But these strange references to what appeared to be another Semitic nation within a loose Mesopotamian confederation were of no help to the students of the Elamite language, which, in any case, still continues to puzzle philologists as to its origins and provenance.

One of those who worked at the problem of deciphering Elamite was Georg Grotefend who had less success with this language than he had had with Persian, where his discoveries, in any case, had been limited by his inadequate knowledge of the ancient oriental languages. The Danish scholar Niels Ludvig Wester-gaard, on the other hand, made better progress: he estimated the number of separate characters at eighty-two or eighty-seven and was thus able to classify the script as partly alphabetic and partly syllabic. But his attempts at translation were mostly guesswork. Dr Hincks, the Irish scholar, quietly working away in his study at Killyleagh, County Down, made his usual penetrating contribution to the subject and identified with reasonable approximation forty-eight out of the 113 signs in which the language is written.

In the meantime Henry Rawlinson had published largely at his own expense his copy of the Elamite text inscribed on the Behistun rock-face, leaving the editorship and translation of the work to Edwin Norris, another of those extraordinarily erudite and gifted scholars so typical of Victorian England. Norris was a Cornishman who specialised in the Cornish, African, and Asian languages, as a glance at his books will show: *Outlines of a Few of the Principal Languages of Western and Central Africa*; *Dialogues and a Small Portion of the New Testament in the English, Arabic, Haussa, and Bornu Languages*; *Sketches of Cornish Grammar*; and *An Assyrian Dictionary*. Norris's greatest contribution to philology remains his decipherment and translation of the Elamite inscription and his recognition of the syllabic character of the script. Whether his argument that this oriental language was related to Finnish is conclusive nobody can definitely prove or disprove, since the origin of both languages is equally obscure.

Now two of the languages of the Behistun memorial had been almost mastered, thanks to the combined efforts of orientalists exchanging views and sharing discoveries as best they could. The third language which Frédéric de Saulcy had called Assyrian was to prove the most difficult of the three and, at the same time, the most important. For once it was fairly certain that it actually was the language of the Assyro-Babylonian civilisation, the whole world, both scholars and laymen, were impatient to discover the contents of the tens of thousands of inscriptions which excavators like Botta and Layard were now sending back to Europe. If one looks at the Foreign Members of the Royal Asiatic Society of the mid-nineteenth century, one can see the universality of interest in the emergent science of Assyriology, not only throughout Europe but more and more in the United States where Washington Irving and Martin Van Buren were the principal representatives.

The story of how the last and most important of the three languages of the Darius inscription was ultimately deciphered is long and complicated and belongs to the years of patient and devoted labour of scholars like Westergaard, de Saulcy, Oppert, de Longperier, Rawlinson, and Hincks—particularly the last of them, the Irish linguistic genius who scarcely ever left his country parsonage. In brief, by 1850, the mystery of the Assyro-Babylonian language had been nearly solved: the task of translating the vast literature dug up in the royal palaces by Botta, Layard, and others could now begin.

Yet, despite the brilliant and convincing arguments put forward by Hincks and Rawlinson, there were still a number of eminent orientalists who could not accept either the theories or the translations of the British decipherers. In Rawlinson's case his critics contended that a language in which the same sign signified half a dozen different sounds would be impossible to read even by the people who wrote it. Moreover, where a written word is derived from signs whose origins are pictures, the translator can never be certain of the *exact* meaning of that word. Some idea of the enormous difficulties the Assyro-Babylonian cuneiforms present to the orientalists can be gauged from the examination of any one of the 627 signs used in the script. Take, for instance, the sign ⊢╪╤⌐ the original pictograph of which was ≫≫ ◁

One expert thought that this pictograph represented grain falling from a vessel; another, a penis with testicles; another, a tent door; another, the male and female organs in conjunction. All of these theories are put forward to explain the various assumed meanings of the sign as *whirlwind, conception, enter, dig, clothe, god Marduk, sickness, dove, venereal disease*, and so forth. It is no wonder that Frédéric de Saulcy, the leading French orientalist of the mid-nineteenth century, asked what one was to think of a script in which, for instance, the same sign could mean so many things and be pronounced indifferently, *a, ha, pa, bu, i, ya, nit, ku, du* . . . et cetera? The implication was that Rawlinson's translation of the Babylonian rock was largely guesswork.

The controversy between the supporters and the opponents of the Rawlinson-Hincks theory was finally resolved in a dramatic fashion by a mathematician called William Henry Fox Talbot (1800–1877), a pioneer of photography and the inventor of the 'calotype', the system of printing from negatives still in use, in a perfected form, today. His book called *The Pencil of Nature*, incidentally, was the first volume illustrated with photographs ever to be published (1844–6), and is now only obtainable in the great national libraries. A brilliant mathematician, particularly in the field of Integral Calculus, an enthusiastic astronomer, philologist, antiquarian, and Member of Parliament, he was a truly great Victorian; and so diverse and yet profound was his scholarship that it is not surprising to find him working on the Assyro-Babylonian inscriptions and, after a few years of intensive study by way of an intellectual hobby, producing a translation of an Assyrian cylinder from the reign of Tiglath-pileser I (1116–1078 B.C.). Fox Talbot sent his translation to the President of the Royal Asiatic Society in a sealed envelope with the unusual request that in order to test the worth of the Rawlinson-Hincks system, these two scholars should independently make their own translation of the Tiglath-pileser cylinder, place them in sealed envelopes, and await the verdict of the learned world as to the similarity of the translations, or lack of it. The Asiatic Society not only agreed to this interesting proposal, but invited the celebrated German orientalist Dr Jules Oppert also to submit his version of the cuneiform text. So there were to be three additional translations to compare with that of Fox Talbot in order that nobody could charge the Royal Asiatic Society with duplicity.

The four sealed packets were opened on May 29th, 1857, by two examiners and the following report was submitted by the Egyptologist J. Gardner Wilkinson:

> My impression, from a comparison of the several passages in the different translations, is that the resemblance (very often exactly the same, word for word) is so great as to render it unreasonable to suppose the interpretation could be arbitrary, or based on uncertain grounds.*

Scholars and, for that matter, the general public could now decide the matter for themselves on the publication of the four versions by the Asiatic Society. Here are the opening lines of the Assyrian text as translated independently by the four experts:

* Inscription of Tiglath-pileser I, as translated and published by the Royal Asiatic Society, 1857, p. 7.

Rawlinson

In the beginning of my reign, Anu and Vul, the great gods, my lords, guardians of my steps, they invited me to repair this my shrine. So I made bricks; I levelled the earth . . . I laid down its foundations as a mass of strong rock.

Talbot

At the commencement of my reign, Anu and Yem, the great gods, my lords, the upholders of my footsteps, gave me a command to rebuild their temples. I made bricks; I levelled the site (?) I laid the foundation on a lofty mound of earth.

Hincks

In the beginning of my reign, Anu and Iv, the great gods, my lords, the guides of my feet, commanded me that their temple should be rebuilt. I formed crude bricks, I cleared out its rubbish, and reached the bottom thereof. I laid its foundations on a great artificial hill.

Oppert

In the commencement of my reign, the gods Anu and Ao, the great gods, my lords, ordered me to exact my force and to destroy their buildings. I moulded the bricks; I surveyed the ground; I made its foundations strong as to resist to the shaking of mountains. . . .

It is obvious from this sample of the four versions that the Assyriologists, in particular Rawlinson and Hincks, had found the key to the Babylonian cuneiform, even though some words, and particularly the names of persons, animals, objects, and so forth, were still uncertain. Yet the opponents of the polyphony principle upheld by Rawlinson (who meant by the term the use of the same system of writing by different peoples speaking different languages) continued to challenge his translations, and one of them, the learned French diplomat the Comte de Gobineau, once famous for his racialist theories (he was one of the precursors of the Nazi Aryan creed), published his own renderings of various Babylonian inscriptions. De Gobineau founded his readings on purely Arabic roots and, as a result, transliterated the royal name Nebuchadnezzar into *Nnnemmmmmresusus*, an even more bizarre form of the name than Hincks's *Nabiccudurrayuchur*.

The truth was that quite a considerable section of the learned world continued to doubt the work of Rawlinson, Hincks, Oppert, and other leading Assyriologists until almost the end of the nineteenth century. In France especially the greatest scepticism prevailed concerning the genuineness of the translations. In addition, Rawlinson was personally attacked by certain Continental scholars as deliberately withholding his copies of the Behistun inscriptions from the world of learning, Isidore Löwenstern going so far as to claim that the explorer had done so for reasons of self-glorification—a serious charge to make against an English officer and gentleman who had risked his life and later used his personal fortune to present the Behistun memorial to the world. Yet even in England itself men of the intellectual calibre of Sir George Cornewall Lewis and Lord Macaulay rejected Rawlinson's translations from the Babylonian as utterly spurious.

By the end of the century, however, Rawlinson's theories were vindicated, and so was his brilliant intuitive observation that the Babylonian script was based on a still older language which he called variously Scythic, Turanian, the Hamitic language of Babylonia, Proto-Chaldean, and Akkadian. Rawlinson states that it is 'an ancient and most difficult language' which he is inclined to trace back to the uplands of Central Africa! He was, of course, floundering about in a veritable philological quagmire, for at this date, 1887, the very existence of the Sumerian people and civilisation was unknown and undreamt of. It was Rawlinson's brilliant 'discovery' of their language that, in time, led historians back to the most ancient culture in the world, back to the land of Sumer where Western civilisation originated.

F

7

The Discovery of the Sumerians

THE SUMERIANS WERE 'DISCOVERED' so recently that it is scarcely surprising they remain the mystery people of history, so mysterious, in fact, that until recently their existence was denied altogether, even after their principal cities had been excavated and the names and dates of their kings recorded. Indeed, the search for the 'Sumerians' led historians so far back in time that new problems of analysis and interpretation were raised, and not even the eventual decipherment of their language solved the central problem of who they were and whence they came.

Even so, we know now that there was a race of people who preceded the Babylonians in Mesopotamia and passed on their highly developed culture to those semi-barbarians who appear in history for the first time about 2225 B.C. We know that they occupied the lower plains of the Tigris and Euphrates and that by 3000 B.C. they had built cities of burnt and unburnt brick, cultivated the surrounding fields, irrigated them with canals and water-courses, and had grown rich in sheep and cattle. Even more important, they had developed a system of writing which proves beyond doubt that they must have been undergoing the civilising process for hundreds of years before we first meet them among the ruins of their cities.

The significance of the Sumerian invention of writing cannot be over-emphasised, for it represents man's greatest achievement since his discovery of how to make and use tools. Once a system of recording his knowledge acquired from the experience of previous generations has been found, his development becomes enormously accelerated, so that we can see for ourselves that he has advanced more rapidly in the last 5000 years, since the Sumerians first began to keep written records, than he did in the previous 50,000. Therefore any assessment of the Sumerians and of their place in history must begin with at least a glance at this extraordinary intellectual achievement which they alone of the inhabitants of our planet at this stage of history seem to have been capable of.

It is, of course, axiomatic that as soon as man was intelligent, he drew pictures for purposes of communication: it is this need to transfer information across space and time which is surely the key to the prehistoric rock art of southern Europe and Africa.* But from picture-characters, as of a star, to ideograms where the star now stands for the concept of heaven is a very long step, and still longer the transition from ideogram to phonogram in which the original star ✷ has become ►━┳, with the sound AN meaning 'god'.

Writing, then, as we know it, was systematised, even if not actually invented, by the Sumerians, who certainly adapted simple pictographs into ideograms which could express actions and ideas as well as objects. To take an example. Primitive man could, of course, draw a picture of running deer or running men, and his viewers could interpret the pictures to mean deer in flight or warriors attacking an enemy. But he could not draw the pure action 'to run' or 'to drink' without using the picture of a man or animal in the process of running or drinking. The genius who ultimately devised a sign for pure action—e.g. the verb 'to drink'—simply combined the picture for *mouth* with the picture for *water* running into the mouth and produced the ideogram *drink*, thus:

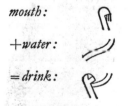

mouth: picture of a head, with the *mouth* emphasised by means of vertical strokes

+*water:*   picture of a stream, hence an ideogram for *water*

=*drink:*   combined picture of *mouth* with *water* flowing into it, meaning therefore *drink*

The next phase in the development of Sumerian writing was the speeding up of the recording process and, as with our writing, signs which were once carefully drawn as pictures were eventually 'scrawled' hurriedly, particularly if the scribe were taking dicta-

* See James Wellard, *Lost Worlds of Africa* (1968), Chapter 2.

tion. Moreover, since his pen or stylus was a straight, wedge-ended tool it could not easily make curves on soft clay, as the clay would tend to pile up and blur if the amanuensis tried to use the stylus to produce cursive or flowing script. The solution to the scribe's problem, therefore, was a stylised rendering of the original pictograph, the form being determined by the wedge-ended stylus. Hence from the original drawing of a bird there eventually developed a stylised version probably in this form:

For some reason which is not altogether clear, despite the various explanations, this sign was turned on its side and appears as:

and the simplified bird-drawing after the passage of an unknown period of time became this shorthand version. Thus:

which is the sign for *bird* in early Babylonian. This, in turn, was later simplified to:

It can readily be seen from this brief sketch of the development of the Sumerian script that the language has not been easy to decipher. In fact, it was some time before the philologists recognised the existence of a Sumerian language at all: they simply guessed at the meaning of the texts by a process of decoding key words with the help of syllabaries compiled by the Babylonians and Assyrians. For these later people, having conquered and absorbed the Sumerians into their empires, adopted the cuneiform script and even learnt the language: hence they had need of Babylonian-Sumerian word-books, some of which have survived. Sumerian, in fact, survived in Babylonia much as Latin survived in medieval Europe, as the language of religion, law, and international diplomacy. However, there was an important difference. Since Sumerian does not belong to the Semitic family of languages, the Babylonians and Assyrians, whose language, like Hebrew and Arabic, is Semitic, ran into difficulties when they tried to write down their own speech in Sumerian cuneiform script. Their problem can perhaps best be appreciated if we think of the inconvenience of writing English in Chinese ideographs, or in any script which is not strictly alphabetic.

Who, then, were these mysterious Sumerians who had invented this system of writing? The eventual decipherment of their language and the excavation of their cities revealed that they were a highly advanced people who inhabited southern Mesopotamia at the dawn of civilisation. At some time in the second millennium B.C. they were invaded by Semitic tribes who possibly came from the Syrian or Arabian deserts. What is certain is that these Semites found a people far superior to them in every field of human endeavour except in the art of war, which explains why the more civilised urban-dwellers fell easy prey to the desert nomads. But as so often has happened in history, it was the victors who were eventually to be conquered by the vanquished, as the barbarians surrendered to the superior culture which the Sumerians had developed over long centuries—the art of writing, the codes of law, the sciences of building and farming, and the politico-social structure of civilised people.

And so today, irrespective of who the Sumerians were (i.e. Aryans or Semites) and from whence they came, we at least know what they looked like, how they lived, and what they believed in, for they left behind comprehensible records of the civilisation they had created. For instance, we know from their sculptures that they were a shaven-headed, large-eyed, and curly-bearded people, smiling enigmatically like Greek masks personifying Comedy. True, they remain somehow remote and alien, despite their large eyes and benign smiles and comfortable paunches, always some 5000 years away from us in time, oriental and unfamiliar. Indeed, oriental was their way of life, as their records, found on literally thousands of tablets, steles, cylinders, and monuments, reveal in detailed descriptions of every phase of both their civic and private activities.

Their country, the Land of Sumer, or the lower half of what was later to become Babylonia, contained a number of city-states ruled over by a governor who was also the high priest of the local god. Where these cities were close together, and hence rivals for the available land and water, a war was fought until one of the towns was brought under the domination of the other. The governor of the victorious city thereupon became semi-deified and assumed the title of king and founded a dynasty. If this royal personage subsequently conquered the king of another group of cities, he became a 'great king' and a 'king of kings'. Further, as a monarch's military and political power grew, he was regarded as more and more godlike, for the government of the ancient oriental kingdoms was invariably theocratic. All laws, all policies, and all decisions were directly subordinate to the local god whose decrees were passed on by the king-priest. It was a simple, effective, and invincible politico-social system which was never questioned in the ancient world from its beginning somewhere around 6000 B.C. to its end with the rise of Greek democracy. The best that the ordinary citizen could ever hope for in Sumer, Babylonia, Assyria, Persia, or any of the other oriental kingdoms was that their king would be either a reasonable or a merciful ruler, for if he was a tyrant there was nothing they could do to remove him. The overthrow of a king was always the result of a murder committed by an ambitious usurper, himself a potential tyrant. Political revolution, in brief, was unknown in the ancient world. Continuous wars brought about the only changes in rulers and government.

The strength of the autocratic system was the unquestioned belief in the god or gods of the region, a belief so strong and all-pervading that it nullified all political and social dissension: in other words, there was no opposition to the reigning monarch or his establishment on ideological grounds, any opposition that arose being invariably based on the personal ambition of a rival. So the foundations of society were never shaken so long as the citizens accepted, with genuine faith, the supremacy of the god and the divine right of his representative on earth, namely the king.

It was this total acceptance of authority which was the strength of Sumerian society, as it is the strength of a highly disciplined army: in other words, the individual was wholly integrated into the community and so acted with a corporate mind and will. He did so because the survival of his social organisation depended on his surrendering his personal whims and wishes for the sake of the security of the group. To this there was, of course, no alternative in a region like Lower Mesopotamia where floods, droughts, the encroachment of the sea, storms, and earth tremors made survival a collective effort. Agriculture was not possible without a system of irrigation; and the canals and irrigation channels could not be dug without the work of every able-bodied man, woman, and

child. This spirit of co-operation permeated every aspect of
Sumerian life and none more so than in religion, the proof of
which are the colossal temples, or 'houses of the gods', as the
Sumerians preferred to call them, which could only have been
built, in view of the absence of proper materials and sophisticated machines, by the unremitting labour of the entire
community.

The gods of Sumer, therefore, like those of Babylon, Assyria,
and Persia, are of paramount importance, for they were not ab-
stractions whose function lay outside the events and activities of
everyday life. Their power and influence were felt in all aspects of
creation, for to the Sumerians there was no other possible explanation of the phenomena of the universe—the regular rising and
setting of the sun and of all the heavenly bodies, the coming of the
seasons, the rhythm of birth and death—than that of some super-
human lord or king who ruled over the cosmos as earthly kings
ruled over their domains. And just as an earthly king had his
wives and children and courtiers, so the principal lord of the
universe had his entourage, which was the pantheon of pre-
Christian religions. It follows that the chief god, together with the
lesser divinities, was conceived of in strictly human terms; and
this is how he is always portrayed in pagan art, as a super-man and
super-king whose power it was foolish to question and disastrous
to defy.

The Sumerians originally had many such gods—in fact, as
many gods and godlings as there were cities. Fara, for instance,
had its god Sharuppak; Lagash its Ningirsu; Eridu its Enki; Ur
its Nanna; Larsa its Babba; and so on. They are all as dead as the
dodo, of course, and are now regarded as linguistic curiosities.
Most of them died by killing each other off in battle, until only the
strongest were left, and these, of course, were the gods of the
victorious city-states. There survived a shadowy figure called An,
the King of Heaven; his son Enlil, once the tutelary deity of the
city of Nippur; and Enki, Lord of the Earth. The consort of An
was Ki, the earth-goddess, Enlil being the offspring of their
union. It is interesting to note that the celestial god was a male,
the terrestrial a female. As is usual in primitive theogonies, the
male is the dominant deity and the female is relegated to a vague
rôle behind the scenes, as in human society. The Sumerians do
not appear to have gone to the extent of the Hebrews, the Greeks,

and the Christians, however, by blaming woman for all the woes
mankind is heir to.

It thus becomes obvious from even a casual study of the
Sumerian pantheon that the gods multiplied and prospered in
accordance with the military conquests of the kings, their chief
representatives on earth. So, too, these divinities became more
remote and unapproachable, exactly as a 'great king' must have
become to his subjects. And, again, just as the earthly monarch,
the more powerful he became the more he surrounded himself
with courtiers and sycophants, so the gods were screened off from
the common people by priests and hierarchs. In time the 'royal
family' of the Sumerian pantheon reads like the genealogies of
European monarchs in Victorian times, and it takes a specialist to
know the relationship between the different branches. In addition
to An, King of Heaven, we now have Utu, the sun-god. Ki, the
earth-mother, seems to yield her position as head-woman to the
goddess Nammu, 'the mother who gave birth to the universe'.
A moon-god also appears on the scene, variously called Sin and
Nanna, the son of Enlil and the father of Utu and of the love-
goddess Inanna. Here, then, are the roots of the Sumerian theological family tree:

```
                    Nammu m. ?
                         |
          An [= Heaven] m. Ki [=Earth]
                         |
                Enlil m. Ki (his mother)
             (the air-god)
                         |
              Sin or Nanna (the moon-god) m. ?
                    |           |
        Utu (the sun-god)  Inanna (the love-goddess)
```

It can readily be seen that the complications in the genealogy
of the Sumerian deities necessitated a staff of full-time specialists
to ensure that each god was accorded his rightful due in terms of
the size of his temple, the splendour of his retinue, and the length
of his rituals. Thus arose the priesthood which was as essential to
a theocracy as a civil service to a democracy, both organisations
becoming more numerous and bureaucratic as they multiplied
their function. By the third millennium, in fact, the priests were

responsible for scores of deities, most of whom had their temple, their holy day, shrines, rites, prayers, sacrifices, and so forth.

Consequently, religion in the form of ritualism dominated the whole of Sumerian life and society; and whereas the worship of a divinity has become a subject about which modern man tends to argue in a 'scientific' spirit, to the Sumerians the gods and the homage due to them were incontestable, like the ebb and flow of the tides. In brief, the Sumerian accepted the fact that, as a mere servant of the gods, he was as expendable and insignificant as an animal was to him. Any good fortune, any talent or virtue, any wealth he possessed were gifts of the gods who could just as easily take away what they had given. What is crucial in this concept of divinity is, of course, the nature of the gods themselves, for if the deities are cruel, rapacious, merciless, and unjust, their worshippers will automatically exhibit the same characteristics. This is clearly shown in a number of pagan religions—the Phoenician cult of Baal, the devourer of children, being the classic case. Conversely, where men civilised their gods, as the Greeks civilised Apollo, originally the Destroyer, their own lives and conduct became more merciful and humane.

Fortunately for the Sumerians, their gods appear to have been moral beings, extolled as lovers of truth, justice, and virtue. At the same time, men had to recognise the existence of evil, of falsehood, injustice and vice; and since the mere human had no free will and, therefore, no say in the matter, certain wicked gods were made responsible. Indeed, this simple logic was the strength of the religion, for it is impossible to love and trust a god who is responsible at one and the same time for good *and* evil; for mankind's happiness *and* his misery; for the blossoms of spring *and* the death of a baby. In other words, God without Satan is a mere ethical abstraction and quite inadequate for a wholly credible religion.

The Sumerians, then, had in a sense solved the principal theological and philosophical problems which beset us today by postulating as first principles the infallibility of the gods, the helplessness of man, and the inevitability of fate. Such beliefs have always seemed to sterner moralists to be the essence of spiritual cowardice. On the other hand, the Sumerian, recognising that he was mortal and therefore like other living creatures, not destined for immortality, accepted whatever fate brought him and devoted his energies, mental and physical, to the end of making life on

earth as enjoyable as possible. One can see the results of this philosophy in the portraits of this exotic people with their large sensual
eyes, enigmatic smiles, bald heads, curly beards, and tendency to
womanish fat. It is as though they felt that as there was nothing
they could do about the universe, they might as well enjoy their
food, their women, and their sleep, since every phase of life was
regulated by divine law. The ordinary man could do nothing about
his fate and so was content to leave the interpretation of the god's
wishes to the king who was at the same time the pope. Again, as
in all theocratic communities, all land and, in theory, all possessions were the property of the god; and all men had their specific
duties in the service of that god. Consequently there were in Sumer
few of the problems of modern capitalist societies. Unemploy-
ment, social unrest, and poverty on the scale and in the form that
we know it were unheard of. For just as the citizens regarded it as
obligatory to work for the god (=the state) by ploughing the
fields, tending the farm animals, fishing the rivers, serving in the
shops, building the temples, and so on, so they regarded the duty
of their king, as the god's representative, to provide them with
adequate food, shelter, and protection.

Sumerian society, in brief, has certain resemblances to the large,
well-organised, and prosperous monastic communities of Christian Egypt in the seventh century. And just as a Christian settlement in the Thebaid flourished under the rule of a benevolent
bishop, so a Sumerian community prospered under a righteous
king like Urukagina of Lagash (*c.* 2400 B.C.) whose maxim was
'the mighty must not do injustice to the orphan and the widow'.
In actual practice, Urukagina restrained the ubiquitous and rapacious tax-collectors, suppressed the usurers and the petty inspectors
who harried the farmers and fishermen, arrested thieves and murderers, and forbad discrimination against the poor and weak.
And for a period of ten years, at least, Lagash appears to have
been as free, prosperous, and well-run a city as any we know of in
history. Its idyllic period was eventually ended by the internecine
wars characteristic of the period, but not before the precepts and
example of Urukagina had become part of the social conscious-
ness of civilised communities, and, in time, the basis of the
Babylonian legal code.

Within the framework of this theocratic government, then, the
city-states rose to great heights at a time when Europe was still in

the Stone Age, its population living in caves or lake villages, with very little art or architecture. By 2600 B.C. Sumerian builders were erecting structures of brick sixty-five feet high, making use of the arch, the vault, and the dome. They were living in some cases in two-storeyed houses not so radically different from the residences of well-to-do merchants in the provincial towns of Iraq today. It is notable, however, that their art and architecture, like every other public activity, were a manifestation of religion, much as it was in the cathedrals of medieval Europe: in other words, craft and skill were exploited for the greater glory of God and not of man. The result in ancient Mesopotamia was the erection of those 'Towers of Babel', ziggurats, or temple-towers, which the Jews hated as the personification of heathenism and Greeks like Herodotus admired for their architectural achievement. The ziggurat at Ur is, of course, the most famous of these lofty temples, since enough of the vast ruin survived for the archaeologists to be able to reconstruct the size, shape, and function of these characteristic Sumerian temples. That of Ur, for instance, was a three-storeyed erection, built entirely of brick, the core being of rubble cemented with bitumen (the pitch found in Babylonia) and the outer face of kiln-baked brick. A long stairway led up to the shrine of the city-god, Nanna, the moon-deity and divine patron of Ur. But it is not simply the size of this 4000-year-old temple which astonishes us today, but the skill and artistry of the architects who designed the building, for since it consists basically of rectangular blocks piled on and against each other like children's building bricks, the ziggurat could have been like a modern 'office block': that is, a huge monolith with the minimum concession to aesthetic principle. It is not so, for the Sumerian designers appear to have discovered the part played by optical illusion in architecture, a discovery, or rediscovery, of the builders of the Parthenon. In effect, there are no long straight lines at all in the Ur ziggurat, but the line of every wall and of every superstructure is imperceptibly curved or convected, so that the observer, by the principle of entasis, receives an impression of both strength and lightness, instead of (as in the case of the modern 'egg-box' construction) weight and deadness. Moreover, the use of the converging staircases leads the eye upwards towards the tower wherein lies the shrine of the god midway between heaven and earth. It is a masterpiece of architecture, and

we are not surprised that Herodotus, who had seen the temples
of Greece and Egypt, was impressed by the ziggurat of Babylon,
which he seems to have visited about 450 B.C. He states that this
ziggurat was *eight* storeys high and that the visitor ascended by a
path which wound round the outside of the structure. Halfway to
the top there was a bench where sightseers could rest and catch
their breath before going on to the topmost platform, which was
the shrine of the god. One can visualise the Greek traveller climbing up to the temple in order to see what was inside. But, he says,
there was nothing except a couch of unusual size, richly adorned,
and flanked by a golden table. On this couch, apparently, sat or
lay a woman said to be the wife of the god who came down from
heaven in person to cohabit with her. 'For my part I don't believe
it,' says the historian, who was something of a sceptic where
religions were concerned. It is not surprising, therefore, that he
scoffs at the custom whereby every woman in the land had to
prostitute herself at least once in her life in the temple of Ishtar
(the Inanna of the Sumerians, the Astarte of the Semites, and the
Aphrodite of the Greeks). He reports that wealthy women took
all the precautions they could to avoid a too-unpleasant experience by surrounding themselves with a whole army of attendants
so that strangers could not conveniently approach them. No doubt
they had made their own arrangements to fulfil their religious
obligations before they set out to the temple. The majority of
women, however, having adorned themselves in their best finery
for the occasion, seated themselves in the holy enclosure and
awaited their partner. Herodotus remarks, no doubt with con-
scious irony, 'and here there is always a great crowd, some coming
and some going'. A man, having chosen the woman who pleased
him, had only to toss a silver coin into her lap to be entitled to her
favours. The value of the coin made no difference, for provided
the man had uttered the correct formula—'The goddess Ishtar
prosper thee'—he could not be refused, for refusal was forbidden
by religious law. 'Such of the women who are tall and beautiful
are soon released, but the ugly ones have to stay a long time before
they can fulfil the law.' In fact, Herodotus found on inquiry that
some women had been waiting for four years to do their duty,
while others were no doubt in and out of the holy enclosure
within a matter of hours.

   It is an interesting story, and characteristic of Herodotus, but we should probably accept it with some reservations. The Greek historian was probably confusing the harlots who plied their trade in and around the venereal temples with the women worshippers. From what we know of Sumerian society, certainly, it seems unlikely that respectable women would be forced to prostitute themselves in the name of religion, though we still don't know enough about this ancient people to make positive pronouncements. Thus it was a considerable shock to admirers of Sumer as the exponents of a benign civilisation to see what came out of the Royal Tombs of Ur, particularly that of Grave 789, which obviously belonged to a very important personage, possibly a king. His tomb, though robbed in antiquity, was found to contain the skeletons of sixty-three men and women and six oxen. Included among the men were six helmeted guards. Now it is obvious that all these people and animals were not buried in this royal grave *after* they died, and the fact that the skulls of both the guards and the female attendants had been crushed by a heavy blow tells us what had happened when the great man was buried in Grave 789 four and a half thousand years ago: the guards, attendants, draught animals (oxen), and food supplies were buried with him. The evidence of this practice which we associate more with savage than with civilised people (an Ashanti queen was buried with 4000 sacrified retainers) is confirmed in Grave 1237, the so-called 'Great Death Pit' in which seventy-four bodies were found neatly laid out in rows. What is strange about these corpses lying on their sides with their legs slightly bent and their hands covering their faces is the absence of any signs of violence or even of terror. To the contrary, the women, who far outnumber the men, lie with their head-dresses and ornaments still in place, so they could not have struggled when they died. Sir Leonard Woolley, who excavated the royal tombs, suggests that the sacrificial victims walked to their assigned places, lay down, and took some kind of drug, perhaps opium, which induced sleep and possibly death. The pit was then filled in.

It must have been a very gaily dressed crowd that assembled in the open, mat-lined pit for the royal obsequies, a blaze of colour with the crimson coats, the silver and the gold; clearly these people were not wretched slaves killed as oxen might be killed, but persons held in honour, wearing their robes of office and coming, one hopes, voluntarily to a rite which would in their belief be but a passing from one world to another, from the service of a god on earth to that of the same god in another sphere.[1]

One feels that the archaeologist is somewhat out of his depth here, or is, perhaps, falling back on the age-old justification of murder in the name of religion. Unfortunately for his theory, the preponderance of women to men in the Great Death Pit—sixty-eight women to six men—suggests that these unfortunate victims were concubines buried alive with their lord and master, whether they were 'coming voluntarily to a rite' or not. One suggests concubines rather than slaves since all the women were adorned with precious ornaments, including gold and silver hair-ribbons, earrings of gold, and necklaces of lapis lazuli—not the jewellery of slaves. Neither did the soldiers 'come voluntarily', for the six guards in Grave 789 all had their skulls crushed. We must conclude, therefore, that the Sumerians of 2500 B.C. believed in human sacrifice, which is, after all, at the basis of all religions, including the Christian, where it has been sublimated into the metaphorical eating of Christ's body.

But it is, as we have pointed out in the case of the Greeks, also an axiom of religion that as men civilise themselves, they civilise their gods. Human sacrifices, like those we find in the Royal Tombs of Ur, are unique throughout Mesopotamia and must belong to a remote period in Sumerian history when such practices were still regarded as pleasing to the gods. We do not meet with it again in the annals of that nation—and certainly not among the Babylonians or even, for that matter, with those masters of cruelty, the Assyrians. The rite seems in later periods to have been restricted to the Phoenicians and Carthaginians, though we should not forget that the Greeks indulged in the practice at the time of Troy, as the Jews did in the time of Abraham. But in Sumer it is now generally agreed that human sacrifice was limited to the first dynasty of Ur (2500–2300 B.C.), after which homicide was dealt with by the law of the land.

This change in attitude and the recognition of the value, if not the sanctity, of human life was due to progress and prosperity, due to organisation of agriculture and trade. Canals and irrigation channels brought abundant water to the outlying fields and groves. The two rivers, the Tigris and the Euphrates, were the highways of international trade. Thousands of clay tablets dealing with financial and commercial contracts indicate the prosperous and complex nature of the Sumerian business world. And the artefacts found in the graves and tombs prove that the ruling caste was rich and luxurious.

Side by side with this wealth and prosperity of the larger Sumerian cities like Ur, Larsa, Lagash, Nippur, Sippar, and so on went the extraordinary cultural development which differentiates the lower Mesopotamian valley from the rest of the world—so much so that here, in the orchards and gardens of a town like Eridu, may have originated the legend of the Garden of Eden. The word 'Eden' itself, which has in its Hebrew form the connotation of 'pleasure' or 'delight', may be derived from the Akkadian word *Edinu*, meaning a fertile plain. Originally, then, Eden must have been a particularly lush oasis which to desert-dwellers would be the nearest thing to an earthly paradise they could conceive of. And so it is described in Genesis, as a well-wooded and watered garden made fertile by four rivers, one of which is actually named as the Euphrates. The other three rivers—Pishon, Gihon, and Hiddekel—are not so easily identified, though Hiddekel is described as 'going in front of Assyria'—in other words, the Tigris, the second of the Two Rivers which made the intervening plains a rich agricultural land in contrast to the surrounding deserts.

Following up the significant clues that the Garden of Eden was associated with the Euphrates and the Tigris, Biblical scholars are prepared to accept the theory of the Assyriologists that the other two rivers specified in Genesis—namely, Pishon and Gihon—may be the Hebrew names for two of the principal canals which joined the two great waterways. Even so, it is difficult to do more than speculate as to the location of Eden, since the Euphrates and Tigris have changed their course radically since the second millennium B.C., and the old canal system of the Sumero-Babylonian empires has collapsed completely. Otherwise the explorer might find further positive clues of the oasis and the four rivers at the Sumerian town of Eridu, known in ancient times as 'the good city' on account of the shrine of the god Tammuz who dwelt there in the shade of a sacred palm tree, while the goddess Bahu had her couch in the foliage of the same tree. And as if to corroborate this remarkable resemblance between the Hebrew myth

of the Garden of Eden and the Sumerian shrine of the rustic god
and goddess, we find the latter pair frequently depicted in
Akkadian sculptures, while a cylinder seal now in the British
Museum depicts two figures, a male and a female, seated on opposite sides of a tree with hands stretched towards it. Behind the
woman is an upright snake. Clearly, then, primeval Man and
Woman, the Garden, the Tree, and the Snake are common to
both Sumerian and Hebrew mythology and probably originated
with the former. As a rider to this interesting theory, we note that
the Arabs, who accept the Hebrew version of the Creation as
orthodox, locate the Garden of Eden at the confluence of the
Euphrates and Tigris, in the village of Al Qurnah, forty miles
north-west of Basra. Here they will point out the original Tree of
Knowledge in whose trunk, they say, lives a serpent. Only believers, however, are able to see this personification of the Tempter
who has the power to vanish into thin air at the approach of un-
believers.

The Garden of Eden legend, therefore, must certainly have been
conceived in the minds of these Semitic desert-dwellers who came
out of the arid wastelands of the Arabian and Syrian deserts and
saw before them the bright green fields and leafy orchards of the
Sumerian communities. These desert-men, we should remember,
were savages in the Roman sense: that is, they had neither settled
communities, an agricultural system, nor any form of written
language. They were wholly nomadic and lived by hunting and
obeyed only the law of the tribe. In contrast to these wandering
bands—in contrast, in fact, to the inhabitants of the rest of the
Middle East and of Europe itself—the Sumerians were civilised
even by modern standards. Their cities were well built and administered; their fields were properly irrigated and tilled; their
arts and sciences were highly developed. And they had a further
claim to being the most advanced people in the world—a strong
sense of justice based on rational principles and not, as with
savages and barbarians, on the law of the jungle. And so we find
Sargon of Agade (*c.* 2350 B.C.) described as 'the king of justice
who rules by righteousness'. Nammu, the founder of the third
dynasty of Ur (2113 B.C.) is called 'the king who observed the just
laws of the sun-god'. A king of the Sumerian city of Larsa is
termed 'the shepherd of justice'. And so forth. In other words, the
Sumerians in their emphasis upon these concepts were civilised

in an ethical as well as a material sense, and it is this which makes their appearance in remote history so interesting.

In fact, the earliest law code of Ur lays down the first principles of modern justice and jurisprudence: namely, the substitution of fines for the primitive law of 'an eye for an eye'. The Code of Nammu which dates from the twenty-second century B.C. specifically states that the penalty for cutting off another man's foot, whether by design or accident, shall be ten silver shekels. It was this approach to the problem of crime and violence which was ultimately to influence even the neighbouring Semitic peoples who were still at the stage of barbarism, with their cruel and jealous gods, their jurisprudence based on the *lex talionis*, and their national energies devoted to war and destruction. And when the Sumerian dynasty finally fell about 1850 B.C. they bequeathed to their barbarian conquerors a fully-developed civilisation based on a respect for humane gods, a code of law, economic prosperity, sophisticated sciences and arts, an alphabet, and an ethical system which foreshadowed many of the moral principles of future societies.

G

8

Art and Literature in Sumer

IT IS LARGELY BY means of their art and literature that we can best glimpse something of the mind of ancient peoples. For whereas the scientist can live and work apart from the day-to-day affairs, the artist cannot disassociate himself from the life around him. His function has been said to be not merely to hold up a mirror to that life, but to reveal its essence, its outstanding characteristics and, if possible, its inner significance. Yet we have to admit that if the Sumerian and Babylonian artists do this at all, it is by coincidence since (a) their work was a craft pure and simple; (b) its purpose was wholly functional; and (c) there was no concept of 'free' art, or of art for art's sake. True, modern art critics now tend to regard these ancient productions as authentic works of art in their own right and not just as 'museum-pieces', but it is still very much an open question whether these old craftsmen would have thought about their work in this self-conscious twentieth-century manner. They were given a job to do and rigid standards by which to do it. With specific official instructions to guide him, the sculptor picked up his chisel and set to work. His job was to produce the likeness of a god or a king who had to be portrayed not as a puny man but as a mighty life-force, at once majestic and terrible. It was a large order, and one can understand better the Sumerian, Babylonian, and Assyrian sculptures if one realises what the creators of them were required to produce. Their solution to the problem was to fashion what they conceived of as a super-man: and this idealisation of omnipotence accounts for the huge staring eyes of the idols, the great beards hanging in tiers from the uncompromising lips, the wide shoulders, and the impression of absolute immutability. Similarly, the statues of the goddesses manage to create an aura of feminine mystery, the strange wide-eyed serenity of the eternal female. The portraits of kings emphasise their earthly power: as the representatives of god on earth, they, too, are given full beards, wide shoulders, and an aura of majesty, but not the great staring eyes of the all-seeing god.

And so for every kind of creature, divine, human, and animal, these old craftsmen attempted not a naturalistic representation, but an idealised one. To those only familiar with Greek or Renaissance art, the statues, steles, and figurines which have been unearthed in the ancient Mesopotamian cities seem, at first, nearly lifeless; or, alternatively, rigid and inhuman, especially the cold, stern portraits of kings, priests, and state officials. We are delighted, therefore, when we meet with those rarer naturalistic portrayals of men and animals—the Assyrian bas-reliefs of lions, hunting-dogs, deer, and so forth. But what we cannot expect to see in Sumerian, Babylonian, or Assyrian art is the daily activities of the ordinary citizen, for the artists themselves would not have seen the point in wasting their time and talent on such mundane matters. Art was in the service of religion; the lay world was served not by artists, but by artisans who produced the plates, cups, vases, votive figures, jewellery, and ornaments which were used in everyday life.

Many of these objects, humble though they are, come as a relief after the awesome statuary which adorned the temples—idols of gods with great bulging eyes and of their worshippers, some cringing in the act of veneration, some smiling with a smug expression that may seem to us to be deliberately satiric, but is certainly not so. The products of the artisans, on the other hand—of goldsmiths, silversmiths, bronzesmiths, and potters—have much more variety and reveal to us the human side of the people who made and those who used them. The Royal Cemetery at Ur was rich in these artefacts and not surprisingly its discovery, together with the grim mystery of the skeletons in the king's graves, was as exciting to both the learned and the lay world as the discovery of Tutankhamen's tomb. The cemetery at Ur was excavated from 1926 to 1932, a period which resulted in Leonard Woolley's findings being somewhat overshadowed by the fantastic treasures brought out from the Egyptian tomb by Howard Carter from 1922 to 1930. Yet to historians and archaeologists

the artefacts contained in the Royal Cemetery at Ur were, in a
sense, more exciting than those of the pharaonic grave, since
what they represented was the treasure of a civilisation over a
thousand years older than that of the Egyptian king. The Royal
Tombs of Ur date from about 2500 B.C., though Woolley himself
placed them a thousand years earlier than that. Tutankhamen
ruled Egypt about 1360 B.C., by which time Sumer had handed on
its laws, its arts, and its sciences to the whole of the eastern Mediterranean world and had itself passed away.

And so the objects in gold, silver, and inlay which were brought
out of the 1840 graves are unique in the history of civilisation, for
they reveal a standard of art and craftsmanship which was not
thought to be possible at a time when the rest of the world was
still in the New Stone Age. Yet from Grave 789, the one that contained the skeletons of sixty-three men and women and six oxen,
the archaeologists discovered the remains of two four-wheeled
waggons, a sledge, a harp with a sounding-box made of gold sheet
hammered over a wooden core, the jewellery of Queen Pu-abi,
and many other valuable objects which were buried with this
royal dame and her murdered attendants. From Grave 1237, the
Great Death Pit where six men and sixty-eight women were apparently killed and buried in order to keep their royal master
company in the next world, jewellery of gold, silver, lapis lazuli,
and carnelian—all the adornments of the dead women attendants
—were still *in situ*. From this grave, too, came the astonishingly
modern figure of a he-goat standing with his front feet in the
branches of a tree. The body was originally carved out of wood,
gold was hammered to the shape of the head and legs, silver to the
belly, shell to the horns, lapis lazuli for the beard and neck. It is
one of the most charming examples of animal portraiture in the
whole history of art.

Such were the achievements of Sumerian artists and craftsmen
four and a half thousand years ago. The inlaid gaming board, for
instance, made in the form of a wooden box to contain the playing
pieces and encrusted with a mosaic of shells, lapis lazuli, bone,
and coloured paste, would grace any modern living room and the
game itself could be played, assuming it is the same as is still found
in Ceylon. The jewellery which the women attendants of the
Great Death Pit (Grave 1237) wore in death is not fundamentally
different and certainly not inferior in craftsmanship to the most

expensive jewellery worn by women today. An example is the twelve 'beech-leaves' made from gold foil and soldered to a head-band, a masterpiece of the goldsmith's art. As it was found to-gether with many other ornaments by the crushed skull of one of the sixty-eight dead women in the Death Pit, it was possible to reconstruct the head, a work undertaken by Mrs Woolley, who modelled the dead lady's head and face in wax and placed the headband, combs, neckband, necklaces, and ear-rings all in place. 'The reconstructed head,' says Leonard Woolley, 'presents us with the most accurate picture we are likely ever to possess of what she looked like in her lifetime.'[1]

The art treasures which have survived from Sumer can still be seen in considerable numbers in the principal museums of the world—notably the British Museum, the Louvre, the Berlin Museum, the Oriental Institute, Chicago, the University Museum, Pennsylvania, and the Baghdad Museum. But what is astonishing is that so much has survived from 4000 to 5000 years ago: first, because the soil of Mesopotamia, unlike that of Egypt, does not conserve cloth, wood, or even metal; and, secondly, because when the empire was overthrown around 2000 B.C. the conquerors of the great Sumerian cities—Ur, Erech, Uruk, and Lagash—looted what they considered of any value and smashed to pieces the rest. The story of the end is told in a moving poem entitled *Lamentation over the Destruction of Ur*:

How, O Sumer, are thy mighty fallen!
The holy king is banished from his temple
The temple itself is destroyed, the city demolished
The leaders of the nation have been carried off into captivity
A whole empire [i.e. Sumer] has been overthrown by the will
of the gods.

The reference here to 'the holy king' is to Ibi-Sin,* the last king of Ur, a monarch who was deified during his lifetime. Evidently his godhead did not protect him, for an Elamite force crossed the Tigris from the east, overran the land of Sumer, destroyed Ur, Erech, and the other Sumerian cities, and carried off 'the holy king' to Persia. At the same time the invaders sacked the temple of Ishtar, the Sumerian Aphrodite, and stole the idol of the god-dess herself. But her cult was far too deep-seated to be superseded

* Also called Ibbi-Suen. His reign lasted from 2029 to 2006 B.C.

or forgotten, and as the goddess of love she managed, in one form or another, to hang on to her place in the pagan hierarchy until the early Christian fathers killed her off once and for all, though vestiges of her cult are said to survive to this day.

If, in addition to the art that a past civilisation leaves us in the form of statues and pictures, we are able to read what men thought and felt in far-off times, only then can we say that we really know them. Thus we can claim to share fully in the lives of the Greeks and Romans, whereas peoples like the Phoenicians and Etruscans, for instance, elude us except as shadowy figures on the stage of history. Unfortunately little survives of the 'literature' of ancient Mesopotamia, partly because little was written. What we have— in enormous quantities—are official documents of scant interest to any but historians and philologists. The literature proper of Sumer, Babylonia, and Assyria consists of an occasional epic poem, some elegies like the *Lamentation over the Destruction of Ur*, and a handful of folk-tales and folk-sayings. Moreover, be- cause of the language problems, this small corpus of literature is a very difficult and specialised subject, confusing to both the expert and layman alike. The confusion arises over the tremendous problems confronting the translators, and very often efforts to solve these problems result in some very odd results indeed. What, for instance, is one to make of this translation of an extract from a Sumerian poem called *Enki and Ninhursag*?

> Nine days being her nine months, the months of womanhood,
> Like fat . . . fat, like . . . fat, like good princely fat,
> Ninmu, like . . . fat, like . . . fat, like good princely fat,
> Gave birth to Ninkurra.[2]

Surely something has gone wrong here, for would a poet even 4000 years ago refer to the process of parturition as 'like good princely fat'? Indeed, Dr Kramer, the translator, is fully aware of the difficulty, for he changes the word 'fat' in a later version to 'cream', so that the birth of Ninkurra reads:

> Ninmu, like cream, like cream, like good princely cream,
> Gave birth to the goddess Ninkurra.

Thus the Sumerians, so *simpatici* with their bald heads, bland faces, crossed hands, and pot-bellies, seem in their literature, as we are obliged to read it, to be writing the kind of gibberish that passes for poetry among the pseudo-dadaists of our own day. What, for instance, is one to make of this?

> Uttu with joyful heart opened the door of the house.
> Enki to Uttu, the fair lady,
> Gives the cucumbers in their . . .
> Gives the apples in their . . .
> Gives the grapes in their . . .
> Uttu, the fair lady, . . .s for him, . . .s for him,
> Enki took his joy of Uttu,
> He embraced her, lay in her lap,
> . . .s the buttocks, touches the . . .[3]

Once again we wonder whether the dots represent four-letter words or whether the translator simply could not fathom what exactly was going on. Yet disregarding all those cucumbers, et cetera, that Enki brought 'in their . . .', it does not seem beyond the powers of invention to fill in the missing words, especially as the Sumerians apparently had no euphemisms for describing sexual congress and no inhibitions about performing it.

Our bewilderment is even greater in those translations where original words are retained, either because they are untranslatable or unknown. Hence, the layman is confronted with lines like these:

> Thy *mahhu* in thy holy *gigunu* dressed not in linen
> Thy righteous *enu* chosen in radiance, in the *Ekissirgal*,
> From the shrine to the *giparru* proceeds not joyfully.[4]

It should be stated at once, however, that these examples have not been quoted to discount the work of Sumeriologists who have so painstakingly copied, transliterated, and rendered into the best English they could the thousands of clay tablets that have survived for nearly four millennia. Indeed, one can hardly expect a philologist dealing with an obscure language whose vocabulary and syntax are still not fully understood to be also a poet-translator of the calibre of Edward FitzGerald. Yet one can hope that one day a translator will do for Sumerian literature what FitzGerald did for Omar Khayyám and King James's forty-seven translators did for the Bible.

Indeed, there have already been several brave attempts at this difficult assignment. One of the first and most interesting was that of R. Campbell Thompson, who made a poetical rendering of the

Epic of Gilgamesh as early as 1928. Campbell Thompson, a Sumeriologist of distinction, has this to say about his translation:

> Of the poetic beauty of the Epic there is no need to speak.
> Expressed in a language which has perhaps the simplicity, not
> devoid of cumbrousness, of Hebrew rather than the flexibility
> of Greek, it can nevertheless describe the whole range of
> human emotions. . . . Whether there is justification for taking
> the risk of turning it into ponderous English hexameter metre
> is an open question, but in doing so I have done my utmost to
> preserve an absolutely literal translation.[5]

Thirty years after Campbell Thompson's translation Miss N. K.
Sandars, though not a Sumeriologist, made a popular version of
the Epic of which she says:

> It has seemed worth attempting a version which while adding
> nothing that is not vouched for by scholarship nor omitting
> anything of which the meaning is beyond doubt, yet will avoid
> the somewhat uncouth appearance of the line by line transla-
> tion and will give the reader a straightforward narrative.[6]

It is interesting, and, indeed, illustrative of the enormous difficulties facing the translation of Sumerian, to compare the various
versions of the *Epic of Gilgamesh*, which has been frequently done
into English as into other European languages. We take as our
example the incident from the First Tablet describing the seduction of Enkidu, the prototype of primeval man. This incident is,
perhaps, the most significant and dramatic event in the story,
since it is the first description in world literature of the myth of
the loss of man's innocence. The account, then, of how Enkidu,
the Sumerian Adam, met his Eve and how she persuaded him to
abandon his carefree life in field and forest for life in the city is a
much profounder analysis of man's fate than we are given in the
Genesis version of the myth. For even though the language is, by
our standards, lacking in refinement, the story itself is beautifully
told, and its 'moral' powerfully presented. But what is really interesting about it is that for once the primeval Eve is not the
villainess she is made to be in the Hebrew (and Greek) myth,
even if she is a harlot which, in any case, was no disgrace in
Sumer. And how much this tells us about men's attitudes towards
women in those far-off days!

Taking all these facts into consideration, there seems to be no reason to be shocked by the literal translation of this episode, though all the translations hitherto have bowdlerised the original, which is rendered by the Danish Assyriologist, Svend Aage Pallis, as follows:

> The harlot uncovered her breasts and spread her legs, and he [i.e. Enkidu] possessed her luxuriousness. She felt no shyness, but took his penis, loosened her clothes, and he lay on her. She did a woman's work and made him lascivious, and he mounted her on her back.[7]

Understandably, most translators have regarded this as pretty strong stuff, though if that is how the Sumerian poet described the seduction, what can we, or need we, do about it? Yet one of the more recent American translators glosses over what he calls 'the more objectionable passages' (of which this is one) by turning the Sumerian into Latin—or having a Latinist do it for him. Here is the absurd result:

> Him, the wild (?) man, the prostitute saw,
> The savage man from the depths of the steppe.
> 'Is est, meretrix, nuda sinum tuum;
> Aperi gremium tuum ut succumbat venustati tuae.
> Noli cunctari . . . [et cetera, et cetera]'[8]

Miss Sandars, who tells us that she used the Heidel translation among others, does not shrink from at least conveying the general idea of the seduction and renders the 'objectionable passage' as follows:

> She was not ashamed to take him, she made herself
> Naked and welcomed his eagerness, she incited the
> savage to love and taught him the woman's art.
> For six days and seven nights they lay together,
> for Enkidu had forgotten his home in the hills.[9]

Other versions show, too, the problem that confronted the translator looking back over his shoulder at the shade of Thomas Bowdler. But the more one sees to what a level this insipidity has brought Sumerian literature, the more one feels the need for a new and vigorous approach to the subject, for we are not concerned with the niceties of drawing-room conversation but with what the first civilised people in the Western world had to say to us. *Gilgamesh* is one of the great epics of literature—unique among the Mesopotamian writings, it is true, for it is about man and his fate, instead of about those tiresome local gods and goddesses who are as tedious as their names—Sin, Uttu, Nanna, Ninlil, Ninazu, and Nunbarsheguna. After all, these deities, being immortal and presumably invulnerable—and dead as a doornail—cannot interest us very much. Moreover, these Sumerian godlings did not have the humour and humanity of the Greek anthropomorphs whose lives seem to have been one long romp.

But Gilgamesh of Uruk (he is still called 'King of Babylon' in the British Museum catalogue) was definitely human: his destiny was the same as ours in that he was born to suffer and die. He is, indeed, the first tragic hero on the grand scale, the scale with which the Greek dramatists familiarised us 1500 years later. And for this reason the story of Gilgamesh has the power to move us like that of Agamemnon or of Ulysses whom the Sumerian hero in some respects resembles.

Alas! this is not true of the bulk of Sumerian literature which the scholars have so far given us, and one must admit that the task of 'humanising' a great deal of the liturgical poetry is truly formidable. Monopolised, as it were, by a handful of specialists, that literature has hardly reached the outside world. No wonder that one of the most eminent of the Sumeriologists, S. N. Kramer, who has devoted his academic life to copying, reading, and translating the tablets, rather gloomily defines a worker in his field as 'a well-nigh perfect example of the man who knows "mostest about the leastest"—a very limited fellow indeed, who rates "way down" even among the lowly academicians'.[10] A sad commentary on the state in which this branch of scholarship is held, particularly when one realises the enormous dedication the Sumeriologist requires to wrestle with the grammar, syntax, and vocabulary of the Sumerian language itself. It is not surprising that the best we can sometimes expect of a difficult passage turns out to be:

> May I (too) have a favourable *shedu* like that before you;
> May I (too) have a *lamassu* like that which goes behind you.

The unenlightened reader can only grope about in the recesses of his subconscious to guess what these objects, apparently worn front and back, refer to.

However, Dr Kramer explains for us some of the problems he and his colleagues are up against in translating from the Sumerian. He speaks of the complexities, 'treacherous possibilities', and sources of error and admits that many Sumerian words can be only vaguely apprehended. He warns us that:

If the translator starts with a definite bias as to the meaning of the passage, it will often enough be not too difficult to find an equivalent for the particular word involved, which after a superficial examination can be made to fit the sense anticipated.[11]

Quite obviously the layman is out of his depth in any discussion of philological niceties of this sort, and all he can do is await the verdict of the experts. Yet, at the same time, he cannot help feeling that the Sumerians themselves, those shadowy people he wants to hear speak (as we can hear quite clearly Romans, Greeks, Egyptians, and even Babylonians) remain silent. Moreover, if some of these translations we have are their authentic voices, is what they are saying worth the effort of attending to it?

We know from the *Epic of Gilgamesh* that it is. And we know, too, from other sources what we may be missing, for certainly the Sumerians speak to us clearly enough in other artistic achievements—in their portraits, for instance—not so much portraits of the gods and kings as of those citizens like Ur-Nanshe, the singer, with his hair parted in the middle and his eager smile; or Kur-lil, the smug official with his hands clasped comfortably over his paunch. And what they seem to say to us in their portraits and, for that matter, in those snippets of secular literature which resemble proverbs, is twofold: first, enjoy life to the full; and, secondly, it is the only life we have: death is the end for us all. The conviction with which the Sumerians held these views pervades all their non-official literature and art, as the convictions of the writers and artists of our own medieval period account for the sombreness and mysticism of their productions—and the comparison is valid since both ages had strongly theocentric forms of society and both were deeply religious.

This may seem paradoxical until we see that the difference between the Sumerian culture and that of the Middle Ages is the absence in the Sumerian attitude of a sense of guilt, or original sin. It is almost impossible for us to conceive of religious conviction

without a sense of guilt, for we are conditioned by the Hebrew
prophets and the Christian Fathers in the matters of morality.
Hence we tend to equate sex with sin, for instance, a moral stance
which creates all kinds of problems when dealing with alien cultures like those of Sumer. Moreover, to judge a 4000-year-old
civilisation by the ethical standards largely formulated a hundred
years ago can lead us to all manner of historical inexactitudes and
misinterpretations; one thinks of those impressive-sounding catch-
phrases with which anthropologists 'explain away' such phenomena as phallic symbols, temple harlots, and the like as 'fertility
rites', 'maternity cults', 'Mother Earth', and so forth. Yet how
difficult it is to believe that when a worshipper entered the Temple
of Ishtar and selected a girl for an hour or so's dalliance that he
seriously regarded this as an act of piety intended to please the
gods or persuade them to fructify the fields. We simply do not
know whether this was actually the case, or whether, for instance,
the Church was running a licensed brothel as the Methodists, say,
might run a charity bazaar all in a good cause.

The point is, perhaps, that we ought to go and ask the Sumerians themselves their opinion, and we can only have that if we discard our own ideas of what is proper and improper (discard them,
it will be understood, for the purpose of understanding another
culture); and, in addition, we do need an honest and, if possible,
graceful translation of their literature. There are, for instance, a
number of Sumerian poems on the subject of death which remind
us in their philosophy and imagery of the Elizabethans who had
the same melancholy amounting almost to despair at the prospect
of 'Time's winged chariot'. And the Sumerians would undoubtedly have agreed with Marvell's description of the after-world as
consisting of 'deserts of vast eternity'—in other words, nothing
but empty space. A very ancient lament which belongs to a period
as early as 2500 B.C. states categorically:

> He who was still alive in the night, today he is dead;
> Suddenly he is eclipsed, swiftly he is crushed.
> One moment he is singing and playing,
> All of a sudden he howls like a wailing man.[12]

En passant, we quote these lines as an example of how desperately Sumerian literature needs better treatment at the hands of its
interpreters; for the englishing of this lament is manifestly in-

adequate, even the syntax being false. Unhappy, too, is the choice
of words. 'All of a sudden he howls like a wailing man' so jars on
the ear that we are more likely to think of wolves and banshees
than of a man in his death-throes.

Yet one must concede that it is still too early for the outsider
to be in a position to deal with the semantic problems of Sumerian.
Miss Sandars, of course, has made a splendid beginning in her
version of Gilgamesh, and it was largely due to her 'humanisation'
of this ancient epic that our enthusiasm for the earliest of all literature has been aroused. And as a recent example of what can be
accomplished by a translator who interprets the spirit as well as
the words of the original (the essence of the translator's art) we
quote two Sumerian epigrams adapted by Nigel Dennis from the
literal translations of Dr S. N. Kramer.[13]

> My wife is in church (literally, 'the outdoor shrine');
> My mother is down by the river (probably attending some
>   religious rite);
> And here am I starving of hunger.
> (Dr S. N. Kramer)

> My wife is thanking god for all he has given her,
> My mother is prostrate beside the sacred river,
> There is not, I think, much hope of dinner.
> (Nigel Dennis)

and

> The desert canteen is a man's life,
> The shoe is a man's eye,
> The wife is a man's future,
> The son is a man's refuge,
> The daughter is a man's salvation,
> The daughter-in-law is a man's devil.
> (Kramer)

> It is desert fare that makes a man,
> It is a shoe that points the way,
> It is a wife that writes his fate,
> A daughter that consoles his age.
> It is a son that shields his head,
> A son's wife that breaks his heart.
> (Dennis)

All the same, it cannot be reiterated often enough that the
difficulties attendant upon the presentation of Sumerian literature
to the 'general reader' are formidable. To begin with, not more
than a score of orientalists can read the tablets in any case, and we
must be grateful to them for their enormous patience as well as
erudition in giving us our first glimpses of these strange and at-
tractive people. But we still need to know a lot more about them
than their official records concerning the attributes of their gods
and the exploits of their kings tell us. This is why their literature
proper* is so important—not so much for its philological puzzles
as for the philosophy of life it expresses. That philosophy from
the intimations we obtain of it in the more felicitous translations
shows the Sumerians to have a serene and life-enriching view,
despite their fatalism about the hereafter—'the house where
people sit in darkness, with dust as their food'. It is summed up,
perhaps, in the advice an old woman gives to Gilgamesh, who is
in despair at the inevitability of age and death:

> Fill your belly with good things. Day and night, night and day,
> dance and be merry, feast and rejoice. Let your clothes be fresh,
> bathe yourself in water, cherish the child that holds your hand,
> and make your wife happy in your embrace.[14]

A hedonistic philosophy, perhaps, but one that takes into
account the happiness of those one loves. Yet perhaps this almost
over-civilised appreciation of the good things of life would be
called materialism by some, decadence by others. At all events, it
did not take into account the envy of the have-not peoples who
lived a stark desert existence beyond the fertile plains of the Two
Rivers, the nomadic tribes who quickly put an end to the feasting
and dancing by destroying the Sumerian cities and decimating
their inhabitants. And so the world's first civilisation passed out
of history, to lie buried under heaps of rubble for the next 4000
years. All that remained of Sumer was its mind and spirit which
we see reappearing in a new and different form in the next of the
empires of the Middle East.

* Admittedly meagre in quantity compared with the 'literatures' of
Greece and Rome, but sufficient to give us an insight into Sumerian
thinking on secular matters.

9

The Rise of Babylonia

ONE OF THE MOST difficult areas in the history of the ancient Middle East concerns the periodic migrations of entire nations, or federations of tribes, whose names and origins are lost in the twilight world of legend. Yet we know that these waves of barbarian nomads suddenly burst out of the deserts of Arabia or descended from the steppes of Asia and swarmed on to the settled agricultural communities of Mesopotamia. To the Sumerians who had created not only a rich farming economy but an urban civilisation, these warlike hordes must have seemed as unwelcome as the plagues of locusts.

It was one of these periodic migrations around 2500 B.C. that threatened the very existence of the Sumerian city-states. The invaders seem to have come out of South Arabia, though all we know about them was that they were called the Amurru by the Sumerians and were probably the same people the Hebrews refer to as Amorites or Canaanites. The Bible describes the latter people as giants whom the Israelites found in occupation of Palestine on their arrival in that country. But whoever the Amurru were, or by whatever name they are called, it is certain they were a Semitic people who were still living in the Bronze Age when they swarmed into the Mesopotamian plains, captured the towns, killed the local kings, and then settled down to enjoy the advantages of civilised life. It was these people who were to create the Babylonian state whose first chieftain king appears on the stage of history in about 2300 B.C. His name was Sargon I and he ruled not from Babylon, which was at this period an unimportant village and trading post, but first at Kish, then at Agade. This Sargon, who is not to be confused with Sargon II of Assyria (721–705

B.C.), sometimes calls himself king of Kish and sometimes king
of Agade, and he reigned for fifty-five years, from 2302 to 2247
B.C. All we know about him is that he waged a succession of
thirty-four successful wars, principally against the land of Sumer
and eventually united the whole of central and southern Mesopotamia in one kingdom. This region was later to become known
as Babylonia, with the upper half called Akkad after the former
capital Agade, and the lower half Sumer.

Sargon, then, founded a dynasty which lasted from 2303 to
2108 B.C. The rulers and administrators were Semites, as was the
language; everything else was Sumerian: arts, sciences, and religion had been taken over lock, stock, and barrel by the invaders.
It was this combination of the military prowess of the victorious
desert nomads with the intellectual superiority of the conquered
Sumerians which enabled Sargon and his successors to create the
nucleus of an empire which was to reach out through its diplomatic and commercial channels to Egypt in the west and India in
the east. As yet this empire was not the centralised autocracy
which was later to be characteristic of the Babylonian, Assyrian,
and Persian empires, but was still a loose confederation of allied
city-states kept loyal to the most powerful of the kings by a large
standing army. Sargon is probably referring to this force in the
inscription which states that 54,000 men daily took their meals
in his presence. This was undoubtedly an army big enough to
defeat any rivals in the immediate vicinity, though not big enough
to police the entire area, so that the king was obliged to wage
constant campaigns, for no sooner had one insurrection been suppressed in the west than another started in the east. In fact, in
Sargon's old age, at a time when he must have been finding the
soldier's life very strenuous, his enemies united to attack him,
hoping that his senility or death would put an end to his domination. However, the old king rallied and again took to the field
and, as his memorial says, 'he caused their great army to perish'.

Sargon left his empire to his two sons Rimush and Manishtusu,
both of whom were challenged time and again by the petty kings
of other city-states. We must remember that at this stage of history the continual wars were caused principally by the feuding so
characteristic of desert tribes where the prestige of the sheik, the
partition of grazing land, and the ownership of wells keep the inhabitants of the towns and villages, as well as the nomads them-

selves, constantly engaged in, or on the verge of, savage conflict in which no quarter was asked and none given. It was during this type of tribal warfare that Rimush was killed, although his brother Manishtusu was able to avenge him by defeating the national enemies one by one. Once this had been accomplished, even though the resultant peace was only temporary, the Akkadian dynasty was on its way to becoming recognised as supreme by the city-states. In addition, Manishtusu, king of Agade, who was formerly regarded as only one more chieftain of a tribe, was now accepted as a 'great king'.

Such was the status of the next ruler, Naram-Sin (2224–2187 B.C.), grandson of Sargon, who consolidated the territories won by his grandfather and father and styled himself 'king of the four quarters of the world'. It was thought at one time that this title implied that he had pushed westwards as far as the Mediterranean, but it is more likely that his troops made periodic sorties to the coast or escorted the caravans to the Mediterranean ports without actually occupying the territories they passed through. Certainly he undertook full-scale campaigns in the north, and brought what was a thousand years later to become Assyria within his sphere of influence. In confirmation of this, we find both the father Rimush and the son Naram-Sin building temples in Nineveh. These works show not only the piety of the Akkadian kings but their intention of unifying the newly created empire of the 'four quarters of the world', for the ancient monarchs used religion to bind their colonies to the mother country as modern states use political institutions. Officials and agents were now personally appointed by the king, who thus inaugurated a kind of civil service, an institution which was to become a feature of every civilised government from that time on. And as a corollary to the appointment of officials to distant towns, Akkadian, the language of the invaders, became both the official tongue and the lingua franca of the territories, so that Sumerian soon ceased to be spoken at all and became in the course of time a 'dead' language whose use corresponded almost precisely with Latin in the medieval world.

In other words, a new and different form of civilisation had arisen in the Middle East. This new form was based on the concept of imperialism, with a king-emperor who ruled over vassal states from a capital city by means of a professional army and a civil service. Obviously such a system, as compared with the Sumerian

H

concept of independent city-states (a concept later favoured by the Greeks during the period of their greatest political and philosophical achievements), lent itself to the creation of despots and tyrants; and when Naram-Sin was deified within his own lifetime and henceforth addressed as 'the god Naram-Sin, the mighty, god of Akkad', it might be said that the foundations for nearly 3000 years of monarchal tyrannies of one sort and another had been laid. It is interesting to speculate on the reasons which decided even a powerful king to take such a dangerous step as declaring himself divine—dangerous because this would surely seem an affront to the old gods; and also because it must have been doubtful whether any intelligent subject was going to believe it. Everybody knew that the king had to die: so if he was mortal, how could he be a god? One can only guess from this distance in time and space that Naram-Sin had become something of a megalomaniac, or had been made such by his courtiers and sycophants. At all events, by declaring himself to be divine, he had given himself and his successors unlimited power, which was soon accepted as the prerogative of kings by people everywhere and was still accepted up to the time of the French Revolution in the more subtle form of Divine Right.

We shall note the introduction of another revolutionary idea which foreshadows the final domination of Babylon as a world power: that is, the appearance of a quasi-capitalist economy which is alien to the old Sumerian culture. Under the Sumerian system all landed property belonged to the local god and was administered by the priests, while only such things as furniture, slaves, and dwelling houses belonged to the private citizens. It was, we see, a type of theocratic communism. But by 1800 B.C. it is obvious from the enormous number of Akkadian documents dealing with business deals, estate accounts, administrative affairs, and land sales that private capital was a dominant factor in the economy. The Sumerian system of religious communism, therefore, had been abandoned in favour of trade and commerce, which were to become the twin pillars of the Babylonian Empire. In short, the Semites had imposed their ideas of politics and economics on the foundations of the old culture, changing the course of history from a theocentric type of society to a mercantile one. Capitalism had appeared on the world scene in a form not radically different from what it is today. It is also significant that about this

time—that is, with the end of the Third Ur Dynasty *c.* 1900 B.C.—
the Sumerian language began to be replaced by Akkadian for
business purposes and everyday affairs. The old tongue was kept
for church services and literary compositions of one sort or another, as though by retaining Sumerian as the language of temple
ritual the Akkadians were able to make a separation between
church and state, a useful—indeed, a necessary—distinction in a
capitalist economy. In short, there was one language for purposes
of religion and another for those of business, just as today there
is one code of ethics for the former and another for the latter.

At the same time, one must be careful about assuming that
religion lost its power as a result of the conquest of the Sumerian
dominions by the Semitic invaders. Certainly there is no period in
the whole of Babylonian or Assyrian history when the gods were
not officially honoured and their temples restored. Yet we cannot
refrain from asking to what extent this religiosity was the servant
of state policy, as some critics would argue that it was during the
Roman Republic and, again, in Victorian England. Certainly we
see in the history of all religions that the gods are placated during
peacetime by various rituals, services, and sacrifices and become
of enormous importance in times of peril, such as prolonged wars
close to the homeland. This functional attitude towards religion
implies that the worship of a divinity is more of a socio-political
institution than a spiritual process, and it is this attitude which
seems to differentiate the Sumerians from the Babylonians, as it
could be said to differentiate the religion of the Christian ascetics
of the Thebaid from that of the established church of Rome.

We can date the end of the Sumerian Empire to roughly 2000
B.C. with the fall of the Third Dynasty of Ur and the rise of various
other city-states up and down the length of Mesopotamia. The
wars and rivalries, the decline and fall of these cities and petty
empires do not concern us here, especially as they are areas of
ancient history about which the specialists are still arguing and
periodically changing their chronologies and conclusions. What
we are interested in is the radical social and economic revolution
which took place even while the interminable wars between the
kings, Sumerian, Amorite, Elamite, and so forth, were raging
back and forth across the land. As we have seen, one of those
changes was undoubtedly the shift from the Sumerian concept of
religious communism in which all real property belonged to the

god and to this extent could not be bought or sold, to the Semitic
system of limited capitalism with its private contracts covering
the sale of land.

The other important change seems to have been the gradual
development of a new class of *petite bourgeoisie*, or small free-
holders—farmers, shopkeepers, minor officials, and the like—who
were held together as a national group not by the church, but by
the monarchy, which was now the essence of the state. What this
meant was that the god was no longer the centre of community life,
nor was his temple the community house. God had become the
special responsibility of the king; the maintenance and repair of
his temple was his job, undertaken at his expense. The national
anthem, if there had been one, would undoubtedly have asked the
god to save 'our gracious king', not the petitioner and his family
and his city. In other words, religion which in Sumer had been
the business of the whole community had become the monopoly
of the ruling classes. We find the Babylonian kings imploring the
gods to grant them a long reign, an unshakable throne, and an
obedient people, implying that the deity was, or should be, in the
service of the government. The monarchs made quite sure that
the priests were loyal by granting this class special privileges:
in fact, the temple could now be considered as an extension of the
palace to enable the king to exercise the same control over the
clergy that he exercised over the army and the civil service. Under
the Sumerians there had always been a tendency on the part of the
more powerful members of the priesthood to play a leading role in
politics, to the point of sometimes usurping the prerogatives of
the crown. A letter, for instance, from the high priest of Lagash
to a colleague states that he had led the local army against a band
of Elamites who were raiding the territory around Lagash and
that he had put the enemy to flight, capturing 540 of them. For a
chief priest to take command of the national defence forces and to
send a report of his success to another priest indicates the power
of the clergy under the Sumerian system, for certainly no Babylonian king would have permitted any of his subjects, however
patriotic or pious, to get his hands on the army where the final
source of power resided. So one of the changes which the West
Semites introduced was the institutionalising of religion and the
curtailment of the powers of the church. As for the priests who
may initially have resented the loss of their power and prestige,

they were given acceptable compensations in the form of grants of land, tax concessions, grazing rights, and, of course, gifts of food, clothing, women, and jewellery presented to the temple ostensibly for the delectation of the god. It is not difficult to guess what happened to all the food that was set out on the temple altars in case the god came down to earth and got hungry: it went into the stomachs of the priests and their families, and was rightly regarded by them as part of their salary as senior civil servants.

The final change, or reform, introduced by the Semites was the substitution of their chief god for the principal Sumerian deity. The Amurru, or Amorites, had come out of the desert with a very ancient concept of the Supreme Being common to all primitive peoples throughout the world. This Lord of Lords, known by various names, such as Hadad to the Canaanites, Yahweh to the Hebrews, and Marduk to the Babylonians, was, of course, originally a fertility-god who created life by distributing the waters of the earth, so making fields and orchards fruitful. As a storm-god whose symbol was a thunderbolt, Marduk was feared in much the same manner as the Hebrews feared the Yahweh 'who maketh the clouds his chariot', but as the good Shepherd he was dearer and closer to the simple people. Eventually, the kings of the new empire made Marduk the international god, for in this way they were much better able to identify their interests, religious and political, throughout their expanding empire. In other words, their policy now was to have one imperial king and one imperial god, although the members of the old Sumerian pantheon were allowed to survive as worthy pensioners of the state. But they had no authority comparable with that of Marduk, who, by the time of Hammurabi (1792–1750 B.C.). was the undisputed master of both heaven and earth. So Marduk was the god of the nation; the king was his representative on earth; and everybody else was therefore the servant of the divinely appointed monarch.

With the creation of this powerful monolithic society, the Babylonian kings were ready to extend their frontiers first to the south where they conquered the ancient Sumerian cities of Lower Mesopotamia; then to the north in the region that was later to become Assyria; and eventually to the west and the Semitic kingdoms of the Mediterranean coast. It was only to the east across the Tigris that the Babylonian armies did not penetrate in depth. Beyond the great river lay the kingdom of Elam, the mysterious

regions listed in Genesis as one of the sons of Shem, a country
whose history, like its language, is only imperfectly known. The
Elamites, however, appear quite frequently in Sumerian annals as
they were constantly raiding and sometimes conquering the great
city-states of the delta lands. It was the Elamites who sacked Ur
and carried off not only one of the last of that famous city's kings
but the goddess Ishtar, sacrilegiously snatched from her temple.

But Elam was a country of half-barbarous tribesmen who raided
the fertile plains and rich cities of Lower Mesopotamia for loot
and never really stayed long enough in the conquered territories
to secure a firm footing in the area. They were probably incapable
of administering a highly civilised urban society in any case, and
when they did settle in the city of Larsa they probably left the
running of civic affairs to the educated citizens of that Sumerian
metropolis, while they marched about with their army in search
of more booty.

Certainly, by the time Hammurabi came to the throne in 1792
B.C., the Elamites were in partial control of southern Mesopotamia which they ruled from their provincial capital at Larsa. In
the north the Assyrians were more powerful than the Babylonians, so that the new king was really boxed in between two rival
and contiguous states. He bided his time and spent the first years
of his reign consolidating his position and building up his army.
Then, in the thirtieth year of his kingship, he began his military
conquests, and succeeded in conquering his rivals one by one,
reducing Assyria, the last of them, in the thirty-seventh year of his
reign, 1768 B.C. Hammurabi was now master of the whole of
Mesopotamia with its scores of once famous city-states, the names
of which he proudly lists in the Prologue to his famous Code of
Laws. Nippur naturally heads the procession, for Nippur was the
Rome of the pagan Mesopotamian world as the headquarters of
the cult of Enlil, the chief god of the Sumerians. Next on the list
comes nearby Eridu in virtue of the great age and sanctity of its
oracle. Babylon, the capital, is placed third as the centre of the
cult of the new national god Marduk. The other great city-shrines
of Sumer and Akkad follow in order of their religious importance,
and the list ends with Ashur and Nineveh. Twenty-four cities are
mentioned, together with their temples and chief gods, so that we
are given in this fascinating list a gazetteer of Hammurabi's empire and the origins of Babylonia. The other source of our know-

ledge of this remarkable man is his famous Code of Law which he drew up and inscribed on stone for the purpose of 'establishing justice in Sumer and Akkad'. Fortunately for the historian of civilisation, one of these imposing monuments survived and was taken out of the ground at Susa in Persia by the French Assyriologist Jean Vincent Scheil in 1901. Susa, the ancient capital of Elam, is the Shushan of the Old Testament, but it is best known to us as the royal residence of Darius the Great, who built there a palace with timber from the Lebanon, gold from Sardis, lapis lazuli from Sogdiana, turquoise from Chorasmia, silver and ebony from Egypt, and so on. Susa was the scene of one of the most curious spectacles in history—the 'marriage' of eighty officers and 10,000 men of Alexander the Great's army to an equivalent number of Persian girls. One can hardly begin to imagine what that day and night were like as the 20,160 brides and grooms celebrated their nuptials.

But more than a thousand years before Alexander had organised this happy occasion, the official text of the Code of Hammurabi, inscribed on stone, had been brought from Babylon and set up in the centre of the Elamite capital for all men to see what justice was and, further, to see that it was done. *En passant,* it is rather ironic that the so-called marriage of Alexander's troops to the Persian girls would have been considered illegal under a strict interpretation of the old Babylonian code, since marriage by capture, meaning of course forced marriage, was not recognised. But one need not be too literal in these matters, particularly in the case of soldiers who had been a long time in the field and suddenly found themselves in a newly 'liberated' city.

10

Hammurabi, the Lawgiver

THE BABYLON THAT HAMMURABI had created from his conquests of the rival states of Elam, Mari, Larsa, and Assyria was different from all the kingdoms which had gone before in that it survived, though with many vicissitudes, for 2000 years as the most important centre of power, wealth, and culture in the great Mesopotamian watershed of civilisation; and even after its decline and eventual disappearance with the rise of a totally disparate civilisation—namely the Hellenic—its prestige was never wholly forgotten: something of its achievements lingered on in the subsoil, as it were, of Western culture.

That Babylon achieved such a place in history was largely due to the triumphs of a king not in war, but in peace. For Hammurabi the warrior turned out to be one of the great law-givers of his age, worthy to be ranked with Solon the Athenian. In its way the Babylonian's code of conduct for regulating the relations between men was as important a step forward towards a saner society as that which Moses formulated for his people some 500 years later; and the resemblance between the two leaders of their nations is all the more striking since both are reputed to have received the tablets of their law from a god on a mountain-top.

Hammurabi of Babylon, therefore, represents something more than the typical warlord of his age, even though it would be foolish to sentimentalise him as a man of peace imbued with Christian virtues. He lived, we remember, in a brutal age, when 'smiting one's enemies', as we learn from the Old Testament, was the first duty of a monarch, a duty performed with all the violence and cruelty of total warfare, ancient and modern. And so it is not surprising to find that Hammurabi, who came to the throne as a

young and ambitious soldier of about twenty-five, well aware
that he was surrounded by implacable enemies, spent the first
thirty years of his reign in mercilessly attacking the neighbouring
states until their cities were destroyed, their citizens enslaved, and
their kings mutilated and allowed to die in dark prisons. Not even
the idols of the defeated gods and goddesses were spared, but
were kept as royal hostages until all danger of retaliation was
past.

But after thirty years of successful campaigning, Hammurabi,
in the sunset of his life, seems to have decided to make some
retribution for the suffering he had caused, and to make his peace
with the gods and his fellow-men. We find him now busying himself restoring some of the temples he had destroyed or allowed to
fall into decay. He also caused 'to be made splendid' statues of the
gods and goddesses to whom the temples were dedicated, not
omitting to set up flattering idols of himself. If the head found at
Susa, the work of an eighteenth-century B.C. sculptor, is of this
king of Babylon, he was a splendid-looking monarch with large
eyes, a small firm mouth, and a magnificent curly beard, though
showing in this portrait signs of age and perhaps of sickness. For
Hammurabi dedicated himself wholeheartedly to his task of kingship, concerning himself not only with the great affairs of state
but the petty details of his people's welfare, so that we find among
his archives letters discussing the insertion of an intercalary month
in the calendar; the proper procedure for the inspection of the
royal flocks and herds; and a recommendation for the restoration
of a baker to a post formerly held by him. A typical royal command despatched to a regional governor from the king's palace in
Babylon reads:

> Thus saith Hammurabi. You shall muster the men who hold
> land along the banks of the Damarum Canal and set them to
> work clearing out the channels. I want this project completed
> within the month.[1]

In addition to personally supervising every department of public administration, the king devoted himself to the systematisa-
tion and codification of all the laws and traditions of the Mesopotamian world, going back to Sumerian times when law and
order first became a cornerstone of civilised life. The basic principle which Hammurabi chose to guide him was the amelioration

of the ancient tribal law of the *lex talionis*, or 'an eye for an eye'.
He was not able, or did not wish, to abolish altogether the custom
of 'a life for a life', but he did introduce the principle of fines in
payment for misdemeanours which were formerly punished by
death or mutilation. And this change in the administration of justice can be seen as one of the greatest of all advances in the long,
slow process of civilisation, for it foreshadowed the coming of
societies based not only on the force of the law but also on the
power of money to control men's minds and passions. Long before Hammurabi's reign the Sumerians had discovered the principle that social intercourse was much simpler if, instead of waiting to be killed by a person one had offended, one paid him compensation in cash. This sort of arrangement, in fact, became the
foundation of all law as it was thenceforth known and practised,
leading to the establishment of courts of law, lawyers, solicitors,
juries, and the complex apparatus of jurisprudence in civilised
societies.

Hammurabi, therefore, intent on stabilising his kingdom in
order that his dynasty could continue to rule, was anxious to es-
tablish a strong and fair judicial system, for the kings of the Mesopotamian city-states had learnt by this time that even if their subjects would not actually rebel they would collaborate with a rival
if justice was not done and seen to be done. For this reason ancient
monarchs were anxious to add to their honorifics titles like 'king
of justice', 'he who made justice to prevail', and so forth.

The famous Code of Hammurabi, which, unlike the Tables of
Moses, has survived in several steles or bronze plaques, begins
with a Prologue, which sets the tone for all civilised law thereafter. In it the king states that he was commanded by god (Marduk, the tutelary god of Babylon) to give justice to the people and
to grant them good government in order to destroy the evil and
the wicked and to prevent the strong from oppressing the weak.
The 300 laws follow, falling into specific categories beginning
with the administration of justice (false charges, false testimony,
and falsification of judgment) and ending with regulations concerning the purchase of slaves abroad.

Perhaps the most interesting section of the Code from the social
point of view is that concerned with Marriage, Family, and
Property. This section contains sixty-seven paragraphs and begins
as follows:

If a man slanders a high-priestess or a married lady and cannot prove what he has said, he shall be flogged in the presence of the judges and half his head be shaven.

Subsequent laws seem to have been framed to protect women in a humane fashion, even though it is clear that their status was not much higher than that of the house-slaves. All the same, husbands could not treat their wives unjustly, and the divorce laws were both equitable and reasonable.

136 If a man absconds and leaves his wife without proper maintenance and she then goes to live with another man, she need not return to her first husband if and when he returns.

138 If a man wishes to divorce his first wife because she is barren, he must give her the cash value of her bridal gift and make good the dowry she has brought from her father's house before he can divorce her.

148 If a man's wife becomes crippled [with rheumatism, arthritis, etc.] and he decides to marry another woman, he may do so but cannot divorce his first wife who shall continue to live in the same house and to be cared for for the rest of her life.

Additional security for wives, widows, and concubines was written into the Code, the last group obviously requiring special protection as they were chosen from the household slaves and were thus exposed to the possible hatred and persecution of the first wife. However, the law affirms:

170 If a concubine has borne a man sons to whom the father states 'You are my sons', he shall count them as legitimate and they shall take proportionate shares in the property of the paternal estate.

. It is noteworthy that all of these particular laws concerning wives and concubines have been incorporated into the Moslem code regulating marital relationships. Noteworthy, too, is the ethical principle underlying them, namely the recognition that the strong must make concessions to the weak, which was, perhaps, the most important contribution of the Babylonians to

morality and which, in fact, foreshadowed the whole basis of
Christ's teaching. In other words, the concept of justice tempered
with mercy, which was eventually to change the nature of men
and society, was introduced into public life and given official
sanction in law, though it was a long time before it was extended
to cover the treatment of foreign enemies. Indeed, there is no
mention in Hammurabi's Code, or, for that matter, in Moses's
Commandments, of either justice or mercy towards one's enemies:
to the contrary, the Israelites were expressly forbidden to show
mercy to their fellow-Semites; and typical of the Old Testament
morality is the divine command given to King Saul to slaughter
(or, as one would say today, to 'waste') an obscure South Palesti-
nian tribe in the following manner:

> Thus saith the Lord of Hosts, Now go and smite Amalek, and
> utterly destroy all that they have, and spare them not; but slay
> both man and woman, infant and suckling, ox and sheep, camel
> and ass.
>
> (I Samuel 15:03)

But the Israelites were not, of course, unique in this practice
of genocide, which has always been the ultimate atrocity of nations
brutalised by war. We find all the Middle Eastern and Eastern
Mediterranean kings accepting as god-inspired the policy of
slaughtering the non-combatants along with the combatants.
Such was the command of the Lord of Hosts, whether his name
was Yahweh, or Marduk of the Babylonians, Ashur of the
Assyrians, Baal of the Phoenicians, Ahura Mazda of the Persians,
and so forth. So we must not expect to find the idea of compassion
which Hammurabi introduced into domestic law being extended
beyond the walls of Babylon and those cities loyal to the crown.

Yet the seed of this delicate plant had been sown and was to
reach its full flowering in the Age of Chivalry when a soldier, or
so Chaucer tells us, was distinguished by his gentleness rather
than by his brutality; and we can trace its germination back to the
earliest known code of laws, attributed to Ur-Nammu, the founder
of the Third Dynasty of Ur (2113–2096 B.C.), who declared that:

> the orphan is not to be given over to the rich, nor the widow to
> the powerful, nor the man of one shekel over to him of one
> mina.

a principle which underlies the Code of Hammurabi in many of those sections dealing with Marriage, Family, and Women's Rights. For instance, the phrase 'nor the widow to the powerful' is not merely the expression of a pious sentiment, as a politician might talk of 'protecting widows and orphans', but is a basis of specific laws, notably the 136th clause concerning a man who abandons his wife, leaves her without proper maintenance, and obliges her to put herself under the protection of another man. The abused wife is then free to remarry without being involved in the complexities of the civil or the prohibitions of the ecclesiastical courts, as in Western society today.

Yet however commendable some of the clauses intended to protect wives and widows may sound, one should not be led to believe that women enjoyed equality under the law with men in Babylonia, or that they could actually expect justice in a patriarchal society dominated by conservative old men. Both women and their children were, like the flocks and herds, the property of the *paterfamilias*, who could dispose of them pretty much as he wished. Consequently women's role in society was negligible. One can surmise that clever women exerted considerable influence within the house, but they had none outside. Men saw to it that they were kept in the place which had been assigned to them by nature and had become hallowed by custom. Their place was a little higher than that of the household slaves and a little lower than that of the free but insignificant male citizen.

Yet a careful study of the Code of Hammurabi does make it evident that women in Babylon did have specific legal rights as wives, mothers, concubines, and courtesans (a respectable class of society). Thus, they had some protection under the law in cases of desertion or ill health. It was a beginning towards a more just and humane social order, even if it did not liberate women from their traditional bondage. For the laws could not give women the opportunity, let alone the competence, to take part in the political, economic, intellectual, or artistic life of the time, though, come to that, the average male citizen was no better off in this sense than his wife. We can assume that he occupied himself in housing, feeding, and clothing his family while she busied herself with household matters, much as the average man and his wife do today. The real difference between the Babylon of King Hammurabi in 1750 B.C. and the London of King George II in A.D. 1750

was in the greater respect accorded to women, which is a matter
of the moral rather than of the civil law. When it came to asserting
their human rights in the courts it is doubtful whether the Victorian wife was all that much better off than her Babylonian sister.
The divorce laws as set out in the Code of Hammurabi permitted
a man to get rid of his wife more or less at will, while they gave
women no such right to dispose of their husbands on similar
grounds. Legal theory and practice were not all that different in
the Western world up to recent times, certainly not as long as a
wife was legally a man's chattel, even if this did not entitle him in
practice to hand her over as a slave for a certain number of years
in payment of a debt—permitted under the Babylonian but not
the Christian law.

But in one respect the former legal code gave women greater
freedom than the latter which, in the ecclesiastical courts at any
rate, gave her no marital freedom at all. In contrast, the 124th
clause of Hammurabi's Code specifically states that:

> If a woman hates her husband and refuses him his conjugal
> rights, her case shall be examined in the district court. If she
> can prove that she has kept herself chaste and has no fault
> while her husband has been unfaithful and so has demeaned
> her, she shall not be punished but may take her dowry and
> return to her father's house.

This, by any standard, is a remarkably liberal law, and, unlike
most legal documents, it takes into account the reality of human
emotion which, in marriage certainly, is the all-important factor.
Thus it is assumed that a wife can hate her husband, just as the
converse is obvious, whence the problem of what to do about it
has to be considered and, if possible, solved. No such provision
is found in the legal code of any Western nation; to the contrary,
the refusal by a wife of conjugal rights, even if she does hate her
husband, is a heinous crime in some quarters. One has to admit,
of course, that the Babylonian law as stated was probably unwork-
able, since while it might have been comparatively easy for a wife
to prove that she had kept herself chaste, one wonders what her
husband's lawyer would do to her if she claimed in a public court
that 'she had no fault'. In fact, experience must have forewarned
many women as to the dangers of challenging their husbands in a
court dominated by elderly judges, for if the verdict went against

a wife and she was shown to have some fault (like being an execrable cook?), she paid a terrible penalty for her temerity: her husband was entitled to drown her.

Yet, in the final analysis, it would be unrealistic to assess the Code of Hammurabi by the legal standards of 4000 years later, particularly in the matter of women's rights. What we can conclude is that the firm beginnings of law, and of the social order that distinguishes civilised from barbarous communities, were first clearly laid down in Babylonia; and that it was largely as a consequence of Hammurabi's wise rule that Babylon progressed from a small village on the banks of the Euphrates into a world capital. Unfortunately for the progress of mankind, it was not able to retain its position of dominance for long, for the period immediately following Hammurabi's reign was one of chaos, as barbarians from outside the frontiers of civilisation swept over the cities and territories of the established and orderly kingdoms between the Two Rivers. Babylon's downfall was to result in the rise of its sister state, Assyria; and the Assyrians, as we shall see, had no time for the liberal views of the Babylonian Hammurabi or for the idea of mercy even towards their own people, let alone their enemies.

11

Social Life in Babylonia

THE CONCEPT OF A society based on a written code of law administered in public courts and not arbitrarily interpreted behind closed doors was, perhaps, the greatest contribution made by the Babylonians to the conduct of civilised life. It is true that some of the moral principles on which the Babylonian jurisprudence was based had been formulated by several of the more humane kings of Sumer. The condemnation of the oppression of widows and orphans by Ur-Nammu, the founder of the Third Dynasty of Ur, is an example which we have already noted. But in social relations pious exhortations are one thing, properly enacted legislation is another. It was Hammurabi who first systematised and codified the vague principles of justice which had hitherto served to regulate conduct.

But the Code of Hammurabi is unique not only as the oldest model of jurisprudence in history but even more for the light it throws upon the every-day activities and affairs of ordinary people. It is obvious that we are woefully short of evidence as to this aspect of the ancient Mesopotamian world, which we know almost exclusively in terms of the reigns of kings with exotic and unpronounceable names, of their endless wars of extermination, and of the rise and fall of numerous petty city-states. In addition, nearly all the artefacts recovered from the hundreds of mounds that litter the landscape between the Two Rivers come from the tombs of royal personages or high officials; and the written records largely concern affairs of state or business contracts.

The Code of Hammurabi and the legal documents, in comparison, often give us a glimpse of the daily life of the ordinary citizen, just as the streets of Pompeii and Herculaneum suddenly bring alive Roman history to those who only know it from school texts of Caesar's Wars. Now it so happens that the Sumerians, Babylonians, and Assyrians were all assiduous keepers of legal records. Evidently all lawsuits were inscribed on clay tablets by a clerk of the court, who wrote up a summary of the case together with the names of the principals and witnesses, enclosed it in a clay envelope, and filed it away for future reference. From the tens of thousands of these tablets recovered in the last hundred years of excavations a general picture of the societies which flourished five to three thousand years ago can be drawn, just as, presumably, it could be of modern societies by an analysis of our contemporary lawsuits.

What is immediately obvious is the rigid structure of those early societies—a structure first validated by the Code of Hammurabi and so passed on down through history to our own day. In other words, we see that an essential difference between civilised and tribal social structures is the innovation of class distinctions in the former. Thus Hammurabi makes it quite clear that there are three distinct groups in the Babylonian world, and one of the main objects of his legal code is to regulate relations between them. The names used in the Akkadian text of the *Laws* are difficult to translate, but the connotations are quite definite. The upper class are called *awellum*, literally 'men', but obviously implying a well-born personage, superior to the others by reason of his birth, ability, and wealth. The second class are called *mushkenum*, which can be translated as bourgeois, or burghers. And the third and lowest class are known as *wardum*, meaning slave, or serf. This stratification of society could be said to have prevailed down to our own times; and even though various régimes have made attempts to change it and have succeeded in their initial stages, it is apparent that the divisions reassert themselves as the accidents of birth, education, office, and ability undermine in practice the philosophical, religious, or political theory of a classless society.

In Babylonia, where we first find these rigid social divisions, the upper class was composed of the conservators of law, order, and tradition: in other words, officials ranging from the king to the army officer, with the priests, magistrates, courtiers, and the like, combining to create and perpetuate the ruling class. The business, or middle, class consisted of merchants, farmers, professional men, and skilled artisans. Members of this group were free

I

men, separated from the patricians not necessarily by wealth, education, or intelligence but rather by their voluntary acceptance of their inferior social status. The lowest class, composed of slaves, had no rights except those conceded by their masters. They compared with the serfs of the Middle Ages and the wage-slaves of nineteenth-century industry, for it could be argued that there was, in real terms, very little difference between the life and the status of a house-slave in Sumer, 2850 B.C., and a British factory-worker in A.D. 1850, though the evidence of the conditions under which the two men lived and worked would suggest that the former was better off than the latter.

In order to regulate this class structure, the Babylonians had very early in their history devised a legal code which they felt best served the system: for instance, an offence against a member of the upper class was considered more serious than one against a member of the middle or lowest group and hence was liable to be punished more severely. The modern concept of 'equality before the law' would have seemed irrational to the ancient Mesopo-tamians, for in their view a king, nobleman, commanding general, or high priest with all his responsibilities to the state was a more valuable member of society than, say, a shopkeeper. Therefore the punishment for killing the former was more severe than for killing the latter. At the same time, as if to emphasise his superi-ority, the aristocrat had to pay more for services rendered than did the burgher; and it was quite understood that he would have to pay the doctor a higher fee than a shopkeeper paid. Slaves, of course, paid nothing at all.

The status and treatment of slaves in these Mesopotamian societies are difficult for us to understand, since we associate the iniquitous system of human bondage with the enslavement of African Negroes by white men from the beginning of the fifteenth century of our era almost to the end of the nineteenth century. But slavery in this period was different from the ancient practice to the extent that the moral and racial issues which so deeply con-cern, and continue to concern, us scarcely troubled the ancients at all. Certainly racial discrimination had nothing to do with the institution which, in the pre-Christian world, was originally a means of organising labour in the absence of heavy machinery and also an expedient for disposing of prisoners of war. More-over, where small nations were constantly fighting each other and capturing each other's citizens, common sense dictated the need to treat captives with discretion, just as during the Middle Ages chivalry combined with the expectation of ransom softened the atrocities of the battlefield.

The evidence of the relatively humane attitude towards slaves first in Sumer, then in Babylonia, is seen in the legal protection written into the early codes of law. Thus, the enslaved had the right to challenge his master in the courts and to give evidence against him, though one suspects that legal theory was one thing, practice another. It is difficult to comprehend how a system of exploitation could work if the exploited were able successfully to protest. Some such rights were supposed to be given to the black slaves of the British colonies and of the American South, but it is doubtful whether the slave-owners in either case paid much attention to them. Moreover, inasmuch as slaves in Sumer could be branded, flogged, and even killed with impunity, one must be careful about condoning the ancient system. Yet the laws do make provision for slaves to submit their complaints to the courts; own property; engage in business; buy their freedom; and marry free men or free women; so presumably there was always hope for such a bondsman of becoming both free and prosperous. One surmises that a great deal depended upon the ability or talents of the slave. A clever man could set up in business, buy his freedom, and marry a free woman. A pretty or clever woman could no doubt make herself the darling of her master and, if the wife was compliant, become the real mistress of the household.

As for the relations between the sexes, we can safely assume that women, as a class, were at a hopeless disadvantage in a society created by and for men. Since they could never control the affairs of state, religious or political, their influence was confined to the four walls of their home. It is true that we occasionally have a reference to some famous or notorious woman reigning as the queen of one of these ancient empires, Semiramis of Assyria being such a royal personage. Her regency was short, however, and after four years she was replaced by her son Adad-nirari III (810–782 B.C.), and Semiramis passed into the twilight zone of legend. The last we hear of her is that having handed over the royal authority to her son, she flew out of the palace in the form of a dove and was never heard of again. We learn little about the place of women in Assyrian society from these folk-tales.

We learn much more from a document like the Code of Hammurabi, as we have seen in the previous chapter. Marriage, for instance, was a legally binding contract which gave a wife a sense of security, particularly as her husband could not divorce her without compensation. But any hope that she could achieve a superior status through marriage was denied her inasmuch as custom permitted a man to keep as many concubines as he could afford, while, at the same time, the state provided him with a public harem in the institution of the temple brothel. In such circumstances it would be too much to assume that a wife could expect a lifetime of love and devotion from her husband.

The converse is also evident, since women were not expected to have the kind of relationship with the opposite sex that we associate with strict monogamy on the one hand or romantic liaisons on the other. In a word, the function of sex for the Babylonians was either procreation or pleasure, and nowhere in their literature do we find any prohibitions on sexual intercourse or, for that matter, any refinements of the male-female relationship which are the quintessence of what we know as 'love'. Obviously it would be foolish to deny that boys and girls, and sometimes adult men and women, formed deep attachments for each other in which sexual desire was sublimated; but, if so, we have no record of it in either the public or personal literature that has come down to us. On the other hand, prostitution for religious purposes was sanctioned on the grounds that the indulgence of lust contributed to the spiritual as well as the physical needs of the citizens. And if one asks how this was considered possible, let alone desirable, the answer can only be that since the gods who laid down the rules for human conduct were themselves anthropomorphs, their humanity rather than their holiness was the operative force in their lives, whence their need for a comfortable home (their temple); devoted servants to look after them (priests); a well-born wife (the chief priestess of a cult); desirable concubines (sisters of a religious order); and competent domestics (lay sisters). It was expected of a god that he would make use of all the facilities and people put at his disposal—eating the food put out for him on the altars; cohabiting with his wife (a king's daughter was chosen for this office at Ur); diverting himself with his concubines; also, if he felt so inclined, with his male servants, the temple priests. The latter were often catamites, and, like their sisters, submitted themselves to the desires of the god. And so, what was considered good for the god was held to be good for men.

From all this one gets the impression that the essence of morality in Sumer, and later in both Babylonia and Assyria, was not the repression of earthly desires in order to be worthy of the greater rewards of heaven, but, on the contrary, the uninhibited enjoyment of physical delights here on earth. For the ancient Mesopotamians do not seem to have believed in an after-life, or not in the sense of a heaven where the deserving spent eternity. In fact, where we have references to another world it is described as a most depressing place where the ghosts eat clay and flutter about like wounded birds. The normal healthy man had no wish whatsoever to visit this land from which there was no return, though, realising that his going there was inevitable, he made what preparations he could for his physical comfort, like a travel- ler who has to take a protracted and tedious voyage. In practice, then, the Babylonians bent their intellectual, moral, and technical energies to the end of attaining a full and prosperous life, which they succeeded in doing within the limits imposed by the time and place. Their wealth depended on agriculture, because at this early period international trade was restricted and the physical require- ments of the ordinary citizen were, in any case, quite simple. All their needs were supplied by the land which was enriched by the alluvial soil brought down by the Two Rivers. Water, too, was vital, and one of the first duties of every king was to maintain old canals or dig new ones so that there should never be a shortage of water.

The principal crop was barley, which was used for both human and animal food, for making beer, and even for paying wages. Wheat seems to have been grown in smaller quantities than barley. Root crops were cultivated and fruit trees encouraged, as they provided not only extra food but much needed timber in a treeless land. The scarcity of wood and of stone naturally dictated the building materials and techniques of Mesopotamia—now as then —so that the houses of the ordinary citizen as well as the palaces of kings were built of mud bricks, were windowless, and devoid of everything but the simplest furniture. They corresponded al- most exactly to the mud huts one finds today in any Iraqi village. Yet to anyone who has lived in such a primitive domicile the mud-brick house is quite comfortable: its lack of sun and light is precisely what a desert climate requires, while an open courtyard, where the family can sit in the cool of an evening, is an acceptable alternative to mechanical air-conditioning.

Within this type of dwelling the family lived in a simple fashion. There was not much choice in food, for instance, since the staple diet seems to have been barley-bread, porridge, cakes, biscuits, and so forth. Vegetables and fruits were grown in abundance on the extensive farms. Meat and fish were in good supply. All this food was eaten fresh and obviously constituted a healthy and well-balanced diet. For this reason it is possible that the general health of the Babylonians was good, though we have no way of knowing, since no statistics were kept and the diagnoses of the diseases as set forth in the prescriptions for curing them are so mixed up with magic and superstition that it is not always possible to estimate their nature. Take, for instance, this description and cure for a sickness which may have been appendicitis, peptic ulcers, indigestion, flatulence, or simply belly-ache:

> If a man's stomach is hot, you shall bray together the seven drugs [their names are missing or not identifiable]. Then strain, steep in beer, bring to the boil, strain again, and cool. Add barley water and sprinkle with rose water. Introduce this brew into his anus [by means of an enema] and the sick man will recover.

Presumably the object was to empty the bowels, but why the enema should be quite so elaborate and take so long to prepare is a mystery. One can guess, however, that doctors surrounded themselves with magic and mumbo-jumbo, and the more complicated the treatment, the wiser the physician must have appeared and the larger his fee if he accomplished a cure.

Judging from the number of medical texts, prescriptions, diagnostics, and so forth that have come down to us, there was no shortage of physicians in ancient Mesopotamia, despite Herodotus's report to the contrary. For the Greek historian maintains that the Babylonians in his day had no regular doctors, resulting in a curious and interesting form of socialised medicine whereby a sick man was placed outside in the street so that anybody who came along could listen to his symptoms and offer him advice— particularly useful in cases where the passer-by had had the same complaint and had been cured of it by such-and-such treatment.

Herodotus, however, was obviously badly informed, for the abundance of documents treating of medicine reveal the deep interest of the Sumero-Babylonians in all branches of science. One could conclude, in fact, that these ancient people not only had physicians and surgeons to deal with physical ailments but psychiatrists to deal with mental disorders. The latter evidently relied on omens, as the following list of 'Useful Hints' will show:

If he sees a black pig, the patient will die.
If he sees a white pig, the patient will recover.
If he sees a red pig, the patient will die on the third day (or month).
If he sees pigs with their tails up, the patient will have no cause for anxiety.
If he sees pigs copulating, the patient . . . [rest of text missing].

The doctor was, however, greatly handicapped by the restrictions placed upon him by both the state and the church. Thus, the law punished the unsuccessful physician, particularly the surgeon. It uncompromisingly stated that if a practitioner destroyed a patient's eye in the course of surgery he should have his hand cut off. It is not surprising, therefore, that surgery was not a very popular profession, and there is some doubt as to whether the Babylonians practised it at all. They would never have dared, as Greek physicians did, to slit open a man's gullet in order to remove a fish-bone. Rather, they found it more expedient to rely on the traditional diagnoses and prognoses, for these were recorded and, as it were, registered as the officially approved medical practice. Some of these textbooks of Babylonian medicine have actually survived: the tablets were unearthed in a number of Assyro-Babylonian cities and date from the eighth to the fifth century B.C. They constitute a fascinating chapter in the history of medicine, showing how fashions have changed since the professors first enunciated their theory of diagnosis by colour 4000 years ago.[1] We learn that:

If a patient's buttocks are yellow, he has cause for concern.
If the right buttock is black, his illness will be painful.
If the left buttock is red, his illness will be prolonged.

If his stool is red, he will get well.
If his stool is black, he will die.

If his penis is red, he will have a long sickness but will get well.
If his penis is black, he will die.

If his urine is green, he will have a long sickness.
If his urine is the colour of rose-water, he will get better.

If his testicles are red, he will get better.
If his testicles are black, he will die.

It is obvious to us reading this hocus-pocus that Babylonian medicine was a combination of quackery and empiricism, an approach to disease that actually continued to form the philosophy of medicine and of the medicine-man for the next 2000 years at least, for we find this advice given to physicians of the Salerno school about A.D. 100.

> When called to a patient commend yourself to God and to the angel who guided Tobias. On the way, learn as much as possible from the messenger so that if you discover nothing from the patient's pulse or water, you may still astonish him and gain his confidence by your knowledge of the case.

Yet where superstition was unable to inhibit research, the Babylonians made great progress in their pursuit of knowledge, notably in mathematics and astronomy. In fact, at a time when Europeans were still living in caves and grottoes and probably could not count beyond the number of their fingers, the Sumerian schoolboy was working on quadratic equations. And later the Babylonians, deriving their mathematics from the Sumerians, kept systematic reports of astronomical observations so that Greek astronomers, taking up the study of the heavens in their turn, had available a record of solar and lunar eclipses from 737 B.C. together with tables of the ephemerides for predicting the date of new moons and the rising and setting of the planets.

Such intellectual achievements remind us of our own reliance on science and technology, and may give the impression that we are nearer to these ancient people than we are. But on closer inspection the similarities are seen to be superficial. It is true that the daily life of the ordinary citizen of Babylon did not differ greatly from life today in one of our larger cities. The Babylonian had his regular job, and his place in society; he was subject to the laws of the land which were intended to protect him from injustices; he lived as a family man with simple but adequate housing accommodation; his children went to school; and he sought his entertainment outside his own home in the immemorial manner of Middle Eastern and Mediterranean peoples. But there was an essential difference, for while he was physically a free man, provided he was a fully fledged citizen, he was denied any real intellectual freedom. No member of society was really free in this sense, neither the king nor the commoner, neither the artist nor the scientist. The state was monolithic, whence it follows that the individual was of no more importance than a cog in a complicated machine. If, like a cog, he did not perform his function, he was replaced. And not only did he not rebel against the system, he never even questioned it. Politics, in the modern sense—or, for that matter, in the Greek or Roman sense—did not exist. All activities and all decisions were automatic: one cannot imagine any serious opposition to anything, not even in the field of art or science, let alone of religion or politics. One may be sure that a few men must have had dreams of one sort or another, but if they did, they never realised them. They were never taught to think, but only to obey. And the inevitable result of this system was a way of life which the ordinary citizen had neither the opportunity nor the initiative to change.

A study of the social history of the Mesopotamian empires, therefore, leads us to the conclusion that whatever their material achievements, their régimes were intellectually and spiritually sterile, for the authoritarian system under which they lived conditioned men to think and act like the inmates of a well-run and relatively humane penitentiary. In other words, intellectual freedom in the sense that Socrates knew and practised it was non-existent. Consequently we do not find any original philosophical, religious, or political ideas emerging over a period of almost 2000 years, from the time of Ur-Nammu of the Third Ur Dynasty to Nabonidus, the last king of Babylon. Religion, politics, economics, jurisprudence, architecture, engineering, science, art, even the structure of society itself, had not materially changed in all this time. For those who are interested in such matters, it is an extraordinary comment on the nature of the authoritarian state.

But we have seen how the potentially life-enriching view of the Sumerians as glimpsed in their literature, and how the attempts of the Babylonian Hammurabi to introduce justice into the law, foreshadowed at least the possibility of an amelioration of the human condition. The collapse of the young Babylonian Empire put paid to any hopes of further reforms, and the subsequent history of the region once more consists of the annals of warrior-kings and their continuous wars. There are, it is true, enough of these to keep professional Assyriologists busy compiling the lists of monarchs and the dates of their battles, while there is even abundant visual evidence of the exploits of the war-lords on the friezes from the palaces excavated by the nineteenth-century archaeologists. But Assyrian history, which we shall examine next, is largely another catalogue of atrocities referred to in the royal proclamations as splendid victories and so forth; it has little to do with the advance of civilisation.

12

The Assyrians

DESPITE HAMMURABI'S CONQUESTS AND his creation of an empire, his son, Samsu-iluna (1749–1712 B.C.), was not able to hold the empire together: revolts in the southern region and incursions from the north left Babylonia a small, weakened state whose capital and territory were captured and sacked in 1595 B.C. by the Hittites. This was the end of the First Babylonian Dynasty which had lasted just over 200 years.

The Hittite conquerors of the great cultural centre of the ancient world were a nomadic, horse-breeding tribe of Indo-European stock whose culture seems to have been similar to that of the German, French, and British tribes so well described by Julius Caesar and Tacitus. They were a bellicose people, nearly always on the move (hence the importance of their horses), and led by warrior-chieftains who only called themselves 'kings' and acted like tyrants after they had become quasi-civilised. As a military nation, their creative energies were directed along the lines most useful in war—massive fortifications built with huge blocks of stone, Cyclopean walls, and subterranean tunnels. Otherwise they showed little interest in the arts and sciences, leaving these matters, no doubt, to their priests, much as the tribal chieftains of Ancient Britain left the business of learning and teaching to the Druids and the barons of the Middle Ages left them to the clerics. But the Hittites, as they acquired land and possessions in the course of their raids into the Middle East, assimilated also the intellectual assets of the nations they conquered—the laws and systems of writing of the Babylonians, for instance. As a result, these Indo-Europeans, as they became civilised, merged into the polyglot, multi-national, and basically Semitic world of the Middle

East, into which they finally disappeared altogether, along with even more obscure peoples like the Hatti, the Hurrians, the people of Ahhijava, and the inhabitants of the Lukka Lands.

The Hittites were succeeded by the Kassites as conquerors of Babylon. This latter people supposedly came from the mountains of Persia to the east of the Tigris and they kept control of Babylon for the next 600 years, the period of the Second Babylonian Dynasty. The history of this period is still imperfectly known; and while we have the names of a great many kings—or self-styled kings—the names tell us little. They have, indeed, an outlandish sound to them—Nazi-nugash (1350–1345 B.C.), Nazi-marrutash (1323–1298 B.C.) and Kashtiliash IV (1242–1235 B.C.), followed by ten unidentified monarchs. It is only too obvious why these ten rulers have disappeared from the records from a building inscription erected about 1241 B.C. by Tukulti-ninurta, the Assyrian king and contemporary of the Babylonian Kashtiliash. This inscription states with the customary Assyrian bombast:

> Trusting in the great gods, my lords, and in Ishtar, the queen of heaven and earth, who went at the head of my army, I forced Kashtiliash of Babylon to join battle with me. I defeated his troops and slaughtered his men. In the middle of the battle I personally captured Kashtiliash, the Babylonian king. My feet trod on his royal neck, he was my footstool. I brought him captive and bound before the god Ashur, my lord. All Sumer and Akkad I brought under my sway.

In other words, Babylon was now the vassal of Assyria, and it remained so for the next 600 years when the Babylonians rose and avenged themselves by almost wiping out their oppressors.

But before that happened the conquest of Babylon by Tukulti-ninurta made Assyria the leading power of the Middle East. The Hittite kingdom was perishing; Egypt rapidly sinking into its decline. At the time we are speaking of, that is the thirteenth century B.C., neither the Medes, Persians, Phoenicians, nor the Greeks were world powers. Assyria was unchallenged: it was un-challenged, that is, in the military sphere, for the Assyrians by this time had brought the science of war to its most advanced stage. Their prime weapon was the horse-drawn chariot which they had adopted from the Hittites. It is probable that the other armies of the time, if they had chariots at all, were using asses or oxen to pull them. But the Assyrians, like the Romans after them, made an intensive study of military strategy and were continually improving and reorganising their armed forces. In addition to the tactic of using massed chariots, they introduced cavalry as a separate wing and an engineering corps with siege engines and battering rams as front-line troops. As a result of their military prowess, the Assyrians by the time of Shalmaneser III (858–824 B.C.) were the masters of the whole of Mesopotamia.

It is easy to see why if one examines the reliefs taken from the palaces at Nimrud and Nineveh by Layard and others during the golden period of discovery and excavation of the mid-nineteenth century. The famous series of reliefs from the South West Palace of King Sennacherib, for instance, depict the siege of Lachish, which is so tersely yet dramatically referred to in the Old Testament as one of the disastrous defeats suffered by the Jews during the reign of Hezekiah, king of Judah. From the Second Book of Kings we learn that Sennacherib attacked all the walled cities of Judah and took them all, one after the other. Hezekiah was obliged to surrender unconditionally and to pay the Assyrian king 300 talents of silver, thirty talents of gold, and all the treasures of the synagogue and his palace. The Jews fought desperately to save their cities as the reliefs from Sennacherib's palace at Nineveh show. We see the Assyrians rolling their siege towers up an enormous earth ramp against the walls of Lachish, exactly as the Romans were, a thousand years later, to attack the fortress-city of Masada. The infantry follow the siege towers, ready to scale the walls. And on the walls and the towers the defenders hurl down stones, fire-brands, and even chariot wheels in an effort to contain the massed assault. In vain. The account of the siege given in one of Sennacherib's cylinders tells us why.

I besieged and captured the city by using a well-packed ramp, blows of battering rams, and an infantry attack by means of breaches [in the city walls], mines, and scaling ladders. 200,150 people, old and young, male and female, horses, mules, camels, cattle and sheep without number I brought away and counted as spoil.

We see from the reliefs pictures of some of these people escaping by the city gate of Lachish, others being caught and crucified on the road, others crawling on all fours up to the king's throne

as he sat outside the city (and no doubt well out of range of the
defenders' sling-shots), begging for mercy. Some were spared;
others beheaded; others flayed alive; others literally torn limb
from limb. The sculptor had to be accurate about detail, for we
see from the Nineveh reliefs and we know from the account of the
siege in the Old Testament that Sennacherib was personally present at the surrender of Lachish to receive the defeated Jewish
leaders and to settle the terms of their surrender. Hezekiah was
not, of course, present, for Kings tells us that he sent a message
to Sennacherib saying, 'I have offended. Go away from me. That
which thou puttest on me will I bear'—a not undignified admis-
sion of total defeat. Very different was the Assyrian kings'
language in describing their victories. The phraseology gives us
an insight into their mentality. Typical is this proclamation of
Tiglath-pileser I (1116–1078 B.C.) which states:

> Lands, mountains, cities, and princes I have conquered and
> brought under my yoke. I fought sixty kings and established
> my invincible power over them. I personally was unequalled in
> battle, unrivalled in combat. . . .

Such bombast, indeed, was to become the standard rhetoric of
the Assyrian monarchs, and 400 years later Tiglath-pileser's claims
of personal prowess are topped by Sargon II (709–705 B.C.), who
declares:

> With my select bodyguard and indomitable warriors I advanced
> like a strong wild ox. Gorges, mountain streams and cataracts,
> dangerous chasms I crossed in my palanquin. If the way were
> too precipitous, I proceeded on foot. Like a young gazelle I
> ascended the high mountain peaks in pursuit of the enemy. . . .

Even more revealing of the Assyrian mentality is their treatment of the defeated enemy. The standard formula employed to
describe a military victory reads: 'I despoiled their city, burnt it
down with fire, and converted it into a heap of ruins and deserts'
—a communiqué which (unlike most official proclamations) can
be read as literally true, for the object of the continual military
expeditions was not merely to defeat the enemy but to annihilate
him. Hence the destruction of a city as a physical community; the
massacre of the male inhabitants; the rape of the young females

who, according to a war communiqué issued by Shalmaneser III in 1840 B.C., were afterwards burnt alive along with the children; the cutting down of the fruit trees and date palms; the carrying off of the cattle and all livestock; and the poisoning of the earth itself by strewing it with noxious substances like saltpetre.

The Assyrians, in effect, anticipated the policies and methods of modern total warfare, although their practices were somewhat more extreme in that they deliberately protracted the suffering of their victims for as long as they could. Thus the king of a captured city was led through the streets of Nineveh like a bull, with a ring through his nose or lips; exhibited like a monkey in a cage; and finally mutilated by jailers who hacked off his hands, feet, nose, and ears, and tore out his tongue and eyes. Ordinary prisoners were done to death by the thousands and their heads piled neatly into pyramids on either side of the king and his general officers. And the number of civilians massacred in these ancient wars is, of course, impossible to assess, as it would be impossible to calculate the number who have died in the wars of our own lifetime. Moreover, the official historians, being by the requirements of their profession falsifiers of the truth, cannot be trusted. Hence the claim of Sennacherib (704–681 B.C.) that he captured 200,000 men in one battle need not be taken literally but rather as an exaggeration typical of a press hand-out in wartime.

There is no disputing, however, the pictorial evidence of Sennacherib's campaigns against the Babylonians, Phoenicians, and Elamites, for the battle scenes, as we have noted, are vividly depicted on the friezes of his palace—the advance of his troops by land and water, the besieging of cities, the slaughter of the garrisons, and the flight of the defeated enemies across swamps. A characteristic Assyrian touch is provided by the soldiers holding up the severed heads of prisoners for the satisfaction of the king and the information of his scribes. On the other hand, the massacre of enemies was not in itself sufficient incentive or reward for the troops, who do not appear to have received payment in the form of wages, but only board and lodging during peacetime. Their reward was the spoils of war, whence it behoved the king to wage more or less continuous campaigns in order to support a large professional army. An example of the prizes of victory (again if we can believe the official historians) was Sennacherib's capture during his fourth Babylonian campaign of:

208,000 men and women prisoners
7,200 horses and mules
11,073 asses
5,230 camels
80,050 cattle
100,100 sheep

An interesting feature of this list is the precise enumeration of the animals—11,073 asses, for instance, and the round figures for the 'body count' of the humans. The horses, asses, camels, and so forth, together with such items as the soldiers could loot from the enemy's homes before they were burnt, were more important than the number of civilians killed or enslaved, since booty constituted the principal payment for the army. The really valuable and precious articles like the jewels, ornaments, furniture, and personal belongings of palaces and temples were the property of the god (i.e. Ashur) and hence of his representative on earth, the king himself. All these immense spoils of war were stored for hundreds of years in Fort Shalmaneser near the capital Nineveh, the fortress which was sacked and destroyed in 612 B.C. by the Medes and Babylonians. In that year, when Assyria was finally and irrevocably crushed, the victors burnt in bonfires tens of thousands of ivory statuettes and miniatures the Assyrians had looted from all over the world, together with all the furniture and ornaments stored during 260 years in this royal treasure-house. The archaeologists who excavated Fort Shalmaneser described what they found as 'the biggest holocaust of ivories ever witnessed by man, an utterly vandalistic destruction which the enemy [i.e. the Medes and Babylonians] unleashed upon Assyria when their pent-up hatred sought to avenge the sufferings which their former suzerains had inflicted upon them'.[1]

There can be no doubt from the written and pictorial evidence why the Assyrians brought about their own destruction in this irrevocable manner. Not even their large, well-organised, and efficient army could, in the end, perpetuate the régime, and their empire collapsed in the face of the hatred and fury of the conquered peoples. The tens of thousands of slaves who were employed building the forts, palaces, and temples of the kings, the subject peoples who had to provide tribute, and the Assyrian people themselves who were not of the noble or official classes, must all have been thankful to see the end of a line of monarchs who were heroes in the national annals and murderers in the eyes of the rest of the world.

In addition to the picture of the Assyrians they themselves give us in their military records, we can also judge their national character from a glance at their laws, as we have done in the case of the Babylonians and the Code of their king Hammurabi. Here is a typical example:

> If a married woman has stolen something from a man's house and has taken property of a higher value than five *manu* [= 2·5 kg, or approximately 5 lb.] of lead, the owner of the stolen property is to swear under oath that he did not allow the woman to take the property voluntarily and that theft has therefore been committed. If the husband is willing to settle the matter by restoring the property and bailing out his wife, he is in his rights to cut off her ears. If the husband refuses to settle the matter, the woman shall be declared guilty and the owner of the property shall cut off her nose.

This mutilation of women was typical of Assyrian justice and included disfigurement by cutting off nose and ears; excision of the nipples or the entire breasts; hacking off fingers to prevent a woman from doing the housework and making her unwanted as a wife or concubine; and flogging. These punishments were, in general, unknown to the Babylonians, even though this latter people also accepted the partial serfdom of women as a natural and divine law. The Sumerians, again, were even more generous in their treatment of women and in some respects gave them equal status in the courts. But the Assyrians treated their own wives as they treated conquered peoples, the reason being that the basis of their law was the sanctity of *property* and the worthlessness of human life. A wife and a man's children were his *property*: hence he could do what he liked with them. It follows that the worst crimes in the eyes of the Assyrians were theft, indebtedness, and adultery, particularly where a husband felt that his wife had some value as a household possession. In that case, her loss was like the theft of 5 lb. of lead, entitling him, in the last resort, to put her to death if she were in his view no longer useful as a bed companion, housekeeper, cook, or maid of all work. Alternatively, he could merely cut off her nose if he was more or less indifferent to her

K

charms and capabilities. In the event that she was accused of adultery, her lover, as a violator of *property*, was also punished by being put to death if the wife was considered to be sufficiently valuable and the wrong done to the husband correspondingly serious; or he was castrated and disfigured if she was considered of no special value and therefore expendable.

Again, the Assyrians with their predilection for brutality elaborated the old 'eye-for-an-eye' law to cover sexual offences: thus a woman accused of injuring a man's testicles 'in a fight' was severely punished. The phrase 'in a fight' has an odd sound to it, for it is difficult to conceive of a wife or a mistress or even a prostitute deliberately damaging a man's testicles. But common prostitutes in distinction to temple harlots might in Assyrian times have had a bad reputation for violence; or, alternatively, the damage to the testicles might possibly refer to venereal disease, in which case 'in a fight' might be a mistranslation for 'in intercourse'. In either case, the woman's punishment was to have her breasts *torn* off; so a pair of breasts for a pair of testicles was the Assyrian interpretation of the *lex talionis*.

Nearly all Assyrian justice, then, is based on the uncompromisingly materialistic view that property is the most sacrosanct factor in human society. In a sense, everybody, man, woman, and child, was the property of somebody else, even the king being the servant of the local god. But as in all societies where property is the regulator of conduct, the primary object of the law is to protect the rich from the poor and the strong from the weak, since the poor and the weak are always potential threats to the system which exploits them. In Assyria, for instance, slaves, as the lowest class in society, were denied all civil rights whatsoever; while married women, as another of the weaker groups, were also discriminated against under the law of the land. One method of limiting their freedom as individuals was the ordinance obliging them to be veiled in public. Prostitutes, on the other hand, were *forbidden* to wear the veil at all. This is a perfect example of the thinking of the Assyrians: the married woman was *private* property and therefore had to be kept private; the prostitute was public property, and therefore had to be exhibited publicly, like any other goods on the market. The fact that a young married woman might like to see and be seen was regarded as lessening her exclusiveness as her husband's personal possession; and the possibility that a prostitute might want to take an afternoon off and have a stroll through the streets unmolested by men was of no importance: if she was caught in a veil, her clothes were confiscated, she was flogged, and pitch poured over her head.

It is small wonder that the history of the Assyrian Empire is a continual story of external and internal revolts which the stronger kings—that is, the more ruthless commanders-in-chief of the army —were able to crush by marching constantly up and down and back and forth across their domains. Typical was the reign of Sennacherib (704–681) who came to the throne unexpectedly on the death of his father in a border fight with the Cimmerians, a fabulous people even in Homer's time, described as a race 'on whom the sun never looks': in ethnological terms, a south Russian tribe who crossed the Caucasus and invaded Asia Minor in the eighth century B.C. On assuming the throne, Sennacherib had first to suppress a rebellion of the Babylonians; and having done this at the battles of Kutha and Kish, he marched westwards and subdued Sidon, Askalon, and Ekron. Next he attacked and conquered the Phoenicians and Philistines, put down a revolt in Cilicia, and laid siege to Jerusalem. While all this was going on, another revolt broke out in the Babylonian territories. Sennacherib marched eastward and dealt successfully with that. He recorded his total destruction of Babylon in what we are now accustomed to as the characteristic Assyrian prose-style:

> I threw down the city and its houses from the foundations to the summits; I ravaged them and allowed them to be consumed by fire. I knocked down and removed the outer and the inner walls, and the temples and all the brick-built ziggurats and threw the rubble into the Arahtu canal. And after I had destroyed Babylon, smashed its gods, and massacred its population, I tore up its soil and cast it into the Euphrates so that it was carried by the river down to the sea.

But Sennacherib, having in his time caused tens of thousands of innocent and helpless people to be murdered, was himself murdered by his own brothers. Esarhaddon, his son by a favourite concubine, came to the throne and reigned from 680 to 669 B.C. This monarch was worthy of his great predecessors, Tukultininurta, Tiglath-pileser, Shalmaneser, Sargon, and his father Sennacherib. He devoted himself to new wars of conquest; and since there was no longer any rival left between the Tigris and the Mediterranean and all the petty kings were vassals of Assyria, he decided to conquer Egypt itself. He succeeded in 671 B.C., and an account of his victories was duly recorded in an inscription.

I fell daily on the Egyptians with incessant slaughter as I marched from the city of Ishhupri to the royal city of Memphis, a journey of 15 days.

I surrounded Memphis and captured it in half a day with the aid of breaches in the walls, devastating fire, and scaling ladders.

I despoiled and ravaged it and caused it to be consumed by fire.

The pharaoh Tarku, his queen, the ladies of his harem, Ushanahuru his legitimate son and heir, his other sons and daughters, his goods and possessions, his horses, his cattle, his sheep, I carried away as spoil to Assyria. No one escaped death who would not be subservient to me; and so I appointed new kings, viceregents, governors, commandants, sheriffs, and scribes.

The end of this empire that had been created by continuous wars of conquest, by the total destruction of great cities, the slaughter of their population, and the systematic deportation of whole nations came soon after Assyria had become master of the whole known world. This vast domain was bequeathed by Esarhaddon to his son Ashurbanipal, who began his reign, as many of his predecessors had begun theirs, by suppressing a palace revolt organised by his elder brother who had been made the king of Babylon instead of king of Assyria as he expected and wished. However, Ashurbanipal wasted no time in discussing the merits of primogeniture, but marched with his entire force against his brother, defeated him at the gates of Babylon, and silenced his claims with a stroke of the sword. The victorious king now had only one enemy left in the entire world to destroy—Elam, the powerful kingdom to the east. In 646 B.C. he marched against Elam, and within a year that nation was annihilated as a great power for ever.

For twenty years Ashurbanipal was master of an empire which stretched almost from the Taurus Mountains to the southern boundaries of Egypt, but, for reasons that we do not know, his empire began to disintegrate. One contributing factor, however, is self-evident: the Assyrian tyrants were so hated that revolts must have been and, in fact, were continuous. The Egyptians, though not a warlike people, were still able to resist the foreign overlords—those kings, viceregents, governors, commandants, sheriffs, and scribes appointed by Esarhaddon; and Egypt itself was too far away and the journey overland across the deserts too difficult for the Assyrian army to be able to suppress the rebellion. So Egypt and other territories were lost.

Still another reason for the silence of the official annals for the last years of Ashurbanipal's reign may have been that the king retired from public life—that is, from the military ventures which, up to then, were almost the only form of recorded activity the Assyrian kings engaged in. There were no more campaigns, no great battles to boast of. The royal warrior, it seems, became a scholar, and a bibliophile. He spent his time consulting scribes and reading books, even those in the defunct Sumerian language, which he characterises as 'curious and obscure'. He even sent his agents all over Mesopotamia, to cities which had long been abandoned and hidden under mounds of rubble, to collect rare editions of ancient texts which he had translated into Assyrian. In this manner he collected the largest library in the ancient world. His own words are:

> I wrote on tablets, both wrote and read them, and when I had finished with them, I placed them in my library so that I can peruse them for myself or read them aloud [to my guests].

It is an extraordinarily modest statement for a king and army commander who had spent his life on the battlefield. Yet Ashurbanipal's interest in, and, indeed, enthusiasm for, literature cannot be denied, for the royal library contained tens of thousands of texts, 30,000 of which survived the destruction of the palace at Nineveh.

What, one wonders, was Ashurbanipal's motive for collecting books in this manner, a project which, as far as one knows, had never been undertaken by any of his predecessors? Was it a genuine love of knowledge, reverence for art and literature, or mere vanity? Assyriologists have not tried to explain the strange phenomenon, and it is probably fruitless in any case to speculate on the motives of kings. We have to be content with the extraordinary accident which has preserved Ashurbanipal's library for us. Nearly everything else of his empire was destroyed, for his enemies did such a thorough job of annihilating Nineveh that even the *site* of that city was unknown to Western historians until the middle of the eighteenth century. In fact, its ruins were not even mentioned by Herodotus who was travelling in the region only 150 years after the Assyrian capital's destruction. Such total oblivion in such a short time is almost incomprehensible unless we remember that, according to the practice of the time, what was not carried away as loot by conquering armies was burnt in an enormous bonfire; but in the case of Ashurbanipal's library, the very flames that were intended in apocalyptic fashion to wipe out even the memory of Assyria—of its cities, palaces, temples, and its very name—actually preserved the achievements of the last and greatest of its kings for all time. The clay tablets were baked to an additional hardness; and though a number of them had been fused together in an illegible mass by the heat, enough survived for the history of Assyria to be written again.

In fact, the survival of Ashurbanipal's library, together with the reliefs that covered the walls of the royal palaces, make the Assyrians even more real to us than they appear from the description of them in the Bible. We can, therefore, now read the account of the attack on Israel by the Assyrian invaders in the true context of history. We see that the old Jewish chroniclers made some mistakes in the names and dates of the kings, for we are told that both Shalmaneser III and Sennacherib besieged the cities of Samaria and Judah during the reign of Hezekiah. But Shalmaneser III was king of Assyria from 858 to 824 B.C., and Sennacherib from 704 to 681 B.C., while Hezekiah, according to II Kings, reigned twenty-nine years in Jerusalem. He could not, therefore, have withstood the attacks of both Assyrian monarchs. Now we know from the palace reliefs found at Nineveh that Sennacherib did besiege and capture Lachish, an event which the Old Testament ascribes to the fourteenth year of Hezekiah's kingship. The conquest of Judaea, then, must have taken place when Sargon was king of Assyria, so it seems probable that the Biblical scribe wrote Shalmaneser for Sargon.

But these chronological details are not important compared with the general picture the Bible gives us of this ruthless people who must take their place among the most inhuman nations of ancient or modern history. Perhaps the only excuse for their policy of mass murders and deportations is that the other kings of the Middle and Near Eastern states, including the Israelites, behaved in pretty much the same barbarous manner. And the cause of all these horrific deeds seems to have stemmed from the fanatical religious convictions of the Semitic tribes at this period, with each kingdom dedicated to its own national god who demanded the elimination of the rival deities. We read in the Old Testament how 'every nation made gods of their own, and put them in the houses of the high places, every nation in their cities wherein they dwelt' (II Kings, 17:29). And the very names of these anthropomorphs have a menacing quality to them:

> The men of Babylon made Succoth-benoth, and the men of Cuth made Nergal, and the men of Hamath made Ashima.
>
> And the Avites made Nibhaz and Tartak, and the Sepharvites burned their children in fire to Adrammelech and Anammelach, the gods of Sepharvaim.
>
> They feared the Lord, and served their own gods after the manner of the nations whom they carried away from thence.

And so the Assyrian kings went to war encouraged, and indeed commanded, by their gods, as Sennacherib's ambassadors informed Hezekiah's envoys after the siege of Lachish: 'The Lord said to me, Go up against this land and destroy it.' But, as we are constantly told in the Old Testament, the God of Israel was stronger than the god of the Assyrians, for when Sennacherib attempted to besiege Jerusalem:

> It came to pass that night that the angel of the Lord went out and smote in the camp of the Assyrians an hundred fourscore and five thousand; and when they arose in the morning, behold, they were all dead corpses. So Sennacherib king of Assyria departed, and went and returned, and dwelt at Nineveh. And it came to pass as he was worshipping in the house of Nisroch his god that Adrammelech and Sharezer his sons smote him with the sword: and they escaped into the land of Armenia. And Esarhaddon his son reigned in his stead. (II Kings, 19:35–37)

The rest of the story of the Judaean kings during the last days of the Assyrian Empire is particularly interesting, since we discern by reading between the lines that some of them attempted to appease their masters by accepting the Assyrian gods, which was

tantamount to rejecting everything the Jews had held dear since
the time of Moses. Thus Hezekiah's son, Manasseh, 'did that
which was evil in the sight of the Lord' by raising up altars to
Baal. Moreover, when he was old enough to have children,
Manasseh (who came to the throne at the age of twelve)

> made his son pass through the fire, and observed times, and
> used enchantments, and dealt with familiar spirits and wizards.

Here we seem to have a reference to the Babylonian astral
observations (the 'observing of times') which resulted in the com-
pilation of star tables later used by Greek astronomers. And what
is probable is that the Jewish priests quickly divined the danger
of a rival system of predicting the future, to the detriment of their
own spiritual and political power. They therefore prophesied the
most terrible calamities for their people if they continued to
'observe times and use enchantments', and warned that Yahweh
was so angry that:

> Behold, I am bringing such evil upon Jerusalem and Judah
> that whosoever heareth of it, both his ears shall tingle.
> And I will wipe Jerusalem as a man wipeth a dish, wiping it,
> and turning it upside down.
> And I will forsake the remnant of mine inheritance, and
> deliver them into the hand of their enemies; and they shall be-
> come a prey and a spoil to all their enemies.

The Jewish prophets were to be proved right, though whether
their information came from the deity, or was a shrewd interpretation of contemporary power politics as the Medes and Babylonians prepared for their war of liberation against Assyria, or
whether the dire prediction of the destruction of Jerusalem was
written after the event, we have no way of knowing. But in the
context of contemporary happenings this Old Testament version
of Assyrian history is correct. The empire of Ashurbanipal was
threatened on all sides. His enemies were awaiting the psycho-
logical moment to overthrow him; intense diplomatic activity was
going on behind the scenes. Evidently Hezekiah was invited to
join in the plot, as we learn from II Kings 20:12:

> At that time Berodach-baladan, the son of Baladan, king of
> Babylon, sent letters and a present to Hezekiah. And Hezekiah

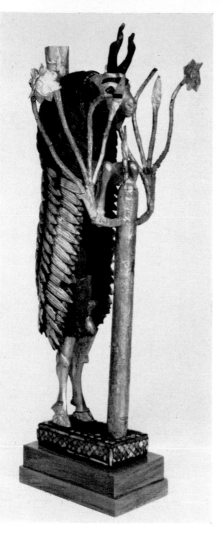

RAM IN A THICKET. Leonard Woolley, who found this famous gold and lapis-lazuli statue in the Royal Cemetery at Ur, suggested that it might be the Sumerian version of Abraham's sacrifice of 'the ram caught in a thicket'. The motif of animals propped up against a tree, however, is characteristic of Mesopotamian mythology, though it is not known why.

BULL'S HEAD. An ornamental figure-head placed on the sounding-box of a Sumerian harp found in the grave of Queen Shubad of Ur, together with 269 other funerary objects and the bodies of the queen's attendants.

DELUGE TABLET, far left. The story of the Flood as told in Genesis is also found in the Sumerian epic of Gilgamesh. This tablet from Nineveh describes how the ark survived seven days of storm, after which a dove was sent forth to find dry land.

WARAD-SIN, KING OF LARSA (1834–1823 B.C.) left, had himself sculpted with a head-pad for carrying a basket of bricks for the building of a temple, thus showing that he was a humble servant of the gods. Similar statues of other Mesopotamian monarchs acting as hod-carriers have survived.

HUNTING DOG, below left. Hounds were used for hunting lions, wild asses, and gazelles. We see in this relief how Assyrian artists who were strictly controlled in their depiction of god and kings expressed themselves freely in their animal studies.

SOLDIERS OF THE ROYAL GUARD, above. These men were archers in the Assyrian army which conquered almost the entire known world during the height of the empire between 900 and 600 B.C. The soldiers were superbly trained and equipped and formed into corps of charioteers, cavalry, infantry, and siege engineers.

DIVINING LIVER, left. Clay models of livers were used for divination, probably by student priests who learnt the science of haruspicy which involved dividing up the organ into sections, each of which represented an auspicious or ill-omened region as found in the actual liver of a sacrificed animal.

JEHU, KING OF ISRAEL, shown on this obelisk making his obeisance to Shalmaneser, king of Assyria (858–824 B.C.). Jehu was the Israelite king who exterminated the seventy sons of Ahab, the forty-two sons of Ahaziah, 'a great multitude' of the followers of Baal, and had Jezebel thrown into the street from an upstairs window, trampled on by horses, and devoured by dogs.

COURT OFFICIALS. The rigid formality of public life in Babylonia and Assyria is epitomised in the posture of these two functionaries with their staffs of office.

hearkened unto them, and shewed them all the house of his precious things, the silver and the gold, and the spices and the precious oil, and the house of his armour, and all that was found in his treasures: there was nothing in his house, nor in all his dominion that Hezekiah showed them not.

In other words, Hezekiah was initially favourable to the Babylonian plot to attack Assyria with the aid of the other dissident states. The plan probably involved a simultaneous attack on Nineveh from the east by the Elamite army, from the south by the Babylonians, and from the west by a Syrian coalition, including the Judaeans. But Hezekiah was dissuaded from joining this alliance by his chief minister, Isaiah, who in his role of prophet commanded the king to 'hear the word of the Lord', which was as follows:

Behold the days come that all that is in thine house and that which thy fathers have laid up in store unto this day shall be carried to Babylon; nothing shall be left, saith the Lord. And of thy sons that shall issue from thee, which thou shalt beget, shall they take away; and they shall be eunuchs in the palace of the king of Babylon.

The prediction of such a calamity was undoubtedly enough to terrorise the old king into giving up the struggle to liberate his country altogether, for shortly afterwards we learn that he slept with his fathers and Manasseh his son reigned in his stead; and when the time actually arrived that the Babylonians with their allies overthrew the Assyrians, Judaea was not part of the alliance and so did not obtain her liberation. On the contrary, she was considered part of the spoils of war, as the victors inherited overnight, as it were, the entire Assyrian Empire. Part of that empire included the small states of Palestine; whence the Jews now became vassals of the Babylonians.

13

The Splendour of Babylon

NINEVEH FELL, AND BABYLON, for 600 years the vassal of Assyria, rose once again as a world power.

This metropolis on the Euphrates—Nineveh was on the Tigris —had never, despite its destruction by Sennacherib, ceased to exist as one of the political and economic centres of the pre-Hellenic civilisations. Its first great king, Hammurabi the lawgiver, had established it as the cultural capital of the diverse Mesopotamian city-states, and it had continued to grow from a little settlement of fishing huts on the banks of a swamp to an immense city encircled by impregnable walls, long considered one of the Seven Wonders of the World. Indeed, according to later Greek historians, Babylon could boast of two of these marvels of men's architectural genius—its walls and the Hanging Gardens.*
We know that the walls enclosed the city in a double line of fortifications. The outer wall was about fifty feet high and ten feet wide. Inside this bastion the builders left a space of about twenty-five feet which probably served as a mustering point and parade ground for the troops manning the walls. In addition to the outer wall, the military engineers built an even thicker inner line of

* The other five were the Pyramids; the statue of the Olympian Zeus by Phidias; the Colossus of Rhodes; the temple of Artemis at Ephesus; and the Mausoleum or tomb of King Mausolus of Caria who married his sister Artemisia. This lady's grief on the death of her brother-husband was so great that in addition to erecting the magnificent monument which was to become the seventh wonder of the world, she used to drink the deceased's ashes mixed with her evening glass of wine, so that her own death two years later, though ascribed to a broken heart, may have been due to a severe attack of colitis.

defence, a bastion some twenty feet in width, so that the outer wall of ten feet, the parade ground of twenty-five feet, and the inner wall of twenty feet gave a defence in depth of about fifty-five feet and an estimated height of fifty feet. All along this huge defensive wall stood watch-towers at a distance of about 100 yards from each other. The circuit of the fortifications was just under ten miles.

The principal problem in the defence of Babylon was the passage of the Euphrates right through the middle of the city, the old part of which lay on the east bank, the new on the west bank. Herodotus mentions this fact, noting that the river was broad, deep, and swift and that the city wall was extended some way downstream and then brought back on both sides to the edge of the banks. The weak point in this system was, of course, the possibility of an armada of enemy boats slipping past the river forts at night and so penetrating to the very heart of the city. Nebuchadnezzar attempted to correct this weakness by building immense forts to the north of the city (from whence had come all the great invasions of Babylonia) and by diverting the water of the Euphrates via a canal into the great moat which followed the line of the city walls.

Inside the defensive system the political life of the capital centred on the palace which Nebuchadnezzar made the most magnificent royal residence in the world, while the equally important religious activities of this theocratic state were directed from the temple of the god Marduk. In addition to this main temple with its gates of solid brass, its inner sanctuaries, containing the couch on which a priestess spent the night in case the god desired some female company, and its solid gold statue eighteen feet high, Marduk had fifty-five other churches dedicated to his cult, while the other gods and goddesses, notably Ishtar, had forty-three. So there were some hundred religious shrines within the one city.

The commercial life of the busy metropolis centred on the river, which was the main highway for trade north to the kingdoms of Asia Minor and south to the land of Sumer. The river at Babylon was spanned by a single stone bridge whose roadway of planks was withdrawn at night—to prevent robbers from crossing from the old town on the east bank to the new suburbs on the west bank, according to some commentators; but more probably to control the passage of smugglers' carts bringing in untaxed supplies from the countryside.

Old Babylon always remained a warren of mud-brick houses and crooked alleys, for that matter not unlike a modern Iraqi village. The houses had no windows and the streets no paving of any sort. But Nebuchadnezzar had far-reaching plans for modernising and beautifying his capital and set about clearing away the old slum dwellings in the vicinity of his palace and the main temples in order to build the great gate of Ishtar and the Processional Way which passed through it. He introduced, too, an innovation in town planning in his project for a park set high enough inside the city walls to be visible to the citizens wherever they might be. This elevated park became known as the Hanging Gardens of Babylon which Nebuchadnezzar was said to have created for the love of his wife Amytis, the daughter of the king of the Medes.

Was there actually such a marvel as gardens that hung in the air? Or was the idea invented by Greek historians long after the fall of Babylon? Certainly Herodotus, who may have visited the city in the fifth century B.C., only some hundred years after the reign of Nebuchadnezzar, does not mention them. On the other hand, several other classical historians give a fairly detailed description of the park, of which that of Diodorus Siculus is the most complete.

> The Garden was 100 feet long by 100 wide and built up in tiers so that it resembled a theatre. Vaults had been constructed under the ascending terraces which carried the entire weight of the planted garden; the uppermost vault, which was seventy-five feet high, was the highest part of the garden, which, at this point, was on the same level as the city walls. The roofs of the vaults which supported the garden were constructed of stone beams some sixteen feet long, and over these were laid first a layer of reeds set in thick tar, then two courses of baked brick bonded by cement, and finally a covering of lead to prevent the moisture in the soil penetrating the roof. On top of this roof enough topsoil was heaped to allow the biggest trees to take root. The earth was levelled off and thickly planted with every kind of tree. And since the galleries projected one beyond the other, where they were sunlit, they contained many royal lodges. The highest gallery contained conduits for the water which was raised by pumps in great abundance from the river, though no one outside could see it being done.[1]

Indeed, the Hanging Gardens of Babylon excited so much interest as one of the Seven Wonders of the World that the German archaeologists who excavated the ruined city were always eagerly looking for evidence of their existence. The important clues were undoubtedly Diodorus's reference to stone vaults which must have been arched; and, again, to the special irrigation system which enabled water to be raised to the highest point of the gardens. So once the rather Arabian Nights fantasy of gardens floating in the air is dispelled, there is no reason to discredit the reports of what Berosus, the native historian of Babylon, described as κρεμαστὸς κῆτος, literally a hanging garden, but no doubt meant to imply a small park supported on the roof of a mansion, exactly as Diodorus informs us it was supported.

We need not wonder, then, that Robert Koldewey was elated by his discovery of a unique vaulted building in the Southern Citadel area of Babylon and that he was convinced that he had found the site of the celebrated Hanging Gardens. For not only was this building, apart from the buttresses of the bridge, the only one in which stone was used (Diodorus makes special reference to the stone beams which formed the roof of the supporting vaults and, at the same time, the floor of the plantation above), but there was also found an unusual well consisting of three adjoining shafts, a square one in the centre flanked by two of oblong shape. The theory is that a chain of leather buckets was lowered down from one of the side shafts, filled with water at the bottom, passed over a wheel, and returned up the other side shaft. At the top, the filled buckets would be tipped into a trough and then passed over another wheel and sent back down the side shaft for refilling, the process being continuous. Perhaps another endless chain of buckets would scoop up the water from the trough at the top of the wall and carry it up to the highest gallery, as Diodorus suggests; but all vestiges of this second stage of the hydraulic system have, of course, disappeared. The square shaft in the centre of the well that has survived was obviously a maintenance tunnel down which the engineers descended to sort out any tangles that took place at the bottom of the well.[2]

Undoubtedly these famous gardens excited enormous interest among the general public at the time of the Babylon excavations and they have kept Assyriologists busy ever since. Thus, though Robert Koldewey, the archaeologist on the site, was certain that he had definitive evidence of the gardens, Wallis Budge, Keeper of the Egyptian and Assyrian Antiquities at the British Museum, was equally certain that they never existed except in the imagination of Greek fabulists. Each man quoted classical sources to support his contention. Koldewey offers us Berosus, Ctesias, Strabo, Diodorus, and Curtius Rufus; Budge counters with Philo of Byzantium, Antipater of Sidon, Hyginus, and Pliny.

It was Philo of Byzantium, incidentally, who first listed the Hanging Gardens as one of the Seven Wonders of the World. What is surprising is that he did not include the great temple tower or ziggurat of Babylon as another, except that this immense seven-storeyed building was in utter ruins by the time Philo came to draw up his list. In fact, by the time of Alexander's conquest of Babylon, nothing remained of this marvellous temple but the rubble which the Macedonian king attempted to clear away. Strabo says that he expended 600,000 working days in removing the debris. Already, then, we begin to see that the Biblical description of the Tower of Babel was not so exaggerated after all. 'And they said to one another, Go to, let us make brick and burn them thoroughly. And they had brick for stone and slime [=asphalt] had they for mortar. And they said, Go to, let us build a city and a tower whose top may reach unto heaven . . .' And this poetical description of the Great Tower is not at all unreasonable in view of the dimensions of the Babylonian ziggurat dedicated to Marduk, the national god—which is the sort of tower referred to in Genesis. This famous shrine was known as 'The House of the Foundations of Heaven and Earth' and, according to Herodotus, it consisted of eight stages, each a different colour, surmounted by the god's private chapel, and reaching 297 feet up into the sky—certainly the highest and most impressive building on earth at the time and inevitably a symbol to the exiled Jews of the hated Babylonian oppressors and of their triumphant god. The Biblical account of the collapse of the great temple appears to be a mixture of actual historical fact on the one hand and of religious bigotry on the other: historically, the tower had been destroyed by Sennacherib of Assyria in 688 B.C., an event which the Jewish chroniclers interpreted in their own mystical fashion and according to their own orthodoxy.

And so, as with many other stories in the Old Testament, some scholars with the scepticism which was characteristic of the so-called Higher Criticism of the mid-nineteenth century were inclined to doubt the historicity of the Tower of Babel, the very existence of which, let alone the whereabouts, was a matter of continual controversy among archaeologists and historians, but all doubts were finally resolved by the appearance of a tablet which decided the matter once and for all. In 1876 George Smith, the brilliant young Assyriologist and 'discoverer' of the Chaldean account of the Flood and the site of Carchemish, published a letter in the *Athenaeum* stating that 'I have discovered a Babylonian text giving a remarkable account of the Temple of Belus at Babylon, and as my approaching departure for Nineveh does not allow me time to make a full translation of the document, I have prepared a short account for your readers, giving the principal points in the arrangement and dimensions of the building'.[3]

George Smith's statement was, in fact, extremely mysterious, since he gave no indication of the provenance or whereabouts of this extraordinarily important tablet, and had it not been for his great prestige (he was celebrated in Britain of the 1870's as the author of popular novels is today), the affair would have been regarded as an elaborate hoax. As it was, nobody could conceivably doubt the integrity or the scholarship of the much loved disciple and collaborator of Henry Rawlinson himself; and so the letter and description of the tower were avidly read throughout the world of learning. Particularly fascinating were the measurements of the tower, of which George Smith has this to say:

The Babylonian measures used are principally the cubit, equal to about one foot eight inches English, and the *gar*, or *sa*, equal to twelve cubits, or twenty English feet; but there is another series of numbers consisting apparently of numbers of barleycorns arranged in sixties: thus the first number is a length of 11.33.20, which consists of 11 × 3600 + 33 × 60 + 20 barleycorns, in all 39,600 barleycorns, or 1155 feet 7 inches. The barleycorn was the standard unit of measurement among the Babylonians, and for this reason was sometimes used in measures of length without the other terms.[4]

The barleycorn, incidentally, was a semi-official English measure of length almost up to the end of the nineteenth century. In Shakespeare's day 'three barleycorns, dry and round, shall make up an inch'.

What was this tablet the young archaeologist claimed to have seen? It was not possible to question George Smith, because he left for Baghdad immediately after the publication of his letter and died, the same year, of 'the plague', as did his companion, the Finnish archaeologist Charles Eneberg. Smith was thirty-six years old; Eneberg twenty-eight. Such were the hazards of archaeology a hundred years ago. But some years later, after Smith's death, the tablet turned up again and was actually offered to the British Museum at what was called at that time 'an extravagant price', so the Trustees rejected the offer and the precious tablet finally found its way to the Louvre where it is now part of the French museum's oriental collection.

The tablet exists, then, is genuine, and is dated by the scribe who wrote it on the 26th day of the month of Kislimmu in the 83rd year of Si-lu-ku; in other words, 12th December 229 B.C. A relatively small document, $7\frac{1}{2}$ in. long and $3\frac{1}{2}$ in. wide, it gives the dimensions of the temple by stages, seven stages in all. The bottom stage measured 300 feet by 300 feet, an area of 10,000 square yards; and 110 feet in height. The top or seventh stage (the shrine of Marduk) measured 80 feet long, 70 feet wide, and 50 feet high. The total height was about 300 feet and on the flat plain of Babylon could thus be seen from sixty miles away in every direction, perhaps as far as the place where Baghdad now stands on the banks of the Tigris.

Another and still older document throws light on the building of the ziggurat or tower which Genesis calls Babel. This is an inscription ascribed to Nabopolassar, founder of the neo-Babylonian Empire and father of Nebuchadnezzar. It says:

The lord Marduk commanded me [i.e. Nabopolassar] concerning Etemenanki, the staged tower of Babylon, which before my time had become dilapidated and ruinous, that I should make its foundations secure in the bosom of the nether world and make its summit like the heavens. [Compare Genesis 11:3: 'And they said, Go to, let us build a city and a tower whose top may reach unto heaven.'] I caused baked bricks to be made. As it were rains from on high which are measureless, or great torrents, I caused streams of bitumen to be brought by the canal Arahtu . . . I took a reed and myself measured the dimensions [to be given to the tower]. Accepting the counsel of the gods

Shamash, Ada, and Marduk, I made decisions and kept them in my heart: I preserved the measurements in my memory, like a treasure. I deposited in the foundations under the bricks gold, silver, and precious stones from the mountains and from the sea. I caused to be made my own royal likeness wearing the *dupshikku* [?] and placed it in the foundations. For my lord Marduk I bowed my neck, I took off my robe—the sign of my royal blood—and on my head I bore bricks and earth. As for Nebuchadnezzar my first-born son, the beloved of my heart, I made him bear the mortar, the offering of wine and oil, in company with my subjects.

In other words, the king and the crown prince worked on the building site of the temple, just as in the Middle Ages kings and nobles drew by hand the first cartloads of stone to the site of the cathedrals that were a-building, an ancient ritual that has become today the unveiling of a plaque by minor royalty to the accompaniment of polite clapping. But Nabopolassar carried a hod of bricks on his shoulder and a basket of earth on his head, and so began the re-erection of the Temple Etemenanki, which had been destroyed by the Assyrian Sennacherib fifty years before and was to be destroyed again by the Persian Xerxes 150 years later. But the greatest destruction was inevitably caused by time, after the city of Babylon had been abandoned to wild beasts, as St Jerome tells us it was. From that time on, the walls of the city, and especially the great mound of the fallen Tower of Babel, served as a brickyard for the local peasants who built their huts out of the debris which Alexander had tried to clear with thousands of forced labourers. And so by the time Robert Koldewey arrived on the scene in 1897 the destruction was complete. He writes:

The mound [of Babel] rises in a steep slope to the height of 22 metres above the plain. . . . The astonishingly deep pits and galleries that occur in places owe their origin to the quarrying for brick that has been carried on extensively during the last decades. . . . Soon after the commencement of the excavations I had interested myself in checking this spoliation, but that was possible only for the Kasr [i.e. the ruins of the palace of Nebuchadnezzar]; at Babil it still went on. Even at the Kasr I had to drive these workers out of their pits and set them to work in our diggings. . . .[5]

L

Another eyewitness account of the nature and extent of the
destruction of Babylon is given by Wallis Budge who visited the
site in 1888. Wallis Budge had been sent by the Trustees of the
British Museum to purchase antiquities in Egypt and Mesopotamia, for the sale of antiquities had become big business in the
latter half of the nineteenth century and all the national museums
of Europe and America had agents in the field. By this time the
day of the original 'excavators'—men like Rich, Layard, Rassam,
and Botta—was over: it was no longer so easy to obtain a firman
to dig a likely site, tunnel into it, extract the artefacts, and ship
them back to Europe. Both the Turkish authorities and the Iraqi
peasantry, though indifferent to the historical significance of the
buried treasures, had discovered their commercial value. And so
the little clay tablets which the shepherds used to find by the
thousands in the ruins of the Assyrian and Babylonian cities, and
which they used to throw aside as worthless, were now being
bought at good prices in the bazaars; and everybody concerned,
shepherds, dealers, officials, and European agents, knew their
value.

When Wallis Budge arrived at the site of Babylon he found
almost the entire male population of the locality engaged in digging for what they called 'pillows'—that is, inscribed clay tablets
which they smuggled into Baghdad for the dealers to dispose of.
In the old days these men had dug into the mounds for building
bricks, but they knew now that the clay tablets with writing on
them were worth more. Wallis Budge was able to buy whole
basketfuls of these Babylonian records for a few piastres each. (The
piastre in his day was worth about twopence.) He tells of one
smuggler who used to make a regular run from the villages outside Baghdad to the bazaars, carrying a hundred or more tablets
sewn into rows of small pockets inside his cloak. 'He was a capable man with quick intelligence,' writes Wallis Budge, and 'it was
quite clear that he thoroughly enjoyed outwitting Turkish
officials.'[6] On one occasion, however, he appeared to have failed
in this commendable cause, for he was caught by the customs
officials with over 100 tablets in his cloak and turban, a string of
cylinder seals and gold coins tied round his waist, and more
'pillows' in the donkeys' panniers. The smuggler was arrested and
taken to court, but the trial was a nicely arranged farce in which
the judge, the judge's secretary, and the chief of police were well

bribed, sharing, in fact, in the payment which Wallis Budge made
for the entire collection. The tablets and cylinder seals are among
the finest in the British Museum.

The stories told by Wallis Budge and his contemporaries of the
fantastic trade in antiques, especially Egyptian and Babylonian
artefacts, are an indirect proof of the wealth of these ancient
civilisations, for it is clear that literally hundreds of thousands of
statuettes, ornaments, seals, tablets and so forth were taken out of
the sands of Egypt and the rubble of Mesopotamia throughout
the nineteenth century and that as many more artefacts were destroyed in the process of looting the ruins. Wallis Budge points out
that the men who dug for the tablets worked mostly at night to
escape detection and that for every 'pillow' they brought out undamaged they must have broken perhaps as many as half a
dozen with their spades. The dealers, in turn, smuggled out whole
collections with the long-distance caravans, packing the tablets
in boxes without any padding at all, so that it was not uncommon
for the entire consignment to be smashed to pieces on arrival. In
one case a very special assortment of tablets was put into boxes
which were hidden between bales of wool, only for the whole lot
—wool, boxes, and tablets—to be put into the wool-press, with
the obvious disastrous results.

The destruction of the small artefacts was as nothing compared
with the havoc made by the diggers for bricks. This quarrying in
the ruins of the great cities had, of course, been going on for centuries—the nearby city of Seleucia, for instance, having been built
by one of Alexander's generals from Babylonian bricks; but the
pillage reached its climax under the Turks in the last decades of
the nineteenth century when public works like dams or canals
were constructed almost entirely of the bricks taken from the site
of the ancient city. Wallis Budge reports that the Turks were
dynamiting walls and towers in order to sell the bricks at from
three to five piastres apiece, while cartloads of bricks were carried
off to the dam on a nearby canal.

Yet even so the extent of the Babylonian ruins in Wallis Budge's
day was so vast that he was unable to formulate a plan of the city,
and he makes the point that if the mounds adjacent to the city itself were a conurbation of the capital, then Herodotus's estimate
of the circuit of the walls as eighty-six kilometres may not be all
that exaggerated. Only systematic excavation 'with hundreds of

diggers working for ten or twenty years' could lay bare the foundations of Babylon, he concludes, noting that the last excavator of the great mound known as the Kasr was Hormuzd Rassam, who dug down more than forty feet into the rubble during the years 1878–81 and found nothing of note. Rassam, in fact, was the last of the old 'excavators', belonging to the generation of Layard and Botta: that is, of treasure-hunters who wielded the pick and spade in much the same manner and for much the same purpose as the prospector for gold in the Klondike.

Fortunately for Babylon, a representative of the new order of excavators was to appear on the scene in the person of Robert Koldewey, who was to devote the next fifteen years of his life to uncovering the foundations of the Mesopotamian city, working, as he tells us, daily, both summer and winter, with a labour force of from 200 to 250 workmen; and what we see and know of Babylon today is entirely due to his skill and devotion.

Koldewey, then, marks the beginning of an entirely new era in Assyriology. After him the nineteenth-century 'excavators' passed into archaeological history along with the antiquarians of the eighteenth century. It was not that Koldewey and his colleagues suddenly had access to the scientific aids used by modern field-workers, or, for that matter, that they employed the highly sophisticated technique of the specialist—Koldewey still used the pick-axe, shovel, basket, and native manpower in the same manner that Botta, Layard, and the others had done. The difference was: (a) the excavations were now undertaken in a spirit of inquiry and not merely for the quick discovery of museum treasures; and (b) they were made with the same meticulous attention to detail which is now the hallmark of all archaeological digs.

As a consequence, the results were not spectacular in the popular sense, and Robert Koldewey never achieved the fame that Botta, Layard, and Rawlinson achieved in the Assyrian field and Schliemann from his finds at Troy and Mycenae. The reason was obvious: the public had been conditioned by the visually exciting finds of the 'excavators' to expect quick, impressive results, especially from an expedition organised on the scale of Koldewey's Babylon excavations. Indeed, this was really the first time the Germans had been able to undertake a Mesopotamian dig at all, though they had contributed enormously to the decipherment of the texts which were now streaming into the museums at an unprecedented rate. But German national pride combined with German scholarship had made it imperative for the Emperor and his people to claim their rightful share of the Assyrian spoils—a claim which was advanced by Professor Friedrich Delitzsch, one of the most eminent orientalists of the period. Professor Delitzsch had worked as a student in the British Museum Oriental Department with the greatest Assyriologists of the age—Henry Rawlinson, Samuel Birch, George Smith, Julius Oppert, Austin Layard, and others. Wallis Budge reports of him, not without some understandable acerbity, that when he was asked by none other than Rawlinson what he was doing, he replied that he was compiling an Assyrian reading book for students.

'A good project,' the English explorer replied. 'And you are welcome to use my *Cuneiform Texts*.' (These were the Babylonian tablets which Rawlinson and his assistants had copied out, edited, and published in the great five-volume edition sponsored and financed by the British Museum.)

'That is impossible,' Delitzsch answered. 'They are too full of mistakes. But I will correct them all.'

Budge reports that all those surrounding the great man gasped in alarm and astonishment, but Rawlinson's reply was quite mild and very revealing of the man who was known as 'the Father of Assyriology'.

'That may well be,' he said. 'I am only a pioneer and not a scholar.'

It was this Professor Delitzsch who inspired his compatriots and succeeded in organising the German Orient Society under the patronage of the German Government. With this kind of sponsorship it was possible to mount an expedition that would have all the funds necessary for a *proper* excavation of a site, instead of a fast scrabble in the earth in search of museum exhibits. The German Orient Society, in fact, spent fifteen years working at Babylon under the direction of Robert Koldewey, assisted by a succession of German scholars and archaeologists.

Robert Koldewey himself, in contrast to an academic like Friedrich Delitzsch, belonged to the old school of explorer-excavators, with many of whom he was warm friends. And like his British and French colleagues in the field he was not a trained archaeologist in the modern sense. He was a professional architect and an archaeologist by predilection. Even as a young man in 1880 he was digging around in the Greek islands at a time when almost any amateur with a passion for ancient history was free to excavate pretty much where he chose. So Koldewey dug in Greece, Syria, Italy, and Sicily and learnt the many disciplines of his science more from experience than from books. And it was this experience much more than his academic qualifications which decided the directors of the German Orient Society to appoint him as the leader of the first scientifically planned and organised Mesopotamian expedition. Koldewey's assignment was to unearth Babylon, then thought to be the last important Middle Eastern site awaiting the archaeologist's spade.

We can see how slowly and meticulously Koldewey and his team cleared away the rubble from the ruins of Babylon when we read that the German expedition employed from 200 to 250 workmen throughout the entire year for fifteen years without uncovering more than half of the buried city. Moreover, the annual reports of the expedition's work were written for and circulated to professional Assyriologists, leaving the general public somewhat indifferent to the results, for Babylonia was now thought of in terms of great bearded god-kings, enormous winged bulls and lions, and vast libraries containing splendid stories like that of the Flood and the *Epic of Gilgamesh*. Koldewey's careful plans and drawings and his emphasis on architectural detail did not excite much popular interest.

Indeed, after fifteen years of digging, he himself had almost reached the conclusion that the magnificence of Babylon had been greatly exaggerated; and if he had been animated by the same motives as Botta and Layard, he might have abandoned his vast project after a couple of seasons. He admits that he felt like doing so at times, so disappointing were the excavations of the temples, which proved to be of unburnt brick, drably decorated with a thin limewash on the walls.

But in the spring of 1902 he was able to announce the sort of spectacular find which rekindled the enthusiasm of the lay public: he uncovered the Processional Way and the Ishtar Gate. By clearing away the tons of rubble which had hidden this massive portal for 2000 years, he gave to the desolate mound of Babylon something of the 'aura' which the columns of Greek temples and the triumphal archways of Roman cities gave to classical ruins. At last he had found in the Ishtar Gate a monument which made all the panegyrics about the size and splendour of Babylon credible. Almost forty feet high, it spanned the Processional Way along which the god Marduk was borne on the most sacred day of the Babylonian year. The decorations of this gate were particularly exciting, for they brought the first touch of colour into the drab Babylonian world of brick and mud. Moreover, in the inscription recording his repair of the Processional Way and the Ishtar Gate, Nebuchadnezzar himself states that it was he who ordered the blue-enamelled bricks of bulls and dragons to be placed in position—nearly 600 of them—in order that the town gate should 'be made glorious for the amazement of all people'. The famous king whose name was a household word had succeeded in his ambition. His bulls and dragons are from the artistic point of view the most interesting artefacts to come out of Babylon, for whatever else this centre of world culture produced, it did not excel in the plastic or domestic arts. For neither the Babylonians nor the Assyrians seem to have had the aesthetic sensibility of their predecessors, the Sumerians, whose art, like their philosophy of life, was altogether more 'human', and hence more diversified. Assyro-Babylonian art was, in contrast, static, being rigorously determined by convention and dedicated solely to the glorification of the state: i.e. the gods, their priests, and the king. So it could be said that once the viewer has seen the portrait of one Assyro-Babylonian god or king, he has seen the portraits of them all. They all have the same great staring eyes, cold expressions, spade beards, and inhuman appearance. They were intended to look inhuman, of course, for they could not otherwise be expected to awe their mortal subjects. The artists who made them knew the rules and were careful to make the god a little larger than the king, and the king larger than the official. There was no room for inspiration, except in one area, the depiction of animals. Hence the only portraits which have any fluidity, any emotion, are those of hunted and dying animals. This odd fact is significant quite apart from its aesthetic interest, since it implies that artists, who normally count themselves the freest of men, were yet so restricted by the rigid structure of Assyro-Babylonian society that the only safe outlet for their genius was in depicting—surely with intense compassion—the fears and terrors of animals as they raced away from the hunter or lay dying, speared through the neck or flanks. The famous frieze of the Assyrian bas-reliefs from the palace of Ashurbanipal (now in the

British Museum), showing the wild horse, deer, and lion hunts, is an example of an unknown artist's cry of pain tragically caught in the sculpting of the paralysed lioness who roars *her* pain towards the sky while she drags her paralysed back legs along the ground after two spears have transfixed her flanks. Similarly the old lion sinks with a last roar to the ground; the young horse races after its mother showing real terror as the hunting-dogs snap at its legs; and the herd of gazelles, one doe with her twins, trot off into the desert, the buck turning his head to see how near is the danger. But as soon as the artists return to their portraits of men they resume the stiff, feelingless techniques which produced the assembly-line statues of the gods and kings, so that a depiction of soldiers carrying the decapitated heads of prisoners of war, or of torturers crushing the skulls of their victims, is all shown as though enacted by robots.

It is not surprising, then, that the enamelled animals that adorne the Ishtar Gate and the Processional Way are really very beautiful and very pleasant to look upon. The yellow bulls on a blue back-ground are splendid creatures, conceived in an entirely different style from the massive and forbidding winged bulls with human heads which guarded the royal palaces. One feels that they were meant to welcome and amuse the country pilgrims who came to Babylon for the festival of Marduk. Nor were the dragons, silver on blue, intended to frighten them for they are sprightly beasts, not dissimilar to a cheetah. In any case, this mythological beast whose ancestry must have gone back to prehistory before the giant lizards became extinct was the sacred animal of Marduk as we learn from the apocryphal book *Bel and the Dragon*. In this account Daniel blows up the dragon by inserting a lump of pitch, fat, and hair into its mouth and presumably setting it alight with a fuse, for 'the dragon burst in sunder'. The story has the ring of truth to it and was probably based on information learnt by the Jews during the period of their exile—like spotting the trapdoor by which the priests of Marduk and their families used to enter the god's private dining-room to polish off the sacrificial food; or the 'dragon' which the priests exhibited in the semi-darkness of the temple amid clouds of incense actually being a monitor, the fearsome lizard which inhabits the Arabian Desert, a creature whose genea-logy goes back to the time of the dinosaurs. Such was Marduk's mas-cot, who appears in symbolic form on the walls of the Ishtar Gate.

These discoveries of the German expedition re-aroused some popular interest in Babylon, though the extent to which the layman's attitude had changed to Assyriology is seen in the lukewarm reception given to the English version of Koldewey's book *The Excavations at Babylon* in comparison with the acclaim accorded fifty years previously to Layard and his *Nineveh*. The German excavator's book was really too 'dry' for the average reader; and, in any case, Koldewey was not interested, as Layard had been, in recounting his personal experiences (dangers from bandits, excessive heat, fevers, et cetera) but in presenting an objective report of fourteen years' excavations. In addition, he was very ill-served by his translator, who was obviously not equipped to render the difficult technical German into readable English.

Yet all honour should have gone to Koldewey for the way in which he respected the ruins of Babylon, doing his best to preserve them instead of digging, tunnelling, and boring his shafts this way and that in the hope of finding monuments rivalling the finds of the early excavators. In fact, his extreme care not to destroy what remained of Babylon placed him at a double disadvantage: first, all excavation, however meticulous, is of necessity a process of disturbing and hence destroying the site which is dug over, while, at the same time, if the archaeologist is too conservative in his methods, he may partially destroy without finding anything to reveal a significant picture of the site; and, secondly, being primarily interested in architecture, Koldewey concentrates on the style and dimensions of buildings at the expense of what might be called the social and cultural life of Babylon. In this respect his book is less interesting than the *Lost City of Adab* by the American excavator Edgar Banks or the *Ur of the Chaldees* by Sir Leonard Woolley.

The visitor to Babylon today is very much aware of Koldewey's difficulties in that he left, as the evidence of fifteen years' labour, mere heaps of rubble which even the most imaginative person finds unevocative of the ancient splendour. This was not, of course, his fault. The city, after all, had been built mostly of clay, and what was worth looting had long since been carried away. Consequently, the visitor who has no specialist to guide him is liable to be disappointed. Is this mound of rubble, he asks, the site of the Tower of Babel? And are these undulating heaps running across the plain the mighty walls which were once one of the

Seven Wonders of the World? Where are the temples and palaces?
For all that is left of what a Roman described as 'the greatest city
the sun ever beheld' is the reconstructed Gate of Ishtar, a pile of
brickwork which is pointed out as the site of the Hanging Gardens, and the weather-worn sculpture of the lion of Babylon left
in situ. Otherwise, Babylon, like Nineveh, is a desolate ruin which
one unconsciously compares with the remains of far less splendid
cities like Mycenae and Leptis Magna. Then one remembers that
the Greeks and Romans built in stone and marble, so that many
of their monuments have endured in the shape of a slender column
or a massive triumphal arch, while even the uninformed visitor
can get a glimpse of their daily lives in the market-places, theatres,
and public baths. Nothing like this is to be seen at the sites of the
great Assyrian and Babylonian cities. Their architects and builders were ingenious and industrious, and they built on an immense
scale, but the materials they worked with were perishable, and
what their enemies did not knock down and throw into the canals
the wind and rain have carried away. The prophecy of Jeremiah
was to prove literally true:

> Therefore the wild beasts of the desert, with the wild beasts of
> the islands, shall dwell there; and the owls shall dwell therein;
> and it shall be no more inhabited for ever.

But perhaps the words of the Jewish priest were not so much a
prophecy as an expression of his hatred for a nation that had captured Jerusalem, destroyed the Temple, and carried the flower of
Israel away into captivity. For what Jeremiah was really writing
about was the tragedy of the Jewish exile after the conquest of
Israel by Nebuchadnezzar; and his hymn of hate was the railing of
an exiled patriot condemning his fellow-countrymen who had
first surrendered and then collaborated with the enemy, or, as the
prophet puts it, 'have brought their necks under the yoke of the
king of Babylon'. But the king of Babylon—that is, Nebuchadnezzar—was not quite the tyrant that Jeremiah makes him, as an
examination of other Old Testament accounts of Babylon will
show.

14

The Jews in Babylon

THE INVOLVEMENT OF THE Jews first with the Assyrians and later with the Babylonians is perhaps the principal reason for the non-specialist's interest in the ancient empires of Mesopotamia. We have seen how profound that interest was during the nineteenth century when the Bible was a much more potent source of both historical and spiritual revelation than it seems to be today. And because of this familiarity with the history of the Jews as recorded in the Old Testament the discoveries of the excavators and the translations of the philologists were received with tremendous enthusiasm by the Victorians to whom the names of kings and cities mentioned in the Jewish chronicles were better known and, for that matter, were certainly more real than those enumerated in the classical histories. There was probably not a single church-goer in the Western world, however uneducated, who had not heard of Nebuchadnezzar, whereas very few indeed had heard of Priam of Troy. Nebuchadnezzar, in other words, was a real historical person, and what he personified was the epitome of ancient kingship. The average man, indeed, had a certain sympathy for a monarch who was finally driven to 'eat grass as oxen'.

This is all the more understandable when one considers not only the fact that the Bible was, as it were, prescribed reading in the home as well as the church, but, even more important, the book's extraordinary fascination as a collection of short stories: a prime example, the account in the Book of Daniel of the hand that suddenly appeared out of nowhere and 'wrote over against the candlestick upon the plaster of the wall of the king's palace'—an account worthy to take its place with the world's best ghost stories. It is no wonder that ordinary people who had no interest whatsoever in Assyriology were eager to hear more about this world of magic in which a king called Belshazzar, the 'son of Nebuchadnezzar', gave a feast to a thousand of his lords, their wives, and his concubines, only to be frightened out of his wits by this ectoplasmic happening. It was first-rate melodrama.

So nearly everyone a hundred years ago had a general idea of what went on at Babylon, for they could read in the Second Book of the Kings and the books of the Prophets how Jerusalem was captured and the Jews carried off into exile and who were the kings and the kings' sons involved in the struggle which was fought not only between earthly monarchs but between the rival gods, the Yahweh of the Jews and the Merodach (Marduk) of the Babylonians. It made exciting reading, even if it was manifestly biassed, as all nationalistic histories are bound to be. What, then, was the truth of these ancient goings-on?

The discoveries of the Assyriologists were soon to give another version of Jewish-Babylonian relations, and, not surprisingly, it was apparent that the Biblical account of Nebuchadnezzar's reign, for instance, does not correspond with either the records of the cuneiform tablets or the archaeological evidence. To begin with, the Book of Daniel in which the events purporting to relate to the Babylonian Exile are found is a very perplexing document in that its early chapters are written in Hebrew which suddenly changes into Aramaic only to change back again into Hebrew. Does this have a bearing on the book's authenticity? Nobody knows, especially since the contents of the book are even more puzzling than its text. For while the actual account of the Exile does have an authentic 'feel' to it, yet it is full of inaccuracies, like making Belshazzar the 'son' of Nebuchadnezzar, whereas Nebuchadnezzar's son and successor was Amel-Marduk, referred to in the Old Testament itself as Evil-merodach. Elsewhere, Darius the Persian is called a 'Mede'. But even more dubious than these errors of detail is the characterisation of Nebuchadnezzar as a weak, vacillating monarch who, we are asked to believe, 'fell upon his face and worshipped Daniel' after the latter had interpreted the king's dream. Such homage from the conqueror of the world to an obscure Jewish captive is as improbable as the story of Shadrach, Meshach, and Abed-nego walking about unharmed in the midst of the fiery furnace. The account of the writing on the wall, on the other hand, is easier to accept in so far as it is in the best tradition of oriental story-telling; and so, too, is the fairy-tale of Daniel in the lions' den and the 'happy ending', whereby Daniel comes out unscathed and his enemies, including their wives and children, are cast in where 'the lions had the mastery of them and brake all their bones in pieces'.

Yet out of this hodge-podge of legends and exilic revelations emerges a very useful working hypothesis which helps us assess the character of Nebuchadnezzar and of the new Babylon he created; for, reading between the lines of the Jewish account, we begin to see the Babylonian king, however dimly, as an autocrat of considerable intelligence and an administrator of exceptional ability. His foreign and domestic policy, obviously, was based on the attainment of peace abroad and prosperity at home. We are told in both the Second Book of the Kings and the Book of Daniel that he was not vengeful towards his old enemies the Jews, but attempted to make friends with them, once he had put down their revolt, which he admittedly did in the usual brutal fashion of the times, killing the sons of the Judaean king Zedekiah before their father's eyes and then blinding the old man.

Nebuchadnezzar's regard for the Jews, then, explains how Daniel, Hananiah, Mishael, and Azariah, 'children of Judah', came to be reared at his court, as later Jehoiachin, king of Judah, was released from prison and given royal prerogatives by Nebuchadnezzar's successor, Amel-Marduk. And so it seems clear from the Hebrew version of the Babylonian story that both Nebuchadnezzar and the subsequent kings were prepared to accept the Jews as citizens of the new empire in the hope of assimilating them as fellow-Semites, though race was of no consequence at this period of history. The Jews were obviously highly respected by the Babylonians as magi, or wise men, whence Daniel had been made 'master of the magicians, astrologues, Chaldeans, and sooth-sayers'. To have been set over the Chaldeans of all people as a master wizard is incontrovertible proof of the Jews' unchallenged superiority in the field of medicine, which, as we saw in an earlier chapter, was largely based on elementary psychology. This being so, one has the impression that Daniel would have proved himself a first-rate psychologist even today, for, according to the Old Testament account, he undertook to treat Nebuchadnezzar after the royal physicians had admitted they were baffled by the king's condition. And no wonder! For the monarch had not only had a dream which he could not remember, but one which he insisted on having interpreted. Evidently Daniel was the only one astute enough to diagnose paranoia and from this to base his treatment on the assumption that if the king couldn't remember his dream nobody else could; whence he, Daniel, could safely invent one to suit the occasion. His stratagem was to invent a really portentous dream that would flatter this unstable and irascible monarch, and this he managed to do, drawing on his imagination for the symbolic picture of the 'great image' with the head of gold, the breast and arms of silver, the belly and thighs of brass, and the feet of iron and clay.

> This is the dream; and we will tell the interpretation thereof before the king.
>
> Thou, O king, art a king of kings, for the God of heaven hath given thee a kingdom, power, and strength and glory. And wheresoever the children of men dwell, the beasts of the field and the fowls of the heaven hath he given unto thy hand, and hath made thee ruler over all. Thou art his head of gold.

Nebuchadnezzar was no doubt flattered and impressed by the self-possession of this young Israelite, though it is absurd to imagine that he went so far as to grovel on the ground, as the Bible tells us. Nor can we reasonably believe that he immediately deposed his own god Marduk in favour of Daniel's god Yahweh, since he was probably unable to distinguish between the two, both of whom were the orthodox national divinities and supreme lords of the universe. What is more likely is that the Babylonian monarch, a man committed to the reconstruction of his country so long ruined and oppressed by the Assyrians, was glad to make use of the Israelites' talents and to accept their god as a potentially useful addition to the Babylonian pantheon. Nebuchadnezzar, in brief, was undoubtedly far more interested in the efficient administration of his domains than he was in Hebrew theology.

But the Biblical account of this interesting monarch is valuable because it makes him human, despite the Jews' hatred of their conqueror. The other kings appear to us out of the mists of time more like monuments than men, and one has only to look at the portrait of Sennacherib on the frieze found in his palace at Nineveh, where he sits stiffly on his throne as his soldiers bring him samples of loot, including the decapitated heads of prisoners, to realise that we have nothing in common with this monstrous tyrant. But the events of Nebuchadnezzar's reign recounted in the Second Book of the Kings, the Book of Daniel, and the apocryphal Judith, familiarise us with many real flesh-and-blood people who are described three-dimensionally as compared with the dehumanised portraits of the Babylonian statuary. Judith, for instance, who decked herself out in all her finery and 'washed her body all over with water and anointed herself with precious unguents', then braided her hair, put on her bracelets, necklaces, rings, and earrings, and sallied forth to meet Holofernes, the commander-in-chief of Nebuchadnezzar's army, brings a sudden touch of much needed colour to history largely recorded in stone. The description of her departure from the Jerusalem gate is one of the most graphic vignettes in literature:

> Judith went out, she, and her maid with her; and the men of the city looked after her until she was gone down the mountain and till she had passed the valley, and could see her no more.
> Thus they went straight forth in the valley: and the First Watch of the Babylonians met her.

What happened next is another example of the discrepancy between the facts as given in the Jewish account and those found in the Babylonian records. Whether a beautiful matriarch called Judith existed or not, we have no way of knowing, but Nebuchadnezzar certainly did not have a general in command of the siege of Jerusalem called Holofernes, a name which cannot possibly be Babylonian. But the encounter between these two, none the less, makes memorable reading, for it is probably the first time that we meet in literature a woman who appears as a national heroine to some and a villainess to others—a Joan of Arc, or a Lady Macbeth. The Babylonian commander-in-chief, it will be recalled, gave a courteous reception to his visitor from the enemy camp, only to have his head severed from his body by two mighty swings of Judith's right arm while he was asleep. The rest of the story, too, is indicative of the mentality of the period, for not content with despatching her host, Judith passed his severed head out of the tent to be secreted in the maid's 'bag of meat'; and bearing this gruesome trophy back to Jerusalem, she was congratulated by the High Priest and declared 'blessed above all women'.

The Babylonians evidently knew nothing of Judith or a general called Holofernes. They knew, rather, that Nebuchadnezzar's army successfully besieged and captured Jerusalem in 598 B.C. In that year the eighteen-year-old king Jehoiachin surrendered to the Babylonians without putting up any fight at all, which was wise of him and his advisers (notably his mother) in view of the practice of cutting off a captive king's nose, tearing out his tongue, and blinding him before finally putting him to death. Happily, the young king and his entire court lived to retire with dignity and peace in the Babylonian capital where they had their own quarters and, as the Second Book of the Kings tells us in the last chapter, Jehoiachin had precedence over all the other hostage-kings, and was given a royal pension for the rest of his life.

In contrast, those of his fellow-countrymen who continued to resist the Babylonians were, after the destruction of Jerusalem, sent to the labour camps, where their anguish is recorded in the great lament of the 137th Psalm, *By the rivers of Babylon, there we sat down, yea, we wept when we remembered Zion.*

An interesting detail of this psalm is the reference to 'the *rivers* of Babylon' (translated in the King James version from the Greek ἐπὶ τῶν ποταμῶν βαβυλῶνος), since Babylon was not only built on the Euphrates itself, but was in the middle of a network of canals, some of them wide and deep enough for the passage of large boats. Alexander the Great, we are told, sailed his fleet on the Babylonian canals. We may be reasonably sure, then, that many of the 7000 Israelite soldiers and the thousand craftsmen and smiths who were carried off after the fall of Jerusalem were set to work maintaining the irrigation system as well as building the palaces and temples erected during Nebuchadnezzar's reign. In fact, the specific reference in the Second Book of the Kings to 'all the men of might, even seven thousand, and craftsmen and smiths a thousand' is particularly significant, since it attests to the historicity of the Bible in this phase of Babylonian-Israelite relations. Why? Because we know that Nebuchadnezzar inherited a capital that must still have been in ruins after its total destruction by the Assyrian Sennacherib, who boasted that he tore down the city to its foundations and threw the rubble into the river.

In short, Nebuchadnezzar had an urgent need for both skilled and manual workers, and hence the thousand craftsmen and smiths who must have totalled about the entire technical population of Israel. It is probable that the skill of these men who were put to work on the building sites and the muscle-power of the 'men of might' who helped maintain the canals resulted in their acquiring a status of some privilege, as Daniel and his companions did in the administrative sphere. What is certain is that the Israelites, alone of the conquered people, kept alive their religious and moral traditions throughout the period of exile, and they could only have done this if the Babylonian authorities had allowed them to live as a privileged group among the thousands of other prisoners of war from all over the empire. That this was so is confirmed by the report in the Second Book of the Kings of the very special favours and concessions made to Jehoiachin, the captive king of Judah, a report confirmed in one of those finds which delight the heart of scholars: namely, tablets discovered in the royal palace of Babylon stating that certain rations were to be provided for *Ya-u-kinu* (the Akkadian spelling of Jehoiachin), 'King of the Land of Judah', and his five sons. Further evidence that the captive Israelites did survive as a homogeneous ethnic and religious group is suggested by a passage in Jeremiah in which the prophet launches upon one of his characteristic denunciations of his fellow-countrymen. After stating that the Lord was his authority, he announces that he was shown in a dream two baskets of figs, one good, one bad; and the interpretation he gives of this vision is that those Jews who had been taken captive and now resided in Babylonia were the good figs who were to be God's chosen people, while those who were left in Judah or fled to Egypt were the bad figs, doomed to be destroyed by sword, famine, and pestilence. In other words, the hopes of Zion were now centred in Babylon where the exiles produced the Priestly Code and laid down the foundations of a new Israel.

In the light of this hope we can understand better the Book of Jeremiah, which is one long tirade not only against Babylon but against his own people. The prophet condemned the latter for their wickedness in accepting foreign gods and foreign ways, but he was really trying to rally them to continue the war against Babylonia. Then it becomes evident that he must have received reports from the captives in Babylon that not only was their treatment tolerable under Nebuchadnezzar, but that they were able to conserve their national and religious identity and even to bring pressure to bear on the king to consider the claims of Yahweh to be as powerful as Marduk. It was, of course, unthinkable that

M

Nebuchadnezzar would ever substitute the Jewish deity for his
own national god, but it is quite possible that he was prepared to
admit the Hebrew Lord into the Chaldean pantheon, just as he
admitted Hebrew soldiers into the ranks of his personal body-
guard. So it was perhaps these developments which explain Jeremiah's sudden switch in foreign policy, for after the fall of Jerusalem he sent a secret letter to the elders who had been carried
away as captives, and to the priests, the prophets, and all the
people held as prisoners and hostages in Babylon. The letter instructed the exiled Jews to co-operate fully with Nebuchadnezzar
in the following manner:

> Build ye houses and dwell in them; and plant gardens and eat
> of the fruit of them.
>
> Take ye wives and beget sons and daughters; and take wives
> for your sons and give your daughters husbands that ye may
> bear sons and daughters; that ye may be increased there and not
> diminished. And seek the peace of the city whither I have caused
> you to be carried away captives, and pray unto the Lord, for in
> the peace thereof shall ye have peace.

However, Jeremiah was certainly not recommending total surrender, nor was he betraying the Jewish cause. To the contrary,
the object of this apparent outright collaboration was much more
subtle than this: it was to preserve and increase a future fifth
column within the gates of the enemy city, ready when the day
came to liberate themselves and their homeland. This day is prophesied in a codicil to the letter in these words:

> For thus saith the Lord, That after seventy years be accom-
> plished at Babylon, I will visit you, and perform my good word
> toward you, in causing you to return to this place [i.e. Jeru-
> salem].
>
> And I will be found of you, saith the Lord; and I will turn
> away your captivity, and I will gather you from all the nations
> and all the places whither I have driven you; and I will bring
> you again to the place whence I caused you to be carried away
> captive.

We do not know whether Nebuchadnezzar's spies were aware
of what was being plotted against him, but it is probable that he
closed his eyes to these threats and prophecies provided that his

Jewish administrators, technicians, and labourers worked well and skilfully on his numerous projects which included the rebuilding of the temples of the gods all over Babylonia and of the royal palace. Watching his captives sweating under their loads, the 'king of kings', as Daniel called him, was unlikely to have been greatly disturbed by Jeremiah's prophecy that Babylon should 'become a heaps, a dwelling place for dragons, an astonishment and a hissing, without an inhabitant'.

The End of Babylon

THE BABYLON THAT KOLDEWEY unearthed was the capital of an empire created almost solely by one of its last and greatest kings, Nebuchadnezzar the Second. This final phase of Babylonian imperial history lasted from 605 to 538 B.C.; and within this brief span of sixty-seven years Babylon ceased to be the centre of the civilised world and ended as a decaying provincial city, depopulated, partly ruined, and finally abandoned altogether.

What, then, were the forces which brought about the decline and fall of Babylon?

The answer may be in part that a nation is only as strong as its leaders, or this was certainly so in the age of military despots. In the case of Babylonia during the sixth century B.C. there seem to have been only two such autocrats capable of controlling the course of history to the advantage of their nation—Nabopolassar, who reigned from 626 to 605 B.C., and his son Nebuchadnezzar, 605–562 B.C. Both before and after the reigns of these two remarkable men the kings of Babylon were puppets either of a foreign power or of the local priests.

When Nabopolassar come to the throne, Babylon was still a vassal state of Assyria, as it had been for over 200 years. During that period Assyria had conquered most of the known world and earned as a result of continuous wars enormous territories and the undying hatred of the conquered peoples. The Medes in particular were growing restless under the Assyrian yoke, and Nabopolassar, casting around for allies, settled upon Media as the most incipiently powerful state in the Middle East. Certainly the Medes had been fighting the Assyrians off and on for several centuries and had a reputation for being expert cavalrymen and brave soldiers;

and Nabopolassar, therefore, was delighted when the Median king Cyaxares agreed to cement an alliance by giving his daughter Amytis as a bride for the Babylonian crown prince Nebuchadnezzar.

The two kings, Median and Babylonian, now felt strong enough to wage what was to be total war on the hated Assyrians. The Medes appear to have undertaken the major assault and actually besieged Nineveh for three years before they could break through the mighty walls and achieve their object of utterly destroying the Assyrian capital, a task in which the Babylonians gladly joined. And so, after the destruction of Nineveh and the dismemberment of Assyria, Nabopolassar as the ally of the victorious Median king was given the southern districts of Mesopotamia as his share of the spoils. Babylon had thus acquired both independence and new territory from Assyria as a result not so much of any military conquest as of its king's political astuteness. Military triumphs came later with the campaigns of the crown prince Nebuchadnezzar, who decisively defeated the Egyptian forces at the Battle of Carchemish in 604 B.C., the Jews at Jerusalem in 598 B.C., and the Phoenicians in 586 B.C.

Nabopolassar, then, by his diplomatic skill and Nebuchadnezzar by his military successes re-created the Babylonian Empire and made of their capital the largest, richest, and strongest city in the world. Unfortunately for the peace and security of their subjects, these two strong men were succeeded by a certain Amel-Marduk, described by the Babylonian historian Berosus as 'an unworthy successor to his father [Nebuchadnezzar] and restrained by neither law nor decency'—a curious indictment of an oriental monarch when one recalls the atrocities of the old despots. The defamation of Amel-Marduk, however, as 'restrained by neither law nor decency' was made by a priest, and it was the priests who plotted this king's death, replacing him by a soldier called Nergal-sharusur, or Neriglissar, the general who was present at the siege of Jerusalem in 597 B.C., according to the account given in the Book of Jeremiah (ch. 39, 3):

> In the ninth year of Zedekiah king of Judah, in the tenth month, came Nebuchadnezzar king of Babylon and all his army against Jerusalem, and they besieged it. And in the eleventh year of Zedekiah, in the fourth month, the ninth day of the month, the

city was broken up. And all the princes of the king of Babylon
came in and sat in the middle gate, even Nergal-sharezer,
Samgar-nebo, Sarsechim, Rab-saris, Nergal-sharezer the Rabmag, with all the residue of the princes of the king of Babylon.[1]

We note that there are two Nergals included in this list, not surprisingly so since the name means 'May Nergal protect the king!'.
The second of them, 'the Rabmag', was some sort of court official;
the first was evidently the son-in-law of Nebuchadnezzar, whose
actual son, Amel-Marduk, he killed in a rebellion. Little is known
of this Neriglissar except that he reigned only three years (559–
556 B.C.)—his son only nine months. Then the priests placed another of their candidates on the throne, Nabonidus, himself the
son of a priest.

This Nabonidus appears to have spent his entire reign of seventeen years in restoring the temples of his country and in tracing
back its history to the origins of the nation. He travelled all over
his kingdom with a retinue of historians, archaeologists, and architects, watching the progress of his building programme and apparently indifferent to political and military matters. In fact, he
made his headquarters in a remote oasis in the Arabian Desert, at
a place called Taima, leaving the administration of the empire to
his son Bel-shar-usur, the Belshazzar of the Bible. He speaks of
Belshazzar as 'my firstborn son, the offspring of my heart'.

As we so often find—in the orthodox history books at least—a
pious, scholarly, and peace-loving monarch is doubted rather than
admired for his virtues. What the Babylonian people themselves
thought about this nice old gentleman, whose manner to all
accounts resembled more that of an absent-minded professor than
of an emperor, we have no way of knowing. The thoughts and
opinions of the Babylonian 'man-in-the-street' are, in any case, an
absolutely unknown quantity in the overall picture of the ancient
Mesopotamian society, but we can guess with reasonable accuracy
that the ordinary citizen had no great interest in church history,
or, for that matter, in the restoration of temples in faraway places,
both matters of absorbing interest to Nabonidus. And, in particular, the king was determined to rebuild the shrine of the god
called Sin, the old Sumerian moon-god, son of Enlil, the air-god,
and Ki, the earth-goddess. He was eager to build this shrine in his
native city of Harran, and it is more than likely that his devotion

to Sin and to the city of Harran sowed the seeds of unrest among
the Babylonian priesthood and commercial circles; in other words,
they felt that their god and their interests were being neglected,
and neglected by the very man they had placed on the throne to
uphold them.

Whatever the reasons, Babylon, the most impregnable city in
the world, fell in 538 B.C. to the Persian invaders led by Cyrus the
Great, with scarcely a drop of blood being spilled—a source of
regret and even indignation to contemporary and later historians,
since up to that time besieged cities had always fallen amid fantastic scenes of destruction, slaughter, rape, and general horror.
Indeed, the peaceful surrender of Babylon to the Persians also
runs counter to both the Old Testament account of the actual
events and the hate-inspired prophecy of Jeremiah. The story of
the 'King' Belshazzar and the writing on the wall must be read as
a fable: Belshazzar was not the son of Nebuchadnezzar, as the
Bible tells us, but of Nabonidus; he was not the king, but the
crown prince; he was not slain in Babylon; and he did not surrender to 'Darius the Mede'. The facts are that he was killed in battle
on the western bank of the Tigris fighting against the army of
Cyrus the Persian.

Likewise the dire predictions of the Hebrew prophets that
Babylon would become a desolation and a wilderness were not
fulfilled as a result of Yahweh's partiality for the Jews but as the
consequence of continuous wars and invasions over several centuries. For despite reverses, the great city continued to flourish
under its new ruler Cyrus whose victory memorial partially explains how this was possible:

> I am Cyrus, king of the world. . . . After I had made my gracious
> entry into Babylon, with exceeding joy I took up my abode in
> the royal palace. . . . My many troops marched peacefully into
> Babylon, and I gave heed to the needs of the capital and its
> colonies and released the Babylonians from slavery and oppres-
> sion. I quieted their sighings and soothed their sorrows.

The inscription is, of course, characteristic of wartime despatches, ancient and modern, but it tells us, by implication, what
actually happened at the siege of Babylon in 539 B.C.—namely that
the city was turned over to Cyrus by collaborators; otherwise
Nabonidus's son, Belshazzar, would not have continued fighting

to the east on the banks of the Tigris. Additional details are fur-
nished by Herodotus, who may even have heard an account of the
siege and fall of the city from an actual survivor. The Greek historian tells us that Cyrus invested the capital for a considerable
time without making any impression at all on the mighty double
walls of Nebuchadnezzar. In the end, the Persian resorted to the
old strategy of turning aside the Euphrates into lateral canals in
order that his shock-troops could penetrate the city by wading
along the river-bed both from the north and the southern
entrances. And so vast was the city, Herodotus adds, that the inhabitants of the centre were ignorant for a long time that the out-
skirts had been captured, but continued dancing and revelling in
celebration of some national festival. So fell Babylon.

Cyrus, then, was able to capture Babylon without first destroying it, perhaps a precedent in the history of ancient warfare,
though one that has seldom been repeated. In fact, there is no
doubt that after the Persian conquest life went on in the city and
the neighbouring countryside exactly as it did before, with daily
sacrifices in the temples and the endless rites and rituals which
were the basis of all public life; and Cyrus himself was intelligent
enough not to trample on the pride of his new subjects. He lived
in the royal palace, went to church, worshipped the national god
Marduk, and was properly respectful to the high priests who still
controlled the politics of the old empire. In addition, he did not
interfere with the trade and commerce of the city, or impose a
heavy tribute on the Babylonians, for it was these unjust and
burdensome levies exacted by venal tax-collectors which had always led to rebellion by subject states.

This peaceful and prosperous state of affairs would no doubt
have continued indefinitely if it had not been for the ambitions of
pretenders to the Babylonian throne during the reign of Cyrus's
successor Darius (522–486 B.C.). Two of these pretenders claimed
to be the sons of Nabonidus, the last independent king of Babylon; whether they were or not we have no means of knowing,
except from what we are told on the great slab of stone 160 feet up
on the cliff-face at Behistun where Darius set up his enormous
victory memorial. From the inscription celebrating his victories
we learn that this pair were defeated in battle and that the first of
them, Nidintu-Bel, was killed in Babylon, and the second, Arakha,
was crucified in the same city. Their portraits on the rock at

Behistun show Nidintu-Bel as the second in the line of nine pretenders and rebels who are roped together by the neck in the presence of Darius. Arakha is the seventh in line. The former is
depicted as an elderly, possibly white-bearded, man with a large
fleshy nose; the latter is portrayed as a younger and more vigorous
man. The Persian text referring to these two aspirants to the
throne of Babylon reads as follows:

And a certain Babylonian named Nidintu-Bel, the son of Aniri,
raised a rebellion in Babylon: he lied to the people, saying, 'I
am Nebuchadnezzar, the son of Nabonidus'. Then did all the
province of Babylonia go over unto that Nidintu-Bel and Babylonia rose in rebellion. He seized on the kingdom of Babylonia.

Thus saith Darius the king. Then did I march against Babylon, against that Nidintu-Bel who was called Nebuchadnezzar.
The army of Nidintu-Bel held the Tigris. Here they were
posted, and they also had ships. Then I divided the army: some
I made camel-drivers, the others cavalrymen.

Aura Mazda brought me help; by the grace of Aura Mazda
we crossed the Tigris. Then did I utterly overthrow the host of
Nidintu-Bel. On the twenty-sixth day of the month Atriyadiya
[18 December] we joined battle. Thus saith Darius the king.
Then did I march against Babylon, but before I reached Babylon, that Nidintu-Bel who was called Nebuchadnezzar came
with a host and offered battle at the city named Zazana on the
Euphrates. . . . The enemy fled into the water; the water carried
them away. Then did Nidintu-Bel flee with a few horsemen
into Babylon. By the grace of Aura Mazda I took Babylon and
I captured that Nidintu-Bel. Then I slew that Nidintu-Bel in
Babylon. . . .

Thus saith Darius the king. While I was in Persia and in
Media, the Babylonians revolted from me a second time. A
certain man named Arakha, an Armenian, the son of Haldita,
rebelled in Babylon. At a place named Dubala he lied unto the
people, saying 'I am Nebuchadnezzar, the son of Nabonidus'.
Then did the Babylonian people revolt from me and went over
to that Arakha. He seized Babylon; he became king in Babylon.

Thus said Darius the king. Then did I send an army unto
Babylon. A Persian named Vindefrana, my servant, I appointed
as their leader, and thus I spake unto them, 'Go smite that

Babylonian host which doth not acknowledge me!' Then
Vindefrana marched with the army unto Babylon, By the grace
of Aura Mazda Vindefrana overthrew the Babylonians. . . .

On the twenty-second day of the month Markazanash [27
November] that Arakha who called himself Nebuchadnezzar
and the men who were his chief followers they seized and
fettered. Then I made a decree saying: 'Let that Arakha and the
men who were his chief followers be crucified in Babylon!'

According to Herodotus, writing only some fifty years after
these events, the Persian king destroyed the city walls and tore
down the gates, though he used the palaces and houses of the
town to quarter his troops during the winter, so we can assume
that he did not altogether wreck the city. Apart from weakening
the defences, he was satisfied with crucifying 3000 of the leading
citizens, which gives us a hint of the size of the population of
Babylon in 522 B.C. If 3000 represented the civic and religious
dignitaries, or, say, one-hundredth part of the citizenry, we arrive
at the figure of 300,000, to which perhaps should be added another
300,000 children, slaves, menials, foreigners, and the like. In view
of the density of the population in Middle Eastern towns, we can
think in terms of a million people inhabiting Babylon and its
environs.

Despite the damage done to Babylon's defences by Darius, the
city still continued to be the commercial centre of the Middle East,
for it stood midway between both the north-south and east-west
trade routes. But the Persians were gradually destroying the prestige of the place as a sacred city until Xerxes (486–465 B.C.), after
another rebellion, decided to reduce it to the state of a provincial
town not only by knocking down what was left of the great walls
but, much more significantly, by destroying the great national
shrine of Marduk and carrying off the god himself.

The significance of this last act of Xerxes cannot be over-
emphasised since it was basic throughout the Middle East that a
nation's survival depended on the survival of the patron-god. We
have seen how the Sumerian city-states collapsed once their chief
god had been captured and carried off by an enemy. The great
elegy called *Lamentation for the Destruction of Ur* ascribes all the
woes that befell the population of the city to this one event: there
is no mention of the defeat of their army, of the incompetence of

their commanders, and the military and economic causes to which modern nations ascribe their defeat in war. All was due to the overthrow of the god.

We are most familiar with this identification of the national divinity with the fate of the people who proclaim him as omnipotent from our close knowledge of Old Testament history in which the destruction of the Temple and the carrying off of the Ark symbolised the eclipse of Israel. For the Ark was not merely the shrine of Yahweh, it was also a war palladium comparable with the eagles of a Roman legion (the loss of which was equivalent to the annihilation of the legion); a chest for containing a fetish stone, possibly from Mount Serbal in Sinai; and the abode of Yahweh when he decided to come down on earth among men. The gods of the other Semite nations all had similar temples and 'arks'. All, too, had military as well as religious functions, so that the Hebrew Yahweh and the Babylonian Marduk were, in most respects, interchangeable, notably in their role as the god of battles. Thus Yahweh, who in the earlier books of the Bible is identifiable with the Ark itself, leads the Israelites into battle, is given the credit for victories, but is never blamed for defeats. The defeat of the Israelites by the Philistines, for instance, is attributed to the absence of the Ark from the field; and the Exile to Babylon is associated with the carrying off of Yahweh inside his container by Nebuchadnezzar. The Babylonians were now to suffer precisely the same national disaster when Xerxes destroyed the Esagila and made off with the statue of Marduk.

So it was inevitable that the overthrow and degradation of the chief god in a theocracy as monolithic as that of Babylon spelt the end of the old order, since kings could no longer be crowned according to the age-old ceremony of the *akitu* festival. This festival, whose nearest modern counterpart is the crowning of monarchs in national religious shrines, was of such weight and importance in the state cult that it is mentioned in the annals in connection with all state victories. What, then, was the *akitu*, and why was it so vital to the survival of the Babylonian system?

In the first instance it was the festival of the New Year which has always had a deep symbolic significance as heralding the return of spring and the rebirth of life. On this solemn occasion Marduk left his temple at the head of an enormous procession and was borne along the great Processional Way to meet the gods from distant cities, notably his former rival and now chief guest, Nabu the patron-god of the city-state of Borsippa. The two gods were then carried into the sacred chamber or holy of holies, where they decided in conference with all the other gods the shape of things to come. Such were the heavenly or divine proceedings of the New Year's festival. The earthly ones were centred on the investiture of the king as the god's vicar, for unless a monarch had 'placed his hand in Marduk's', thus symbolising the passing of divine right from god to man, he could never be spiritually or legally king of Babylon.

And in addition to the conference of the gods when the destiny of man was decided and the king was invested with divine authority, the *akitu* was the annual festival of all the gods, together with their priests, priestesses, and temple servants; and so solemn and symbolic were the resultant ceremonies that no king of Babylon, or of Assyria, or, in the early period, of Persia, failed to be present at this Assembly of the Gods. Gods, kings, princes, priests, and all the population wore special robes for the occasion which was fraught with so much mystery and symbolism, so much pomp and ceremony, that it must have been the most splendid religious festival the world has ever known. The numbers and importance of the participants, the quantity of the 'burnt' sacrifices, the processions in ships and chariots, and, above all, the dramatic rites in the temple were all the quintessence of the deep religious tradition which pervaded the Babylonian state. In view of this, we can readily understand how the humiliation of the god by Xerxes destroyed the whole fabric of Babylonian theocracy and enfeebled the life-force of society itself. For it meant that no Babylonian could again lead Marduk by the hand at the head of the great procession and so identify himself with the divine power, which was the essence of ancient kingship; and it meant that the profoundly symbolic religious drama of Marduk's death and resurrection would never be seen in Babylon again.

The destruction of the 'soul' of the city did not mean, of course, its reduction to a heap of ruins abandoned by its citizens. True, many thousands of its most influential leaders had been crucified or tortured to death, and many thousands of others had been carried off as slaves or as soldiers in the Persian kings' wars against the Greek city-states. But Babylon continued to exist and was even flourishing at the time of Herodotus's visit around 450 B.C., though it must have begun to look more and more dilapidated as the years went by and there was no resident king to rebuild the walls and temples. The Persian rulers were by this time engaged elsewhere, mostly in attempts to subdue Sparta and Athens, where their armies and navies were slowly but irrevocably being defeated and driven back until in 331 B.C. came the final defeat of the last of the Achaemenids, Darius III. In that year Alexander the Great entered the city and proclaimed himself king of Babylon.

Contemporary historians give a fascinating description of Babylon at this time, for as several later writers, and notably the Greek Flavius Arrianus, point out, Alexander, being eager for glory and the perpetuation of his name, nominated several officers as his military historians and these war correspondents kept a record of each day's events called the *Ephemerides*, or Day Book. And so the despatches of the journalists on the spot together with the histories of Alexander by soldiers who accompanied the expeditions make the Macedonian's campaigns the best documented accounts we have of the ancient wars and of the countries, peoples, and cities he conquered.

He did not, however, need to besiege Babylon from which the Persian governor Mazaeus came forth as a suppliant with his wife, children, and the civil leaders. Alexander received this renegade courteously, since he was relieved not to have to attack a city described by the contemporary Greek historians as very strongly fortified, indicating that all the walls which had been destroyed by Xerxes in 484 B.C. had been restored by 331 when Alexander reached the city. However, far from defending their homes, the citizens gathered on the city walls to welcome the Greek invader. As for the civil leaders, they vied with each other in their subservience to the point not only of hastening forth with the royal treasury of Darius but of strewing the approach roads to the city with flowers and garlands and setting up along the way silver altars piled high with frankincense. In short, Alexander, without striking a blow, was given the kind of triumph which was later accorded to Roman generals; and the Babylonians, mindful of the lack of prisoners who customarily solemnised a state triumph by being tortured to death or crucified along the highway, substituted herds of horses and cattle which were gratefully received by the Greek commissary. Caged lions and leopards headed the triumphal procession, followed by the priests, soothsayers, and musicians, with the Babylonian cavalry bringing up the rear as a guard of honour. These horsemen, according to the Greeks, 'had met the requirements of luxury rather than of efficiency'. It was, in short, the kind of oriental extravaganza which at once amused and appeased the unsophisticated Greek invaders, whose object, after all, was the acquisition of loot rather than the conquest of territory. The Babylonians, for their part, had the measure of these semi-barbarian invaders and outwitted them at every turn. It is an interesting example of how to save a city by loving the enemy instead of fighting him. Such was Alexander's reception by the governor and corporation of Babylon, with the triumphal procession led by the wild beasts, symbolic of royalty, the priests, soothsayers and musicians substituting for prisoners, and the Babylonian cavalry providing the colour and, possibly, the comic relief. Alexander himself was taken at once to the royal palace and shown all Darius's furniture and art treasures. His officers were billeted in luxurious homes, the men in more modest but still most agreeable establishments where their physical needs were amply provided for by their hosts. For, says the historian,

> nowhere did King Alexander do more harm to the discipline of his soldiers than in Babylon. Nothing is more corrupt than the habits of that city, nothing more inclined to arouse and attract dissolute desires. Fathers and husbands allow their daughters and wives to prostitute themselves to their guests. Convivial festivities throughout all Persia are dear to the kings and their courtiers; but the Babylonians in particular are lavishly devoted to wine and the concomitants of drunkenness. The women who take part in these feasts are in the beginning modestly attired, then they take off their outer garments one by one and gradually disgrace their modesty. At last—with due respect to your ears— they throw aside the inmost coverings of their bodies. This shameful conduct is not confined to courtesans, but is practised by matrons and maidens with whom the baseness of prostitution is regarded as courtesy. After being pampered for thirty-four days amid such debaucheries, that army which had conquered Asia would undoubtedly have been weaker to face the dangers which followed, if it had had an enemy.[1]

Whether all this is true or not—and we must remember that it was written by a Roman of the old school—it is apparent that

Alexander and his troops had such an agreeable stay in Babylon that the city was spared the usual ravages of Gibbon's 'licentious soldiery'. The Greek king resided longer here than he did anywhere else in his campaigns and he certainly gave orders to have the capital beautified by rebuilding. Quite evidently he intended to make Babylon his Middle Eastern headquarters, and so the city was cleaned up accordingly. Thousands of workmen were set to work to remove the rubble of the ruined temple of Marduk, which he ordered to be rebuilt, and rebuilding was still going on ten years later, two years after Alexander's death in Babylon.

This event occurred in 323 B.C. and it makes curious reading, suggesting that the great king died in his thirty-third year as the result of a drinking bout. From his early adolescence, in fact—and despite the tutorship of the philosopher Aristotle—orgies were a characteristic of Alexander's short life, and it was during one of them that the king, his generals, and the courtesans who were entertaining them deliberately set fire to the palace at Persepolis, the seat of the Persian kings, thus wantonly destroying one of the most beautiful buildings of the ancient world, if not the most beautiful. At Babylon, Alexander indulged in another prolonged drinking session, and this time he was taken seriously ill. Cirrhosis of the liver may have had something to do with his quick death.

Alexander had, of course, changed the course of history during his thirteen years as king of Macedonia and emperor of almost the entire known world, and nowhere more so than in the Middle East and the great Middle Eastern empires. Sumer, Assyria, Media, and Babylonia had by this time already declined or fallen altogether. Now mighty Persia was finished off by the small invincible army of tough Macedonian troopers. Nearly all those cities from Tyre in the west to Ecbatana in the east were razed to the ground, their governors mutilated before being executed, and their citizens massacred or sold into slavery. But Babylon, as we have seen, escaped annihilation by shrewdly exploiting the Macedonians' partiality for wine and women. The great city was to survive a few more hundred years until it died, as if in the course of nature, of old age.

Following Alexander's death there were the usual exaggerated obsequies, the usual public demonstrations of woe, the tearing of hair, attempted suicides, and predictions that the end of the world had come, for how was the future possible without Alexander, now already apotheosised? But behind the scenes the dead king's generals and politicians were already bickering as to who should succeed him, for he had died intestate, without naming an heir. However, he had one legitimate son by the Persian princess Barsine, daughter of Darius III; and another heir was expected from his second wife, Roxane, a Bactrian princess. Before the king had been long in his grave, Roxane, undoubtedly spurred on by her court cronies, had murdered her rival Barsine and her little son. It did her no good, for shortly afterwards she herself with *her* son, Alexander IV, suffered the same fate, both of them being slain by one of Alexander's generals, that same Cassander who had murdered the dead king's mother, Queen Olympias. The *Oxford Classical Dictionary* describes this monster as 'ruthlessly efficient', a somewhat quaint characterisation of a man who slew two queens and a prince in cold blood. Even so, Cassander's liquidation (as it would be called today) of Queen Roxane and Prince Alexander was condoned by the Macedonian veterans, who wanted no foreign prince for their king on the grounds that his blood was tainted. The Greeks, they said, had not fought the armies and navies of the Persians and their allies to bend the knee to even Alexander's son by a foreign woman.

The disposal of the two possible leaders of Alexander's empire, the son of Barsine, the Persian consort and of Roxane, the Bactrian wife, left the succession open to all the ambitious generals who had fought their way across Asia in Alexander's fabulous campaigns. Inevitably the rivalries between these power-hungry men led to almost continuous wars in which Babylon played only a small part as the armies of the pretenders fought it out in distant parts of the empire.

Hence, the death of Alexander really marks the end of Babylon as the world's greatest city. It was not that the citizens themselves lost heart over the untimely death of their latest king—they had no more love for the Greeks than they had had for the Persians—but what they had had as a result of the Greek occupation was the expectation of a prosperous future—first, because Alexander had declared that Babylon was to be his eastern capital; and, secondly, because he had decided to rebuild the Temple of Marduk. The realisation of these two proposals would have meant that Babylon would again be the political, commercial, and religious capital of the East. But Alexander died, and what followed must have quickly convinced the more far-sighted citizens that their city had lost its last chance of revival. Indeed, anybody could see that the death of the world conqueror was leading to chaos as lesser men fought among themselves for the spoils of his empire. Various sons, wives, friends, and generals of Alexander now contended for the prize of Babylon which was finally won by a general and friend of the dead king, Seleucus Nicator.

Under this Greek soldier, who, along with the others, had to fight his way to power, the old city had a few peaceful years. Alexander's project of making it once again the capital of the Middle East was even reconsidered by the new governor. The rubble of the ruined Temple of Marduk continued to be carted away, though there was so much of it that the clearing of the site was never completed. This in itself was a symptom of the decline of Babylon. The vitality was draining out of the city: a sense of hopelessness cast down the citizens as they realised that their city would never again be the capital of the eastern empire, the Temple of Marduk would never be rebuilt, and that continuous wars would inevitably destroy the old order. And, worse, in 305 B.C. Seleucus decided to found a new town to be called by his name. The town was Seleucia, built on the left bank of the Tigris, forty miles north of Babylon and just far enough away from the old capital to rival it as an international cross-roads on the east–west trade routes. As a final blow to the hopes of the populace, Seleucus ordered the principal government officials to leave Babylon and take up residence in the new city. The chief merchants and tradesmen soon followed them in the natural course of events.

Seleucia, then, was an artificial town in that it was 'run up' quickly, more to satisfy the egotism of Seleucus Nicator than to meet the needs of the countryside. In fact, its population was drafted from the old city, while a great deal of its building material was taken from the streets and squares of Babylon. But with the weight of the royal support behind it, and the transference of the local administration from Babylon, Seleucia quickly became the more important city of the two, its population rapidly increasing to some half a million. The surrounding countryside was fertile and well watered by the trans-Euphrates-Tigris canal, or the Royal Ship canal, so that it is not surprising that 200 years after its founding Seleucia became the greatest commercial entrepôt in the East. It did not remain so for long, however. The wars in the

N

region were almost continuous, and the city was repeatedly sacked
and looted by invaders until it was completely destroyed by the
Romans in A.D. 165. This time its bricks and mortar, which had
been taken from Babylon, were ferried across the Tigris to build
still another new town, Ctesiphon, which, in its turn, was sacked
and destroyed in the eastern wars.

During the rise and fall of its rival Seleucia, Babylon continued
to exist as a half-empty city without any special *raison d'être* except
as the religious centre for a cult that was already becoming obso-
lescent. Yet successive rulers of the city contributed towards the
upkeep of the shrines and temples of the ancient gods whose
appeal in the new world of Hellenism must have been limited to
conservatives of the old school. Certainly to the new breed of
Greek philosophers, scholars, writers, and artists—so ultra-civi-
lised in their world-view—old-fashioned deities like Marduk and
the other gods of the Sumerian-Babylonian pantheon must have
seemed slightly ridiculous, like the animal-gods of the Egyptians.
Indeed, it is probable that Babylon by the second century B.C. was
becoming an enormous ruin, visited by interested sightseers and a
few pilgrims: apart from the services which were still conducted
in the temples, little else was going on. Its officials and merchants
had long since gone, leaving behind a corpus of priests who were
responsible for the upkeep of the shrine of Marduk where they
made the traditional ritual sacrifices and offered up prayers for the
reigning king and his family. The more educated of them no
doubt continued to make astronomical observations for the express purpose of predicting the future, astrology being considered
more reliable than haruspication and the other forms of divination.
Indeed, the reputation of the Chaldeans as soothsayers was high
as late as the Roman period when magi were still coming 'out of
the east', as did the Wise Men who brought gifts to the Christ
child, according to the Gospel of St Matthew. These were the
mathematicians and astrologers who were commended by the
great Jewish philosopher Philo of Alexandria for their research
into the facts of the universe, entitling them to the title of 'true
magicians'.

Whether the priests of the last days of Babylon deserved Philo's
--and Cicero's—praise is a moot point, since by the beginning of
our era the 'greatest city the world has ever seen' was nothing
more than a name in the West. Yet it was the priests of Marduk

with the temple-servants (including perhaps the sacred prostitutes) and a few tradesmen who kept Babylon alive after the entire
administration and trade of the area moved away first to Seleucia,
then to Ctesiphon. Indeed, the special privilege that Babylon now
enjoyed as a religious centre tended to make it an 'open city' in
the perpetual wars between the different conquerors of Mesopotamia—Greeks, Parthians, Elamites, and Romans. The prestige of
the city remained such that the succession of petty war-lords who
seized the place continued to call themselves 'King of Babylon'
and, more than that, continued to patronise the gods and temples
with gifts and probably attendance at the revived New Year
festival of Marduk when the king 'placed his hand in god's', thus
confirming his divine right to rule. Whether these later monarchs
believed in Marduk or not is not really important, since in the
pagan world one god was as good as another, and Marduk had
already become identified with Zeus Olympus or Jupiter Belos,
the names being interchangeable according to one's nationality
and language. The important consideration was that the original
shrine of the god should be properly maintained in order that the
king of heaven might have a fit habitation in which to hold court
on his visits to earth; and as long as the cult of Marduk was held
to be of some importance, and there was a body of priests to
attend to the god's needs, Babylon itself survived.

By 50 B.C., however, when the historian Diodorus of Sicily was
writing his account of the city, the great Temple of Marduk was
again in ruins: 'In fact,' (he says) 'only a small part of the city is
now inhabited and most of the area within its walls is given over
to agriculture.' Even so, there is evidence that shrines to the old
gods survived elsewhere in Mesopotamia, and that services were
held in these ruined temples, almost exactly as a thousand years
later they were held in Egypt in the ruined churches of the conquered Christians. The Arab historian El Bekri, for instance, gives
a vivid account of the survival of the Christian ritual at a lost city
called Saint Menas in the Libyan Desert, and though the time and
place are far apart, one feels that the description could apply to
Babylon towards the end of the pagan period.

> Mina [i.e., Saint Menas] is identifiable by the buildings which
> still remain standing [writes El Bekri]. You can see there superb
> and beautifully constructed palaces surrounded by battlements.

They are for the most part built in the form of roofed colonnades
and some of the buildings are occupied by monks. There remain
a few wells but water is now scarce. Further off, one sees the
Cathedral of Saint Menas, an enormous building ornamented
with statues and the most beautiful mosaics. Inside, the lamps
burn day and night. At one end of the church, there is a huge
marble tomb with two camels and, above it, the statue of a man
with a foot on each of the camels: one of his hands is open, the
other closed. Over the church is a dome covered with paintings
which, they say, represent the angels. The whole countryside
round about is planted with fruit trees which produce excellent
fruit and there are also many vines which are cultivated for
wine.

Substitute the Temple of Marduk for the Cathedral of Saint
Menas, the statue of the Babylonian god for that of the Christian
saint, the dragons of Marduk for the angels, and we surely have a
picture of the last days of the Babylonian church.

In a similar reference to the end of the city we have an inscription recording the visit of the local governor to the ruined Temple
of Marduk where one ox and four lambs were sacrificed 'in the
gate'—referring, perhaps, to the Ishtar Gate at the beginning of the
Processional Way, the great monument which Koldewey was
able to unearth relatively undamaged, still standing in places to a
height of nearly forty feet and still adorned with the famous bulls
and dragons. The single ox and four lambs represented perhaps
one-hundredth of the sacrifices which were offered up to Marduk
in the old days when all the gods and kings were carried along the
Processional Way to the shouts of 10,000 worshippers.

The Greek historian and geographer Strabo (69 B.C.–A.D. 19),
himself partly Asiatic and a native of Pontus, a region of Asia
Minor, may have received from travellers first-hand information
as to the state of Babylon which he reports in his *Geography* as
being 'for the most part deserted', with the ziggurat of Marduk
destroyed and only the enormous walls left as witnesses of the
city's former greatness, and still one of the Seven Wonders of the
World. Strabo's specific references to the monuments of Babylon
—he gives, for instance, the exact measurements of the city walls
—are in contrast to the generalised comments of Pliny the Elder,
who in his *Natural History*, written some time after A.D. 50, states

that the Temple of Marduk (Pliny calls the god Jupiter Belos) was still standing, though the rest of the city was half ruined and depopulated. The Roman historian's credibility is, with some reason, often suspect, for he seems to have accepted without proper examination everything he read or was told. On the other hand, he was in a position as an aristocrat and senior official to get at the facts of regions both within and on the frontiers of the empire; and if he was on the staff of Titus in the Jewish War of A.D. 70 he may have heard an eyewitness description of Babylon as it then existed. But inasmuch as Strabo specifically contradicts him as to the condition of the famous ziggurat, it is puzzling to know whether Babylon was still a 'living' city in Pliny's day, though from the manner in which the Romans ignore it, it is obvious that it no longer had any importance. The only time it is ever mentioned, in fact, is in the account of travellers, like that of Pausanias of Lydia (*c.* A.D. 150), who obtained most of his information on the Near East from his own travels and whose accuracy as a guide to the monuments of his age is confirmed in many cases by existing remains. Pausanias states categorically that the Temple of Bel still stood, though of Babylon itself nothing is left but the walls.

Some modern historians find it difficult to accept the evidence of either Pliny or Pausanias, though tablets have been found in the rubble of Babylon showing that sacrifices and services were being held certainly up to within a decade or two of the Christian era. Moreover, pagan worship was certainly continued at nearby Borsippa until as late as our own fourth century. In other words, the old gods died hard, especially among what was left of the conservative Babylonians whose children were still being educated by the priests of Marduk in church schools; while side by side with this dying paganism the Jewish communities which had existed in the region since the capture of Jerusalem by Nebuchadnezzar in 597 B.C. continued to worship their own god and were conceivably becoming converted to the new Nazarene religion in some numbers. If this were so, it would throw new light on the controversial phrase 'The Church at Babylon', referred to by St Peter in one of his epistles, suggesting that the term was not a symbolic reference to pagan Rome, but a greeting to an actual Jewish Christian community which had sprung up in the region of the Mesopotamian city exactly as similar communities were springing up all over the Roman Empire, particularly in the Middle East

and North Africa where the larger Jewish colonies were established. It is true that nothing resembling a Christian church has
been found in the ruins of Babylon, but one would hardly expect
to come across such building. In any case, the first Christians did
not have churches, but met in each other's houses or held their
festivals in fields and groves outside the city walls.

On the other hand, the German archaeologists who excavated
Ctesiphon in 1928 did uncover the remains of an early Christian
church (probably from the fifth century) built on top of an earlier
shrine, so that if there were Christians in Ctesiphon before its
destruction by the Arabs in A.D. 636 there were undoubtedly other
Nazarene communities scattered about Mesopotamia and even a
'Church at Babylon' to whom Peter sent greetings. It is an interesting point, since it can be argued that it was very unlikely that
there was a Christian community in Rome during St Peter's
apostleship, whereas there were *two* actual Babylons in existence:
the fortress-city in Egypt just outside modern Cairo; and the
ancient Mesopotamian metropolis. Both these places did have
Jewish colonies.

It may seem strange to imagine the very newest cult existing
side by side with the most ancient religion in the world. But it
would not have seemed strange in a pagan society where all gods
were tolerated provided they did not usurp the rights of other
gods. The Near and Middle East, in any case, were the breeding-
grounds of new theologies of which Christianity seemed to be but
one more. Underestimating the new creed was a mistake that both
the ecclesiastical and civil authorities of the pagan world made in
the beginning, though they very soon realised that the new sect
of Christians intended to keep themselves as strictly separate from
the rest of the community as their Jewish predecessors had done
before them. Indeed, their separateness, which seemed at first to be
a sign of weakness, was to be their strength, for whereas both the
Jewish and Christian faith survived in Iraq, the cult of Marduk
did not.

If there was a Christian community in Babylon at the time of the
invasion of Mesopotamia by Julian the Apostate in A.D. 363 we
are told nothing about it by the historians who wrote accounts of
Julian's war against the Persian king Shapur I. But Julian was no
friend of the Christians or their churches, but of the old pagan
gods and temples which he tried desperately to revive throughout

the Roman world. So if the great ziggurat of Marduk had existed in 363 when the Emperor passed by Babylon on his way to Ctesiphon he would certainly have gone to see it in order to raise the morale of the priesthood. The fact that not even the name of Babylon is mentioned is indirect proof that the city by this time had been totally abandoned. All that Julian's biographers tell us is that the army on their way to Ctesiphon passed by the huge walls of some ancient deserted city which was now used as a Royal Game Park of the Persian kings.

Omne in medio spatium solitudo est, says St Jerome (A.D. 345–420) in a solemn passage concerning Babylon. 'The whole area within the walls is a wilderness inhabited by all manner of wild animals.' Such was the description of an Elamite Christian who had actually visited the Persian game reserve on his way to a monastery in Jerusalem. It was the demise of a city and an empire which was viewed with great satisfaction by both Jews and Christians alike, for Babylon had become the symbol of God's wrath.

Others see the destruction of Babylon as the consequence of much more mundane factors: the Babylonians themselves after a thousand years as the political, cultural, and religious centre of the world had to bow to the superiority of new gods who were backed by far larger battalions than they could muster, so that Babylon did not die in a great cataclysm as the prophets had hoped, consumed like Sodom and Gomorrah by fire and brimstone, but simply faded away like so many great and beautiful cities of the Middle East. For it would seem that cities and civilisations have their allotted life-span like everything else.

Epilogue

WHAT DID THIS GREAT and wonderful city bequeath to the world? What heritage did it leave to mankind?

It is not easy for us 2500 years after Babylon's decline to answer these questions. There are two reasons for this: the first is that we of the West tend to interpret ancient history through the eyes of the Greeks and Romans, who are, of course, much nearer to us in mind and spirit than the Babylonians. The Greeks, in particular, are so catholic in their thinking that intellectually we have scarcely advanced on them at all: they are still our teachers, and it is still their serene view of life that colours the best of our philosophy and art. And from the Romans we have inherited a very precise view of what constitutes civilisation in terms of law and order, love of country, service to the community, and social stability.

Secondly, it is hardly more than a hundred years since we first knew anything concrete about Babylonia at all. Before the discoveries of the nineteenth-century excavators reached the museums and the decipherment of the tablets the bookshelves of the libraries our only knowledge of this strange people came from their implacable enemies, the Israelites, and an occasional Greek or Roman historian sufficiently curious to inquire about what had happened to the most famous city in the pre-Hellenic world. The result is bound to be that to the non-specialist Sumer, Babylonia, and Assyria are almost as remote as that kingdom of Atlantis which Plato describes in his two dialogues *Timaeus* and *Critias* and which has become the symbol of those Never-Never lands which exist only on the periphery, as it were, of history.

There are also those who would argue that Babylon has no message for the twentieth century in any case, since these ancient

Mesopotamian peoples lived under such totally different technological conditions from us that it is meaningless to try to compare the two cultures. In the first place—so runs this rather superficial argument—the life of an ordinary citizen in Babylon 3000 years ago and the life of an ordinary Londoner or New Yorker today have nothing in common. The Babylonian would, by our standards, be deprived of the everyday mechanical aids that we enjoy —no central heating, no car, no television, et cetera. Much more to the point is the objection that he would—again by our standards—be relatively ill-informed and unthinking, for a society in which he received little, if any, formal education would leave him without the incentive to concern himself with anything outside his own immediate purview. For in this respect every aspect of existence was rigidly defined for him—his relations with his family, his neighbours, the state, the king, and the gods; his duties as a citizen; his functions as a worker; and his rights under the law. Within such a monolithic structure he had neither the chance nor the expectation of ever changing himself or society. Personal rebellion probably never occurred to him; organised revolution was out of the question. And it is this anthill concept of the community which separates the empires of the Middle East, first from the Hellenic societies and then from our own civilisation, thus making it difficult for us to attune our minds to such an intellectually alien world.

And still a third reason for the difficulty we have in identifying with the Babylonians is the absence of any popular art or literature, inevitable in a society where writers, musicians, and sculptors were civil servants, no more necessary or 'inspired' than tax-collectors or bricklayers. The artist's job was to be competent and to produce what the establishment required. Anything which we regard as aesthetically satisfying, like the reliefs of the lion hunt on the walls of the palace of Ashurbanipal, was due to the absence of rules laid down by the authorities for portraying lesser creatures than gods and kings. Only within this very limited area was there anything resembling artistic freedom.

The controlling factor in Babylonian life, then, was the absolutism of the state and not the liberty of the individual, which left only one safe and free area of intellectual enterprise: namely, what can be roughly defined as pure science. In Babylonia and Assyria pure science meant mathematics and astronomy, for medicine, architecture, and engineering, like art and literature, were merely empirical skills in the service of the state. Originally, even mathematics served a purely functional purpose by enabling the surveyor and the architect to make useful calculations in his task of erecting temples and palaces. But eventually the arithmeticians added to their knowledge the principle of quadratic equations, arithmetic and geometric progressions, algebra, and a theory of numbers. Indeed, their level of achievement in the field of mathematics has been compared with that of the early Renaissance, while their astronomy was equal to that of the Greeks and Romans.

It is unlikely that the Babylonians studied the night sky out of a wholly impersonal interest in astronomy, particularly as their astral observations were made by priests who were the only members of the community entrusted with such arcane matters and the only ones with access to the highest platforms of the ziggurats. Hence we may be reasonably sure that these clergy were primarily concerned with astrology rather than astronomy, using their observations of the heavens to interpret and predict events on earth. Their astrology, however, was not of the kind found in the daily newspaper horoscopes, but was of the judicial or political variety, meaning that it was used solely for predicting affairs of state: for instance, the coming of war, famine, regicide, earthquakes, and so forth. Why an eclipse in the month of April should portend the murder of a king by his son (as one tablet from about 1500 B.C. predicts) will never be known, for it is useless to apply logical analysis to any form of fortune-telling, whether it is reading the future from the movements of the stars or from an examination of an animal's entrails. But the significant factor from the point of view of scientific progress is that in order to interpret heavenly phenomena in terrestrial terms (e.g. an eclipse in April = the death of a king), the priests were obliged to become astronomers despite themselves: that is, to make and record their observations of the movements of the planets, the rise of stars and constellations, and the occurrence of both solar and lunar eclipses. Certainly the planet Venus as the symbol of the goddess Ishtar was observed from 1650 B.C. and it is from such observations that historians can begin to determine the chronology of ancient Babylonia. Eclipses had been recorded as far back as 747 B.C. since the Greek astronomer Ptolemy tells us that he had access to these data. In short, it is evident that what began as magic became in time science, as the star-gazers became more interested in observing eclipses and other celestial phenomena than in predicting coming events on earth; for we can assume that men versed in mathematics and astronomy grew sceptical about the old concepts of the universe. They had, after all, begun to plot the night sky, to recognise and name the constellations, to fix with sufficient accuracy the movements of the planets, especially those of the moon, and by this means to postulate a reliable system of time-measurement. For these reasons there can be no doubt that Babylon was the mother of astronomy and that her contributions to both the theoretical and practical aspects of that science profoundly affected the course of civilisation. Thus, on the one side Greek astronomers like Hipparchus of Nicaea (*c.* 190–125 B.C.), sometimes called the founder of scientific astronomy, was heavily indebted to Babylonian star-gazers like Kidinnu of Sippar (*c.* 320 B.C.) who had calculated the difference between the tropical and sidereal year and so arrived at the theory of the precession of the equinoxes. On the other and practical side it is evident that the Phoenicians made good use of Babylonian astronomy in their great sea voyages north to Cornwall for the valuable tin, south down the African coasts, and westwards to Spain. These voyages could not have been made without some kind of aids to navigation based on tables of the sun, moon, planets, and ephemerides, particularly as the Phoenicians did not have the compass to guide them. And this knowledge of astro-navigation partially explains the famous secrecy of the Phoenicians and their colonists the Carthaginians vis-à-vis the Greeks and Romans, who were envious not only of the maritime trade of their rivals but of their skill as navigators. The Punic secret was most probably their familiarity with Babylonian astronomical tables.

It could be asked why, if the Babylonian scientific records were available to the Phoenicians, the Greeks did not make fuller use of them. The answer is that the latter people were unable to read the cuneiform texts, whereas Akkadian was probably the second language of Phoenicia during the Assyro-Babylonian occupation of Tyre and Sidon. In other words, the original script of the Phoenicians was probably borrowed from the cuneiform writing of Mesopotamia, and certainly the correspondence between the pharaoh Amenhotep IV (Ikhnaton) and the Phoenician city-states was written in Akkadian in the cuneiform script—an extraordin-

ary example of the international influence of Babylon, whose
language, like Latin in the Middle Ages, was the diplomatic and
learned tongue of the eastern Mediterranean. Briefly, then,
Phoenicia and, for that matter, all the Semitic nations of the Near
East, including Israel, owed a great deal to Babylon, whence they
drew many of their religious, political, scientific, and social ideas.

The Greeks, on the other hand, perhaps because of their different ethnic origins, learnt little from the Babylonians. Ironically,
the semi-barbarian Macedonians of Alexander regarded the citizens of the greatest and one of the oldest cities in the world as
'lesser breeds without the law', much as the British in the mid-
nineteenth century regarded the citizens of Pekin. Alexander was
content to capture and occupy Babylon and even to make the
metropolis his eastern capital, but neither he nor his soldiers admired anything Babylonian except the compliant and beautiful
women who entertained them so generously. Indeed, on the king's
death his army refused to accept as the future ruler of the Hellenes
his child by an oriental woman, for to this extent the Greeks were
racists and regarded themselves as vastly superior to all the people
they conquered during Alexander's invasions.

Consequently we cannot expect to find Babylon influencing
Greek thought to the extent that it influenced the religious thinking of the Jews, Phoenicians, and other Semitic nations. In any
case, the Greeks were in comparison with the Mesopotamians
'new men', totally different in temperament from the Babylonians.
There can be little doubt that the latter had inherited through
generations of religious, political, and civic tyranny a slave mentality which was in complete contrast to the free-thinking of the
Hellene. This is immediately apparent if we compare any of the
Greek city-states with any of the city-states of Sumer, Babylonia,
and Assyria. It is apparent, too, in the religious concepts of the
two peoples, for just as the Babylonian gods remained the same
terrible and awe-inspiring tyrants throughout their long history
so the Greek gods were very quickly civilised and humanised;
hence even if a man could not really believe in them as deities he
could at least enjoy them as friends. Thus Socrates addresses Pan
in a prayer to the beauty of nature. He has been strolling along the
banks of the river Ilissus with his friend Phaedrus on a spring
morning and at midday pauses to rest under a shade-tree. This is
his prayer:

O beloved Pan and you other gods of this place, grant me to become beautiful within myself so that I may be in harmony with the beauty of the world. And may I seek no other wealth than that of wisdom, the greatest of all treasures.

If we compare this simple supplication with the bombastic addresses to the gods of the Babylonian, Assyrian, and Persian kings, we have the quintessence of the difference between the Hellenic and the Mesopotamian mentality.

Even so, our religious ideas today owe a great deal more to the Semites than they do to the Greeks. We take our basic ethical concepts from the Old Testament, our basic religious doctrine from the New: we are, in brief, disciples of Judaism, not Hellenism. To what degree, then, is Judaism related to the Babylonian cults? Specifically, how many of the myths, moral laws, theological beliefs, rituals, and imagery of the Old Testament are derived from Babylonian originals? Obviously this is a highly controversial subject, particularly to those who believe that the Bible is the word of God and not derived from earthly sources; but the probability that the Old Testament incorporated certain Babylonian myths and beliefs was bound to be suspected when the stories of the Creation and of the Flood were found in the eleventh tablet of the Epic of Gilgamesh and translated by the British Museum's George Smith. Once this connection between Sumerian-Babylonian and Jewish religious epics had been established, scholars began to notice more and more affinities between Old Testament incidents and those recorded on the cuneiform tablets. The many Biblical references to witchcraft, magic, necromancy, and so forth have their counterparts in the ancient Mesopotamian mythology, as, for instance, King Saul calling up the shade of the prophet Samuel by means of the witch of Endor. It is true that witches and witchcraft are native to all races and all religions, but the more sophisticated version of necromancy as related in the First Book of Samuel, chapter 28, is found in a Sumerian poem which tells of Gilgamesh summoning the shade of his friend for advice and comfort.

Some Sumeriologists have gone so far as to suggest that whole books in the Old Testament have been borrowed from Mesopotamian originals, notably the curious book entitled *Nahum*, with its apparent reference to chariot races, lion hunts, and temple prostitutes. The language of this book, with its reiteration of how jealous, angry, powerful, and destructive Yahweh is, reminds us of the Assyro-Babylonian fear of Marduk, also an essentially *national* god. So, too, the language and the subject-matter of the Song of Songs, or the Song of Solomon, as it is called in the King James version, could be an adaptation of a Babylonian poem, for this erotic verse has nothing in common with the remainder of the Old Testament and a great deal with the Mesopotamian cult of the god Tammuz, whom Ezekiel saw the women of Jerusalem weeping for.

And certainly the old Hebrew concept of Yahweh, or Jehovah, is almost identical with the Sumerian-Babylonian personification of the national god, whether he is worshipped under the name of Enlil or Marduk. Enlil, like Yahweh, rules over mankind on the strength of the principle that might is right. All these Semitic gods are, above all, jealous deities, and they are worshipped and obeyed because men fear, not love, them. There is actually an Assyrian inscription from 720 B.C. describing the Babylonian king Mero-dach-Baladan as a fool because 'he did not fear the name of the Lord of Lords'. And as a result of this terror of the god, the Babylonians and Israelites alike were, in their attitude to their 'Lord of Lords', abject, self-accusing, remorseful, and grovelling —with good reason when one recalls the trials and tribulations of Job, a story, incidentally, which has an almost identical counterpart in Sumerian literature. The Sumerian poem, sometimes called *The Poem of the Righteous Sufferer*, takes as its theme the trials and tribulations of a good man who naturally cannot understand why he has been so badly treated by his friends, his enemies, and, above all, by his god. He laments:

> My comrade says not a true word to me,
> My friend gives the lie to my righteous word,
> The deceitful man has conspired against me,
> And you, my god, do not thwart him . . .
> Tears, lamentations, anguish, and depression are mine,
> Suffering overwhelms me like one condemned to weep,
> Evil fate holds me in its grip, carries off my breath of life,
> Malignant sickness afflicts me . . .
> [Et cetera.]

Compare this with these verses taken at random from the Book of Job. Is the similarity pure coincidence? Or has the Jewish writer (if he was Jewish) borrowed not only the theme but the actual words of the Sumerian original? Or is the Book of Job a direct translation made by a captive Jew during the Babylonian Exile, as N. H. Tur Sinai, the Semitist, suggests? At any rate, here are some of the characteristic sentiments from Job to read alongside those we have taken from the Sumerian *The Poem of the Righteous Sufferer*:

> Mine acquaintance are wholly estranged from me,
> And my familiar friends have forgotten me.
> I call unto my servant, and he giveth no answer.
> Why do you persecute me, O my god?
> He multiplieth my wounds without cause,
> He will not suffer me to take my breath.
> My flesh is clothed with worms and clods of dust.
> My skin closeth up and breaketh out afresh . . .
> [Et cetera.]

Indeed, recent discoveries and translations of both Sumerian and Akkadian texts seem to prove conclusively that Job is a direct borrowing either from *The Poem of the Righteous Sufferer* or from similar poems like the so-called *Babylonian Ecclesiastes*, or *A Pessimistic Dialogue Between Master and Servant*. The similarities between all these poems are so marked that it is difficult not to believe that they are all versions of the original Sumerian lament; and, more important, no one can doubt that this ancient Mesopotamian view of life, based on the severity of the gods, the suffering of mankind at their hands, the necessity of abject submission, and the resultant fatalism of the true believer is reflected in Jewish religious thought as we find it throughout the Old Testament and as expressed in the concept of the 'jealous God' who visits the sins of the parents on the children even unto the third and fourth generation

Manifestly the self-abasement verging on paranoia which we find in Job is the result of intense personal fear of a masochistic god and reveals an attitude of mind which accounts for the basic tenets of oriental religion: namely, the tears for sins committed, whether knowingly or unknowingly; the lamentations and sighs; the countenance bowed down to the ground; the body cleaving to the pavement—all the posturings of the slave in the presence

of a despot. Such attitudes did not come into Western culture
from the Greeks, whose relationship with the gods was, in comparison, sober, well tempered, genial, and, in general, aloof.
Certainly no Greek would ever have contemplated winning the
favour of the deity by wailing and weeping and covering his head
with sackcloth and ashes; nor would he have demeaned himself
by calling himself a slave, as in the pious expression 'the slave of
God' (ὁ δοῦλος θεοῦ) frequently inscribed on early Christian tombs.

We note also two other religious attitudes characteristic of the
Babylonians, the Jews, and the Christians, but quite uncharacter-
istic of the Greeks and Romans. The first of these is the counterpart to the fear of the despotic god: namely a wheedling approach
to the divinity which reminds us of an artful child trying to get a
favour from a stern father. This self-prostrating humility in the
presence of the god often manifests itself in the Babylonian litur-
gies in a sickly sentimentality, as it does later in the Jewish psalms,
and later still in the Christian hymns. The Babylonian Tammuz
is cajoled as the 'Lord of the tender voice and shining eyes'; the
Jewish Yahweh is appealed to as an indulgent magistrate whose
judgments are 'more to be desired than fine gold, sweeter than
honey and the honeycomb'; and the Christian Jesus is addressed,
in Victorian hymns at any rate, as meek and mild, love divine,
husband, friend, priest, king, and so forth. Such fulsome compli-
ments belong to the oriental way of thinking, but were alien to the
European mentality until they were introduced into the Western
world from the Middle East, along with other Eastern forms of
ritual—the incense, prostrations, eating of the dead god, and even
holy marriage—all of them rites typical of the Babylonian cults.

Secondly, we have another trait typical of the Semites which
was absorbed into Western culture after the decease of paganism
and the rise of Christianity: that is, the spirit of fanaticism which
displays itself in a variety of forms, not only religious, but also in
the political and social spheres. This fanaticism resulting from the
conviction that the national god is the only true god, whence all
rival deities of other nations must be eliminated, along with their
worshippers, was, of course, utterly alien to Greek and Roman
thinking. It was, however, a fundamental tenet of Mesopotamian
religions and a belief by which the upholders of the cult justified
their merciless foreign policy of wiping out their enemies, even
down to the smallest suckling. It was this sort of fanaticism which

led Ashurbanipal, who first calls himself 'the Compassionate', to boast that he tore out the tongues of the Babylonian rebels, hewed their flesh into small pieces, and flung the scraps to the dogs, swine, and vultures. The Christian nations were later to share with the Assyrians and the Israelites this same zeal to eliminate their enemies for the greater glory of their god.

We see, then, that Babylon, although it is now only a name and a few mounds in a remote region of Mesopotamia, may continue to influence our thinking to some extent, particularly in the prosecution of our wars, which are, after all, one of the predominant features of our civilisation. We pray to God to annihilate our enemies in the same spirit and with much the same ritual with which the Babylonians called upon Marduk and the Israelites upon Yahweh to support their righteous cause.

All the same, it remains hazardous to try to specify precisely the contributions of one civilisation to another. All that we can be reasonably sure of is that the cultural history of the Western world began in Mesopotamia. For assuming that civilisation depends on urbanisation, agriculture, religious and moral law, jurisprudence, and a system of writing, we find them all well developed in Sumer some 5000 years ago; and from Sumer passed on to Babylon; and from Babylon spread throughout the Middle East and Eurasia. The difficulties and controversies begin, of course, with the attempts to trace *direct* cultural links between Babylonia and the emergent European civilisations. There was considerable influence according to some authorities; scarcely any according to others. The supporters of the former theory base their arguments on the contact the Hittites had with Babylonia on the one hand and the Aegean world on the other. The opponents point to the lack of communications between Mesopotamia, cut off by the deserts to the west, and the Mediterranean world.

And yet despite the cultural affinities which we obviously share with Sumer, Babylonia, and Assyria, those empires remain almost as remote to us as they were to the Athenians who were separated from them by only a few centuries. And even though Babylon did take a leading place in the annals of ancient history as a result of the discoveries of the nineteenth century, yet the enthusiasm for Assyriology has waned, or is certainly not comparable to what it was a hundred years ago when the public bought some 10,000 copies of Henry Layard's book *Nineveh and Its Remains*, while tens of thousands of others must have borrowed it from the libraries. In brief, Nineveh, Babylon, and the scores of other cities whose names are not even known to the non-specialist have again become symbols of half-forgotten episodes in the history of mankind, bound up with vague recollections of apocalyptic prophecies in the Old Testament.

There are a number of reasons for this falling off of interest in Babylonia, notably the inaccessibility of the actual sites of the cities of the Mesopotamian plains, as well as the disappointment the ordinary traveller must feel on visiting them. The physical remains of the two most famous, Babylon and Nineveh, present the spectacle of mounds of rubble, left behind by the thousands of unskilled workmen who dug them out with picks and shovels in the great treasure-hunts of the nineteenth century. In comparison, the lover of ruins has all the imposing or beautiful monuments of Egypt, Greece, and Rome to stimulate his imagination and to satisfy visually his historical interest. If he wants to glimpse something of the Babylonians or Assyrians, on the other hand, he can only really do so by studying the artefacts in the national museums of the Near East, Europe, and America. Yet as he gazes on the mysterious man-headed bulls or examines the sculpted reliefs of the old battles or peers up at the statues of kings and priests with their staring eyes, he is liable to have the same response that he has on his first view of the Easter Island statues, also displayed in museum galleries far from their native land. It is natural that he should ask himself what he has in common with these monoliths and the people who made them. And if he then turns his attention to the literature of the Babylonians he will only get a dusty answer from a perusal of the royal proclamations, the hymns to gods with unpronounceable names, and the thousands of legal and commercial contracts. The plain fact is that creative literature of the scope and variety that we are used to in our reading of the Classics will not be found among the tens of thousands of tablets recovered from the rubble of the buried libraries. As we have pointed out above, only the *Epic of Gilgamesh* has this quality of universality which we find in the *Odyssey*. The rest—the lamentations, the occasional animal fable, and the odd folk-saying—are too elementary to impress us today.

Yet the mystery of Babylon lingers on, as it survived even when all vestiges of the city had disappeared. The name itself evokes a sense of wonder and even of regret.

> Babylon,
> Learned and wise, hath perished utterly,
> Nor leaves her speech one word to aid the sigh
> That would lament her.

So wrote Wordsworth before the great discoveries of the mid-nineteenth century. Now, of course, the story of Babylon is so well known that there is scarcely a name or date of a single monarch during all the city's 2000 years of existence that we do not know, from Sumu-abum, the first recorded king, 2225 B.C., to the last native-born ruler, Nabonidus, 555 B.C.—a total of 138 crowned kings of Babylon. And as for speech, there are literally hundreds of thousands of words for anyone with the time and patience to read them. So to this extent the mystery, which was so vividly evoked in the Biblical account of the Exile by the waters of Babylon, has been dissipated, and what, for instance, was once an almost mythical figure like Nebuchadnezzar II has now become as real in the context of proven history as Agamemnon became after Schliemann's excavations of the palace of Mycenae. Thus, we can say with certainty that Nebuchadnezzar reigned from 605 to 562 B.C.; that he ruled over a neo-Babylonian empire whose influence stretched from the shores of the Mediterranean to the confines of Afghanistan; and that he sacked Jerusalem in 587 B.C. This is a very different version of history from what we read in the Bible concerning a king of Babylon who grovelled before one of his Jewish attendants.

But even if a great deal of the mystery which hung over the name of the great city when the first European travellers looked out over the mound-covered plains of Mesopotamia has gone, the fascination of a lost world rediscovered after 2000 years has increased now that we know that it was here, under those shapeless hillocks of rubble, that our own civilization had its beginnings. We know, too, that in all basic respects we have not changed that much in our own lives: the schoolboys in Sumerian times, for instance, left for their classes just as boys do today; the farmer set off for the fields, the magistrate for the courts, and the artisan for his workshop in the same daily tasks that have to be performed by us.

Yet these empires declined and fell, and each reader, after he

has made the long journey back through time, may want to draw
his own conclusions as to why this happened. He may, in company
with the Hebrew prophets, ascribe Babylon's collapse to the wrath
of God. Or he may argue that the people themselves became too
soft and cowardly to defend themselves against their enemies. Or,
again, he may believe that there is a cycle of growth and decay
which governs civilisations as it does all other forms of life.

The Babylonians would not, of course, have accepted any of
these explanations. They could have argued quite justly that they
had done their best to avoid offending the gods: that nobody, in
fact, had ever built them bigger temples, offered more generous
sacrifices, and accorded them greater reverence. Why, then, should
God forsake them? As for becoming soft and cowardly, they
could point out that they had fought in the four corners of the
world for nearly 2000 years, usually victoriously, and, moreover,
that their last heir to the throne, Belshazzar, had died defending
Babylon against the Persian invaders on the banks of the Tigris.
As for their city dying of old age, they would maintain that the
metropolis was actually slowly bled to death by the successors,
and against the will, of Alexander—by men with delusions of
grandeur who built rival cities just far enough away to ruin the old
capital. And so, as a commercial and administrative centre, Babylon became only a shadow of Nebuchadnezzar's rich and magnificent city, and in the end life only flickered on in the vicinity of
the ruined temples.

The Babylonians would also have insisted that they had, after
all, done their best right up to the end. They had made good laws
and administered justice; they had attempted to control men's
unrestricted passions and violence; and they had set up a code of
civilised conduct for their citizens, condemning family discord,
adultery, murder, theft, libel, forgery, commercial swindles, and
hypocrisy. What more could a people do? In the end the Babylonians knew there was nothing they could do once another
nation backed by a more powerful god and a larger army decided
to destroy them. That nation was Persia, destroyed in its turn by
Greece, destroyed by Rome, and so on up to our own day.

References

CHAPTER 1 BABYLON REMEMBERED (pages 17–25)

1. *Narrative of a Journey to the Site of Babylon in 1811*, by the late Claudius James Rich, edited by his widow, 1838, Introduction, p. iii.
2. *The Itinerary of Benjamin of Tudela*, translated by M. N. Adler, London, 1907. Benjamin's account, written in 1178, was printed in Hebrew in 1543 and translated into Latin and printed in Amsterdam in 1575.
3. Leonhard Rauwolff's travels translated into English in Vol. i of *A Collection of Curious Travels and Voyages*, London, 1693. They were originally written in Dutch and first published in 1582–3.
4. John Eldred's *Journal of His Voyage* is found in Hakluyt's *Principal Navigations*, first published in 1599.

CHAPTER 2 THE EXCAVATORS (pages 26–33)

1. J. S. Buckingham, *Travels in Mesopotamia*, 1928, Vol. ii, p. 200.
2. *Narrative of a Journey to the Site of Babylon in 1811*, by the late Claudius James Rich, p. 39.

CHAPTER 3 LAYARD IN BABYLONIA (pages 34–46)

1. The story of the Peters expedition is told in H. V. Hilprecht, *The Excavations in Assyria and Mesopotamia*, 1904.
2. Austen H. Layard, *Discoveries in the Ruins of Nineveh and Babylon*, 1858, pp. 203–4.
3. E. A. W. Budge, *By Nile and Tigris*, 1920, vol. i, p. 45.

CHAPTER 4 THE FIRST AMERICAN ASSYRIOLOGISTS (pages 47–59)

1. Edgar James Banks, *Bismaya, or the Lost City of Adab*, 1912.
2. Banks, op. cit., pp. 190–2.
3. Banks, op. cit., p. 442.

4. Banks, op. cit., p. 371.
5. *The American Journal of Semitic Languages and Literature*, Vol. xx, July 1904, No. 4, pp. 264–5.

CHAPTER 5   THE DECIPHERMENT OF THE CUNEIFORM SCRIPT
             (pages 60–71)

1. Thomas Herbert, *A Relation of Some Yeares Travaile*, London, 1634, pp. 145–6.
2. For readers who wish to follow the curious hoax of the 'Tarku Inscription', see R. W. Rogers, *A History of Babylonia and Assyria*, Vol. i, Ch. 2.
3. William Price, *Journal of the British Embassy to Persia*, second edition, 1832, p. 15.
4. Price, op. cit., p. 34.

CHAPTER 6   HENRY RAWLINSON AND THE INSCRIPTION OF DARIUS
             (pages 72–81)

1. For the original description of Rawlinson's experiences on the Rock of Behistun, see his article 'Notes on Some Paper Casts of Cuneiform Inscriptions', *Archaeologia*, Vol. xxxiv, 1852.
2. op. cit., p. 75.
3. idem.

CHAPTER 7   THE DISCOVERY OF THE SUMERIANS (pages 82–97)

1. C. Leonard Woolley, *Ur of the Chaldees*, 1950, p. 64.

CHAPTER 8   ART AND LITERATURE IN SUMER (pages 98–110)

1. C. Leonard Woolley, *Ur of the Chaldees*, p. 55.
2. From 'Enki and Ninhursag: a Sumerian Myth', translated by Samuel N. Kramer, *Bulletin of the American Schools of Oriental Research*, Supplementary Study, No. 1, 1945.
3. 'Enki and Ninhursag: a Sumerian Myth'.
4. *Lamentation over the Destruction of Ur*, by Samuel N. Kramer, the Oriental Institute of the University of Chicago, Assyriological Studies No. 12, 352–4.
5. R. Campbell Thompson, *The Epic of Gilgamesh*, 1928, Preface, p. 6.
6. N. K. Sandars, *The Epic of Gilgamesh*, 1960 (Penguin Classics), p. 49.
7. S. A. Pallis, *The Antiquity of Iran*, Copenhagen, 1956, p. 681.
8. Alexander Heidel, *The Gilgamesh Epic and Old Testament Parallels*, Chicago, 1946, Tablet 0, Column iv, 6–23.

9. Sandars, op. cit.
10. Samuel N. Kramer, *History Begins at Sumer*, 1958, Introduction, pp. 17–18.
11. Samuel N. Kramer, *Gilgamesh and the Huluppu-Tree*, Chicago, 1938 p. 12.
12. H. C. Rawlinson, *The Cuneiform Inscriptions*, 1861–4, Vol. iv, Tabi-utul-bel.
13. Samuel N. Kramer, *History Begins at Sumer*, Ch. 15. Nigel Dennis, 'Sentiments from Sumer', in *Encounter*, May 1970, p. 37.
14. Sandars, op. cit.

CHAPTER 10   HAMMURABI THE LAWGIVER (pages 120–7)

1. L. W. King, *The Letters and Inscriptions of Hammurabi*, London, 1900, Vol. iii, p. 14.

CHAPTER 11   SOCIAL LIFE IN BABYLONIA (pages 128–38)

1. René Labat, *Traité Akkadien de Diagnostics et Pronostics Médicaux*, Paris, 1951.

CHAPTER 12   THE ASSYRIANS (pages 139–53)

1. M. E. L. Mallowan, 'The Excavations at Nimrud', *Iraq*, Vol. xxi, part 2, August 1959, p. 96.

CHAPTER 13   THE SPLENDOUR OF BABYLON (pages 154–70)

1. Diodorus of Sicily, *History*, Book ii, Ch. 10.
2. R. Koldewey, *The Excavations at Babylon*, trans. Agnes S. Johns, 1914, pp. 95 ff.
3. *The Atheneum*, February 12, 1876 (No. 2520), p. 232.
4. *The Atheneum*, op. cit., p. 233.
5. R. Koldewey, op. cit., p. 10.
6. A. E. W. Budge, *By Nile and Tigris*, 1920, Vol. i, p. 317.

CHAPTER 15   THE END OF BABYLON (pages 180–99)

1. Quintus Curtius Rufus, *History of Alexander the Great*, Loeb Classical Library, 1946, Vol. i, pp. 36–9.

EPILOGUE (pages 200–12)

1. Adapted from Samuel N. Kramer's translation in *History Begins at Sumer*, pp. 169, 170.

Bibliography

In addition to the books referred to in the list of references, the following volumes will be found useful, particularly as most of them contain additional bibliographies, maps, and illustrations.

I GENERAL HISTORIES
Baldwin, John D., *Chaldean Civilisation and Learning*, 1869.
Banks, Edgar J., *The Seven Wonders of the Ancient World*, 1916.
Budge, E. A. W., *The Rise and Progress of Assyriology*, 1925.
Garstang, John, *The Hittite Empire*, 1929.
Huxley, George L., *Achaeans and Hittites*, 1960.
Jackson, William A. V., *Persia, Past and Present*, 1906.
King, Leonard W., *A History of Babylon*, 1915.
King, Leonard W., *A History of Sumer and Akkad*, 1910.
Kramer, S. N., *History Begins at Sumer*, 1958.
Pallis, Svend Aage, *The Antiquity of Iraq*, 1956.
Parrot, André, *Babylon and the Old Testament*, 1958.
Parrot, André, *Nineveh and Babylon*, 1961.
Parrot, André, *Sumer*, 1960.
Pinches, Theophilus G., *The Old Testament in the Light of Excavations in Assyria and Babylonia*, 1908.
Rogers, Robert W., *A History of Babylonia and Assyria*, 1914.
Saggs, H. W. F., *The Greatness that was Babylon*, 1960.
Smith, Sidney, *Early History of Assyria*, 1928.
Woolley, Charles L., *The Sumerians*, 1928.

II CLASSICAL HISTORIANS
Arrianus Flavius, *Works*.
Berosus the Chaldean, *The Fragments of Chaldean History*.
Curtius Rufus, Quintus, *History of Alexander the Great*.
Diodorus Siculus, *The Historical Library*.
Herodotus, *The History*.
Zosimus, *The History of Count Zosimus*.

III SPECIAL EXCAVATIONS, EXPEDITIONS, AND DISCOVERIES
Banks, Edgar J., *Bismya, or the Lost City of Adab*, 1912.
Budge, E. A. W., *By Nile and Tigris*, 1920.
Chesney, F. R., *The Expedition for the survey of the rivers Euphrates and Tigris*, 1868.
Harper, R. F., Report from Bismya, 1–11, 1903, 1904 (*American Journal of Semitic Languages*, XX).
King, Leonard W., *The sculptures and inscriptions of Darius the Great on the rock of Behistun in Persia*, 1907.
Koldewey, Robert, *Excavations at Babylon*, 1914.
Layard, Austen Henry, *Autobiography*, 1903.
Layard, Austen Henry, *Discoveries in the ruins of Nineveh and Babylon*, 1853.
Mallowan, Max E., 'Ur in Retrospect' (*Iraq*, Vol. 22, 1960).
Pallis, Svend Aage, *Early exploration in Mesopotamia*, 1954.
Porter, Sir Robert Ker, *Travels in . . . Ancient Babylonia*, 1821.
Price, William, *Journal of the British Embassy to Persia*, 1825.
Rawlinson, H. C., *The Cuneiform Inscriptions of Western Asia*, 1861–84.
Rawlinson, H. C., 'The Persian Cuneiform Inscription at Behistun, deciphered and translated' (*Journal of the Royal Asiatic Society*, Vol. X, 1847).
Rich, Claudius J., *Narrative of a Journey to the Site of Babylon*, 1839.
Sherley, Sir Anthony, *Travels into Persia*, 1613.
Woolley, Charles L., *Ur of the Chaldees*, 1950.

IV RELIGION, ART, LITERATURE
Dhormer, Eduard P., *La religion assyro-babylonienne*, 1937.
Frankfort, H., *The Art and Architecture of the Ancient Orient*, 1954.
Heidel, Alexander, *The Gilgamesh Epic and Old Testament Parallels*, 1946.
Jean, C. F., *La religion sumérienne*, 1931.
King, Leonard W., *The Letters and Inscriptions of Hammurabi*, 1898.
Kramer, S. N., 'Enki and Ninhursag' (*Bulletin of the American Schools of Oriental Research*. Supplementary Study No. 1, 1945).
Kramer, S. N., 'Gilgamesh and the Huluppu Tree' (*Assyriological Studies*, No. 10).
Kramer, S. N., 'Lamentation over the Destruction of Ur' (*Assyriological Studies*, No. 12).
Pallis, Svend Aage, *The Babylonian Akitu Festival*, 1926.
Sandars, N. K., *The Epic of Gilgamesh* (translation), 1960.
Thompson, Reginald C., *The Epic of Gilgamesh* (translation), 1928.

V CUNEIFORM WRITING AND INSCRIPTIONS
Barton, George A., *The Origin and Development of Babylonian Writing*, 1913.

Booth, A. J., *The discovery and decipherment of the Trilingual Cuneiform Inscriptions*, 1902.

Gadd, Cyril J., *Sumerian Reading Book*, 1924.

King, Leonard W., *The Sculptures and Inscriptions of Darius the Great*, 1907.

Norris, E., 'Memoir on the Scythic Version of the Behistun Inscription' (*Journal of the Royal Asiatic Society*, vol. XV, 1853).

VI   SPECIAL SUBJECTS

Braidwood, Robert J., 'The Near East and the Foundations for Civilisation' (*Journal of World History*, I, 1953).

Driver, G. R., and J. C. Miles, *The Babylonian Laws*, 1952.

Farnell, Lewis R., *Babylon and Greece*, 1911.

Labat, René, *La médecine babylonienne*, 1953.

Parrot, André, *The Tower of Babel* (Studies in Biblical Archaeology, No. 2, 1959).

Thompson, Reginald C., *The Reports of the Magicians and Astrologers of Nineveh and Babylon*, 1900.

Index

compiled by Anthony Raven

IQ 43J

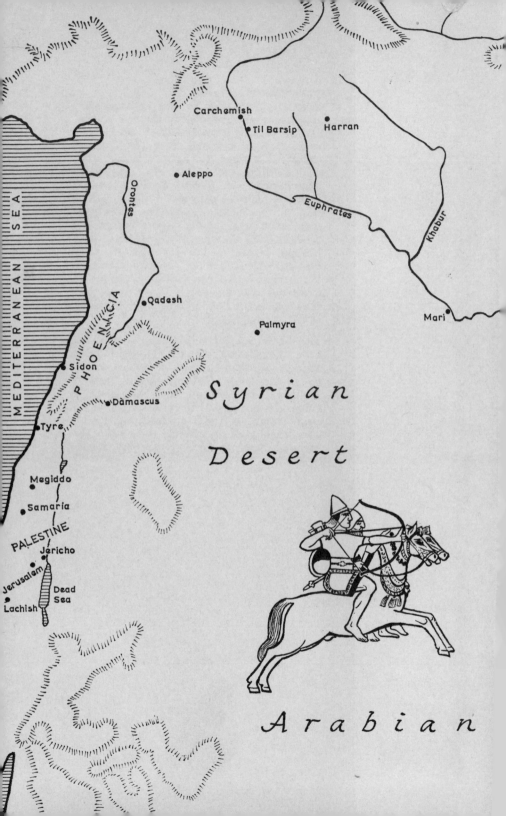

MEDITERRANEAN SEA

Carchemish
• Til Barsip
Harran •

• Aleppo

Orontes

Euphrates

Khabur

Mari •

Qadesh •

P H O E N I C I A

Palmyra •

• Sidon

• Damascus

• Tyre

S y r i a n

D e s e r t

• Megiddo

• Samaria

PALESTINE

• Jericho

• Jerusalem   Dead
              Sea

• Lachish

A r a b i a n